JUDAISM IN THE NEW TESTAMENT

Judaism in the New Testament exp....... how the books of the early church emerged from communities which defined themselves in Judaic terms even as they professed faith in Christ.

The earliest Christians set forth the Torah as they understood it – they did not think of their religion as Christianity, but as Judaism. For the first time, in *Judaism in the New Testament*, two distinguished scholars take the earliest Christians at their word and ask: "If Christianity is (a) Judaism, then how should we read the New Testament?"

The Gospels, Paul's Letters, and the Letter to the Hebrews are interpreted to define what Chilton and Neusner call "Christianity's Judaism" Seen in this way, the New Testament will never be the same.

Bruce Chilton is Bernard Iddings Bell Professor of Religion at Bard College, New York. He has taught and written extensively on early Christianity and Judaism and the historical Jesus. **Jacob Neusner** has published more than 550 books and is an expert on the history of Judaism. He is Distinguished Research Professor of Religious Studies at the University of South Florida and Visiting Professor of Religion at Bard College. He is also a member of the Institute for Advanced Study, Princeton, and a life member of Clare Hall, Cambridge.

JUDAISM IN THE NEW TESTAMENT

Practices and beliefs

Bruce Chilton and Jacob Neusner

London and New York

First published 1995
by Routledge
11 New Fetter Lane, London EC4P 4EE

Simultaneously published in the USA and Canada
by Routledge
29 West 35th Street, New York, NY 10001

Reprinted in 1996

Routledge is an International Thomson Publishing company

Typeset in Garamond by Michael Mepham, Frome,
Somerset
Printed and bound in Great Britain by
Mackays of Chatham PLC, Chatham, Kent

British Library Cataloguing in Publication Data
A catalogue record for this book is available from the
British Library

Library of Congress Cataloguing in Publication Data
A catalogue record for this book is available from the Library of Congress

ISBN 0–415–11843–3 (hbk)
ISBN 0–415–11844–1 (pbk)

In Memory of
Erwin R. Goodenough
and
Arthur Darby Nock

CONTENTS

CONTENTS

CONTENTS

ACKNOWLEDGEMENTS

Both authors express their thanks to Richard Stoneman, our editor at Routledge. His encouragement and advice made the work pleasant and interesting.

Mr Chilton wishes to thank Bard College and the Church of St John the Evangelist, for the time they afforded him to devote to the project. More particularly, three libraries over the years have extended him unusual support for his research: the library of the Yale Divinity School, the *Bibliothèque Nationale*, and the library of the *Institut de théologie protestante* in Paris. Such places make critical reflection pleasurable as well as possible, and hold out the hope that the life of the mind will continue to be nurtured by carefully kept collections of the printed word.

Mr Neusner expresses his thanks, in addition, to the three universities at which he wrote his part of the book, the University of Canterbury, Christchurch, New Zealand, where the first drafts of his chapters were sketched out, the University of South Florida, Tampa, where the work went forward, and Bard College, Annandale-on-Hudson, New York, where the book was completed. Research support has been forthcoming from all three centers of learning. Canterbury provided the Canterbury Visiting Fellowship, USF the Distinguished Research Professorship of Religious Studies, and Bard the Bard Center Fellowship, all providing ample support for research activities as well.

Both authors acknowledge with appreciation the heartfelt support for their joint scholarly activities that has come from President Leon Botstein and Dean of Faculty Stuart Levine at Bard College. Several future joint-ventures, emerging from the authors' shared teaching,

owe their origins to the enlightened academic administration of Bard
College.

Jacob Neusner and Bruce D. Chilton
Bard College,
Annandale-on-Hudson, New York
December 1, 1994

INTRODUCTION

Before we can define "Judaism" for the purpose of our study of the New Testament, we had best say what we mean by any religion, the genus of which Judaism forms a species (and, we shall argue, with earliest Christianity as a subspecies of that same species of religion). Defining religion comes before defining a particular religion, just as defining a particular religion takes priority over defining how two or more religions relate. Alas, as many definitions of religion circulate as there are those who have proposed to define religion.

One responds to the context of definition: for what purpose do we wish to define a religion? Since Christianity and Judaism address not isolated individuals but the entirety of the social order, and since both religions insist that matters of behavior, not only belief, make a great difference, the cases with which we deal dictate a general definition. It is, a religion sets forth a theory of the social order, for which divine or supernatural warrant is claimed, that defines what people are to do and explains how and why they are to do it: a way of life, a world-view, and a definition of the social entity – holy people, church, nation, for example – that embodies the way of life and appeals in explanation to the world-view. That definition presupposes that when we speak about a religion, we refer to a social group, that is, people who form a supernatural community by reason of their shared convictions, attitudes, and actions. So we see religion as fundamentally social, a mode of organizing humanity in community. Others may prefer to define religions as sets of beliefs that people share, still others may choose to emphasize the encounter with God as the starting-point for the definition of religion, and with them we have no argument.

But from our perspective, definitions that focus upon the intellectual or the psychological dimensions of religion pay insufficient attention to religion's power to create community and explain it; and we see as definitive of the religious reality the religious community, not the radically isolated individual facing God quite alone or the questing intellectual, sorting out God's truth. Hence our definition deliberately subordinates the intellectual and the experiential to the communal and the social.

Now we hardly need to wonder how one religion relates to some other, since, by definition, communities are self-sustaining and self-defining. It follows that, in general, the relationship of Islam to Christianity or Taoism to Buddhism hardly demands attention, except for the purpose of comparing and contrasting what each says about a shared agendum of topics, e.g. Islam's God is one, Christianity's triune. Nor does the relationship between one religion and another bear a self-evidently compelling interest for other than this-worldly, political reasons. That is to say, if we show that Christianity relates to Islam in one way, rather than in some other, is more like, or is like, the other in some detail, we do not on that account better understand either Christianity or Islam than we did before we made the comparison. It goes without saying, knowing that they conflict, or that the Nation of Islam and the Mystical Body of Christ have fought wars for a thousand years, conveys no deep understanding of either Islam or Christianity, such that a sustained discussion of how the one relates to the other yields any urgent insight. The upshot is, no self-evident purpose validates the kind of question we raise here, which is how one religion relates to another. That question, represented by the "in" of the title, *Judaism in the New Testament*, presupposes that we shall understand Christianity's first document better because of our grasp of the position of Judaism in the New Testament.

In the study of religion, no premise is better founded, by the testimony of all concerned, than that Christianity emerges out of Judaism. That is precisely how matters are represented from the very beginning. Not only so, but how Christianity relates to Judaism is universally taken to define a principal hermeneutical resource of New Testament studies. And the judgment is not a merely literary one, having to do with the interpretation of holy books. The Founder of Christianity, and all of his disciples and continuators, derived from Israel, believed Israel's Scriptures conveyed God's word, and understood this new way within Israel solely in terms provided by the Judaic setting. The way of life, world-view, and theory of the social entity or of "Israel" that earliest Christianity in all of its complex and rich diversity uniformly found definitive derived from the Hebrew

Scriptures, the Torah for Jesus and Paul as much as for their contemporaries, Hillel and Yohanan ben Zakkai. Scarcely a line of the New Testament is to be fully and exhaustively understood without reference to pertinent passages in the Old Testament. So the inquiry into the practice of and belief in Judaism for purposes of understanding the New Testament surely rests upon deep and sturdy foundations.

Yet the framing of the inquiry on second glance presents a puzzle, and it is that puzzle that accounts for our fresh interest in a much studied question. If it is the fact – and it is – that the Founder of Christianity as portrayed by the authoritative Scriptures saw himself as an Israelite within the framework of the Torah (in secular language: a Jew who practiced Judaism), and if all of his disciples did too, then would they – could they – have understood the question this book proposes to answer? Imagine, if you can, someone who has heard the Sermon on the Mount and has approached Jesus with a personal question: "How does what you say relate to the Torah?" (or, in secular categories, how do your teachings relate to Judaism?). Nothing in the Gospels' account of Jesus is more certain than his reply: "not to destroy but to fulfill," means, what I say is the Torah's message, and what I teach (in secular terms) is Judaism. No sage of the same time or place can have understood the question, since, for all, the Torah conveyed God's exact words to Israel, made God manifest to the world through Israel. Should we turn to the apostle, Paul, with the same question, he too would have responded with that same incomprehension, if perhaps a bit less patience as was his way. For Jesus and all who carried on his teachings saw themselves as Israelites (in secular language, as Jews), and they drew upon that same Torah that all Israel invoked. So the question that strikes us as obvious – what can we say about Judaism in the New Testament? – is one that would have elicited incomprehension among those about whom we inquire.

If that fact is self-evident, then we have to ask ourselves how we have formulated as a standard approach to the reading of the New Testament a perspective on matters that so sharply conflicts with the New Testament writers' own perspective. Insisting that they are Israel and teach the Torah, they would surely have rejected as not so much demeaning as simply uncomprehending a question resting on the contrary premise, namely, this teaching of theirs is not the Torah, and they are not Israel. And yet, two centuries of scholarship of a historical character, following close to eighteen centuries of scholarship of a theological character, sees matters differently. But understanding why that should be so hardly requires sustained reflection.

Because of long-standing divisions the New Testament is rarely understood as its Founder and his disciples conceived it to be, namely, as the Torah, or, in secular language, as Judaism. "Judaism" then is distinguished from "Christianity," and the two distinct religions are ordinarily spelled out, each in its own terms and categories, out of all relationship to the other. Certainly, in the passage of time, that is a perfectly natural path to take, since, after all, Christianity and Judaism do form the foundations of quite distinct and autonomous religious communities, each with its own world-view, way of life, and theory of the social entity (for a Judaism, "Israel"). Why then should anyone ever reconsider the simple and obvious "fact" that the writers of the New Testament composed the foundation-document for Christianity? And if the writings were generated within that setting, it must follow, their relationship to Judaism, their response to its teachings and utilization of its theology and law form valid points of analytical inquiry.

The multiplicity of Judaisms in the early centuries of the Common Era has made ever more parlous the insistence upon a single Judaism, from which Christianity took its leave and against which Christianity is to be contrasted (whether favorably or otherwise, depending on the polemical purpose) that still marks study of Judaism in the New Testament. No one has succeeded in so defining a single Judaism everywhere ascendant, unifying all the Jews and excluding everybody else, as to account for all of the conflicting evidence. A Judaism so general that it encompasses Enoch, the writings found at the Dead Sea, Josephus, Philo, the Elephantine papyri, and the Mishnah – not to mention the (uninterpreted) books of the Hebrew Scriptures of ancient Israel ("the Old Testament") proves trivial. If so many diverse circles, all of them claiming to form "Israel" and to set forth God's message out of the Torah, each of them reaching conclusions not so much in disagreement with everybody else but out of all relationship with those of all other parties, are joined in a single conversation, taken all together, they yield a Judaism that covers everybody and turns out so thin and trivial as not to engage anybody. Whether, then, the Judaism adhered to by all Judaisms consisted of the belief in the unity of God, the Torah, the Temple, covenantal nomism, or what have you scarcely proves consequential when we realize nothing important to the various circles of Judaic faithful represented by the public, preserved documents in hand comes within that definition. A definition that appeals to the lowest common denominator serves in the end to include everything but to explain nothing. By contrast, when we recognize that each set of documents works out of its particular premises and presuppositions, representing a set of choices concerning urgent questions that demand response, self-evidently valid answers that require articulation, we can take into hand the entire corpus of evidence, without homogenization, harmonization, or, worst of all, trivialization.

At issue in the study of *a Judaism* – we can no longer speak of a single governing Judaism, any more than the diversity of earliest Christian writing sustains the view of a single Christianity – is the givens of its critical documents, and how these givens coalesce into an account of (a very particular) Judaism. If we speak of a Judaic system, rather than a Judaism, as we shall suggest in Chapter One and spell out concretely in Chapter Two, our task then becomes, how to describe, analyze, and interpret as a Judaic system a body of writings held by the faithful to cohere. And while the answer in the end proves not so much compelling as self-evident, the perspective turns out quite jarring and fresh. So in these pages we review familiar documents in a different perspective. And, as we shall see, that does make a considerable difference.

The difference emerges as soon as we reflect on how the conception of a single uniform Judaism affects the framing of the question of "the relationship of the New Testament to Judaism," for as soon as we dismiss as hopelessly in conflict with diverse data the notion of a single uniform, operative, ubiquitous Judaism, the relationship of the New Testament to Judaism ceases to define a comprehensible issue at all. We revert here to the ancient insistence of Christianity that Christianity forms the natural next step from Sinai and the fulfillment of Sinai, not so much to precipitate a debate on whether or indeed how that statement is so, as to reflect upon the implication, for the prevailing formulation of matters. How shall we recast the issue of Judaism in the New Testament, practices and beliefs, when the issue is not how a new religion relates to, carries over or rejects an old one? The framing of matters changes when the issue is how a free-standing formulation of a received and shared heritage – the Hebrew Scriptures – has taken over and made its own statement through writings that others, also, have taken over and restated as well. It is no longer to their relationship with a single, alien Judaism "out there" that the New Testament writings attest. Rather, it is to how those writings have cast themselves into a Judaism. And since, as a matter of fact, we can understand a great deal of the New Testament writings out of the pages of what the New Testament handed forward as the Old Testament – not every word by any means, but a great, great deal – the reading of the New Testament's Judaism – its own practices and beliefs – proves more to the point and fits tightly into context.

People take for granted that Judaism contributes a principal formative force for the emergence of New Testament Christianity. We understand the New Testament solely in the setting of Judaism. We propose, by contrast, that we understand the New Testament still better when we regard it *as the statement of Judaism*, that is, from its writers' perspective, the New Testament at every point formed that very same Judaism that the Old Testament had adumbrated. In these pages we propose to examine the premises of a number of key documents, analyzed as we would analyze counterpart writings for any (other) Judaism, and what we uncover is the iron conviction that the writers set forth the Torah of Sinai. That conclusion will not have surprised any Catholic, or, later on, Reformation Christian thinker from the first century to the nineteenth; everyone understood that Marcion's rejection of the Old Testament violated that pattern of Christian truth to which nearly everybody adhered. For Marcion, the second-century heretic, wanted to acknowledge only the New Testament, denying Christianity as a Judaism (or, in today's conventional language, denying Christianity's foundation in Judaism). These days, it is only those unChristian Bible Society editions of the New Testament and Psalms, omitting the rest of Christianity before Christ (in the language of the author of the Epistle to the Hebrews), that conform to Marcion's heretical view. The Pope, for Roman Christianity, and the leaders and governing bodies of all Protestant communions, as well as the heads of the Orthodox Christian churches, unanimously affirm otherwise.

But if as Christianity – Catholic, Orthodox, and Reformation – has always insisted, the two Testaments form one faith, and, in the nature of things, call it Judaism, call it Christianity, it is the single and exhaustive faith of Sinai, then the formulation of matters that presently prevails, which sees Christianity as separate from Judaism and not as a Judaism but an alien and new thing, must give way. Then arguing about the Jewishness of Jesus or of Paul or Peter or the Evangelists emerges as disingenuous; it is like asking about the influence of Judaism upon Aqiba or Hillel, Judah the Patriarch, who sponsored the Mishnah at the end of the second century CE, or upon Yohanan and Simeon b. Laqish, Joseph, Rabbah, Abbayye, and Raba, of the third and fourth centuries, who founded the Talmud and so defined the Judaism that has held the field from their time to ours.

They took for granted that they continued the Torah of Sinai and its tradition, saying precisely what it meant then and for all time, and so did the Evangelists and Paul and the other New Testament writers. They deemed it a fact that theirs was the valid reading of the Torah, and so did their Christian counterparts. The category "Judaism" scarcely pertains, since for none, Christian or Judaic, was "Judaism" a native category.

But what difference does that observation, so entirely coherent with Christian self-understanding throughout history, make? Once we reject the premise that Christianity negates Judaism, and see that Christianity must be placed within its setting as a Judaism, alongside others, what follows is that the description of Christianity from the premise of its essentially alien and estranged relationship with Judaism (that is, other Judaisms, appealing to the same Scriptures) is worthless, because misleading and distorting. Recognizing a number of Judaisms of the same time and place, all of them adhering to a common structure but each different from the others at every important point, we no longer conceive the analytical category, "Judaism versus the New Testament," to define a sensible inquiry. Instead, we try to see matters in such a way that we read the New Testament in its own Judaic context. It defines Judaism – its Judaism, speaking descriptively and after the fact – and how we read the document as a Judaism remains to be seen.

Here we argue that, since, from the perspective of the New Testament writers, theirs was the sole fully authentic statement of the meaning of the Torah (a.k.a., "the Old Testament"), the old premise misleads. For the premise of all accounts of Judaism in the setting of the New Testament rests upon the judgment that Judaism was one religion, Christianity another, different religion, taking shape out of, but against the grain of, the prior and continuing religion. One cannot proceed very far into any of the definitive documents of the New Testament without encountering a given that calls such a premise into question. Christianity did not understand itself as anything other than the natural continuation of the Judaism represented by the Hebrew Scriptures of ancient Israel. The plan of our work is simple. We begin with a clear account of the context in which we investigate the relationship of Judaism and the New Testament, covering Chapters One and Two. We proceed in Chapters Three through Five to take up important New Testament writings, now read as components of a Judaism. Every Judaism starts with the definition of its "Israel," and so does that of our New Testament system. It is appropriate to begin with the earliest documents of the New Testament, the writings of Paul. We turn next to ask some fundamental questions about the way of life of the Christian system of Judaism, and those questions draw us to a rereading of important sayings attributed to Jesus by the Gospels. Here we find the system defining itself, its "Israel," in yet another fashion, now as a way of inclusion and exclusion. Finally, we ask about the system's world-view, and for that purpose we reread the reappropriation of Israel's supernatural history by Christianity accomplished in the Epistle to the Hebrews. No one familiar with how "our sages of blessed memory" in the Rabbinic writings reappropriated that same history and made it their own will find the modes of thought of Hebrews unfamiliar or the result beyond plausibility. In this way we mean to offer an example of the Judaic reading of Christianity, the presentation of Christianity in its original writings as a Judaism. Success for this effort of ours will be signaled by other and different efforts at accomplishing the same exercise of religious history.

It remains to note that Mr Neusner wrote the first drafts of the Introduction and Chapters One, Two, Three, half of Four, and Six, Mr Chilton, half of Chapter Four and all of Chapters Five, Six, and Seven. Each author then revised the chapters initially written by the other. The book speaks for both authors at every point.

1

JUDAISM IN THE
NEW TESTAMENT OR
THE NEW TESTAMENT'S
PARTICULAR JUDAISM?

RELIGIOUS DIVERSITY WITHIN JUDAISM

Diversities within religions come to expression in a variety of ways. Examining all evidences of Christianity or of Judaism, within some broad limits, we find everything and its opposite. The very diversity of the written evidence (not to mention the archaeological evidence) shows what is at stake. Two sets of statements suffice. The Pope, heir of Peter, is head of the Church; all Church authority rests with the local presbytery; there is no Church authority at all. The Torah is the literal word of God in all details, so that, therefore, all who wish to be "Israel" must keep the Torah precisely as it is worded. The Torah expresses God's will and purpose for humanity, but the formulation is this-worldly. The Torah is the work of humanity, the record of aspiration, not revelation. The first three statements clearly belong to any description of Christianity, the issue being a solely, particularly Christian one. But the three statements cannot all be true, since each contradicts the other two. All three in context clearly speak for a Christianity, but not for Christianity in general. That is why we have to take account of not only the definition of Christianity but also the delineation, within Christianity, of Christianities. And the same clearly pertains to Judaism. A statement that purports to state the truth about the Torah obviously belongs to Judaism; but these three statements, all of which cannot be true, certainly require us to recognize that there are diverse Judaisms.

Now the question emerges: precisely where and how, on what basis, shall we identify data that coalesce to form a single Christianity or a single Judaism? How am I supposed to know which statements,

1

which I may find in a variety of writings, speak on behalf of one Judaism, which on behalf of another? And what is the starting-point?

A familiar definition of "Judaism" or of a Judaism responds to the rules of theology: one Judaism is right, another wrong. We therefore define Judaism by selecting those statements of truth, those norms of behavior and belief, that conform to a given theological position, and reject as irrelevant all contradictory statements, dismissing as heretical the books that contain them. So our work of defining Judaism commences with a theological principle, a fundamental idea governing the entire work of description. On that basis, we validate the resort to the-ism, that is to say, "Juda-ism," by which we assume we refer to a systematic, orderly, coherent, proportioned, balanced, and authoritative statement of religious beliefs and norms of behavior.

This same "Judaism" can be analyzed (by appeal to its canon), advocated (by reference to arguments on behalf of its clearly defined propositions as to truth), and set forth in comparison and contrast to other religions, also presented as philosophically cogent theological systems. Indeed, nearly all definitions of Judaism derive from philosophical modes of thought and appeal in the end to a predetermined canon of accepted and authoritative writings. Then, to answer the question just now set forth, the data that instruct me on the positions of Judaism derive from the canon. We know the documents that bear weight because Judaism identifies those documents – and dismisses all others. And our starting-point is the intellectual construct, Judaism, itself.

That familiar, theological approach to the definition of a religion, here exemplified by Judaism, does not serve very well in describing a religion that contains a variety of writings that contradict one another and that self-evidently derive from diverse groups of persons. In the case of Judaism in the first centuries BC and AD, for example, we find a variety of documents that scarcely intersect. If we invoke any criterion we think likely to characterize a variety of writings – a single doctrine concerning the Torah, the Messiah, the definition of who and what is "Israel," for example – we find no one answer present in all writings, and no point of agreement which unites them. Not only so, but both archaeological and text analysis insist that the various writings were produced by diverse groups and do not speak for one and the same community of persons at all.

If moreover we introduce conceptions paramount in prior writings, e.g. Scripture, or later writings, e.g. the Mishnah, Talmuds, and Midrash-compilations, we may well discover that the writings of the first centuries BC and AD do what they will with the former – there being no consensus on what any inherited ideas maintain – and exhibit entire ignorance of the latter. It follows that the theological approach to the definition of a religion, which utilizes philosophical methods in the search for a coherent statement of, and about, a religion, requires us to pick and choose among the data. But what, for purposes of a merely descriptive definition, validates doing so? And how are we supposed to know what to pick and what to discard?

It follows that where we find statements on behalf of Judaism, which clearly contradict other statements on behalf of Judaism, speaking descriptively and not theologically, we address not one right or true Judaism and another wrong or false Judaism but only two Judaisms. And everything that follows rests upon these two foundations: first, the definition of a religion is not a problem in theology, and, second, the definition of a religion takes account of diverse religious systems that all together form the data of that particular, encompassing religion. That is, first, if we hope to describe our data, leading to our work of analysis and interpretation, we shall find our work impeded if we introduce questions of truth or falsity. The reason is that answering those questions requires criteria of right and wrong, e.g. a clear definition of the character of revealed truth and the authority and standing of the Torah in particular. And, second, our task is to encompass all the data pertinent to a given religion, not only those data that cohere or that coincide with a particular theological, and anti-historical, presupposition or premise concerning description in general.

Doctrines of truth or error and the meaning, content, and character of revelation derive from theology; they are particular to the Judaism that appeals to those doctrines to validate its various positions on matters of conduct and conviction alike. If, then, we raise questions of truth or falsity in the description of a Judaism or of Judaism or of all Judaisms, we beg the very questions we propose to answer. This we do by invoking as an answer to the question what is in fact part of the question itself. Stated very simply: description of a religion cannot invoke theological norms, but can only encompass those norms within the labor of description itself.

In our view, we do best to start with documents that enjoy official status, that is, canonical writings. We investigate what those documents say, but then we ask also about the premises upon which their statements rest, the givens and the presuppositions exposed in explicit and articulated allegations. We turn, specifically, to the systemic documents – the writings held to bring to authoritative expression whatever a given religious system wishes to say. A systemic document is canonical writing accorded authoritative standing by a religious community. It contains information deemed both true and important, facts held to be consequential, bearing self-evident implications for conduct and conviction alike. The religious community preserves such a document because the writing stands for the community and sets forth a component of the community's way of life and world-view.

But, in the nature of things, such a document may well convey facts or truths that others, outside of the community that values and preserves the document, accept as well. Not everything contained in canonical writings of a given group needs to be contrasted against opinions held in other circles or communities. Where a number of distinct groups have taken shape within a larger social world, all these groups, as well as the world in which they flourish, may well concur on a broad variety of topics. Consequently, a document that speaks for a specific and distinct group within that larger world may well go over ground quite familiar to others, outside the group itself. What that document says, then, constitutes the religious system's explicit message. What the same document presupposes leads us deep into that system's implicit conceptions, the deep, dense structure of its theory of how things are. In this book and its companions, we aim to identify principal parts of the Judaism – the Judaic religious system – that comes to explicit expression in the canonical writings of the Judaism of the dual Torah.

CHRISTIANITY A JUDAISM

The practice and belief of Judaism in the New Testament – a collection of writings produced for and by Israelites who revered the Torah as God's word or, in secular terms, for and by faithful Jews, educated in Judaism – have long been treated as alien components of Christianity's formative faith and its initial writing. That given of religion is contained in the title, *Judaism in the New Testament*, that is, a foreign body in a familiar one. But the earliest Christians insisted that they formed "Israel" and devoted rigorous thought to the demonstration that theirs was the Torah's sole valid meaning and their Founder its unique medium of fulfillment. In due course they produced the New Testament, but for at least the first hundred years of Christianity their only revealed Scripture was that same Torah that (the rest of) Israel received as God's revealed teaching. So far as possible, these same people appealed to the Torah to validate their faith and studied the Torah to explain it.

So by their own word what they set forth in the New Testament must qualify as Judaism, and they insisted (as vigorously as any other Judaic system-builders) the only Judaism. Judaisms known to us over time follow suit: ours is the Torah, and we form Israel, the holy people. True, early on, the Gospel of John would fiercely condemn "the Jews" and blame them for the crucifixion. But even John valued Israel and certainly adhered to the Torah as he read it. While later on a shift in category-formation distinguished between Judaism and Christianity, even here Christianity insisted on its patrimony and inheritance out of ancient Israel. Not only so, but Christianity would represent itself for all time as the sole valid continuation of the faith and worship of ancient Israel. That is to say, Christianity portrayed itself as (other) Judaisms ordinarily portrayed themselves, and out of precisely the same shared Torah at that.

Consequently, to distinguish between the religious world of the New Testament and an alien Judaism denies the authors of the New Testament books their most fiercely held claim and renders incomprehensible much that they said. Whether Jesus, insisting on his Judaic conception of God's kingdom, or Paul, explaining how in his Judaic conception of Israel through Christ gentiles enter (are "grafted onto") Israel, whether the Evangelists, linking Jesus to the house of David and much that he said and did to Israelite prophecy, or the author of the Letter to the Hebrews recasting the entire history of Israel from an account of salvation to one of sanctification – the picture is uniform. But then how can we grasp the New Testament's Judaism if we do not treat its religion as (a) Judaism?

That simple observation explains why here we see the New Testament as the statement of Judaism (more suitably, a Judaism, among many), and further accounts for our insistence that Christianity's practices and beliefs for its writers and their audience constituted (a) Judaism and are to be interpreted as such. Responding as we do to the self-understanding of the writings before us, how do we effect the simple change that strikes us as self-evidently required? As we shall explain in a moment, we simply bring to its logical conclusion the widely understood fact that, in antiquity as today, many Judaisms competed. Most knowledgeable people now reject the conception of a single Judaism, everywhere paramount. A requirement of theology, the dogma of a single, valid Judaism contradicts the facts of history at every point in the history of Judaism, which finds its dynamic in the on-going struggle among Judaisms to gain the position of the sole, authentic re-presentation of the Torah. Further, along with the notion of a single official Judaism, we give up the notion of a unitary, internally harmonious Judaism, a lowest common denominator among a variety of diverse statements and systems. And logic further insists that we let go of the notion of an incremental, cumulative, "traditional" Judaism. At the same time, and for the same reason, we dismiss as vacuous and hopelessly general the notion of a single Judaism characteristic of a given age, e.g. the first century BC and AD, and we reject as groundless the conception that all documents of said age tell us about one and the same religious community, therefore, a single "Israel" and its Torah. It follows that the sources of a given period of time do not tell us about a single Judaism, characteristic of that time. They tell us about their writers' premises, the Judaic thinking that underpins the Judaic system they have put forth – and that alone.

These closely linked conceptions – singular, harmonious, cumulative, and traditional – contradict the character of the evidence of all Judaisms of antiquity. If we open one set of coherent writings, we find one self-evidently valid answer to a cogent and pressing question, and if we open another set, we find a different answer to a different question. In the one, a given composite of proof-texts will predominate, in the other, a different composite, so it appears that one set of writings speaks of one topic to one group, another set of a different topic to another group. In all, viewed as a conglomerate, the various writings appear to form the statements of different people talking about different things to different people. And that view takes on even greater specificity when we realize that, so far as the diverse writings talk about the same issues at all, they present a mass of contradictions. Archaeological evidence for its part portrays synagogues rich in precisely the images that the written evidence tells us we should not find. So, in all, the conception of diverse, free-standing Judaisms best accommodates the evidence produced in ancient times (in secular categories) by Jews in the name of Judaism, or (in native categories) by Israel in the Torah.

Included in that statement is not only the iron datum that the New Testament writers saw themselves as Israelites teaching the meaning of the Torah, which none can contest, but also the givens of the authors of the documents at Qumran, the writers of the Elephantine papyri, the compositors of the Mishnah, the compilers of the Talmud, and the authorities behind the documentary statements of every other Judaism of antiquity. All writers addressing a community of faithful wrote on the premise that the writers and those who would value, preserve, and conform to those writings formed "Israel" and practiced the Torah (the native category for which the secular one is "Judaism").

Accordingly, we do not conceive that all writings point to a single Judaism, because the points of differentiation and even contradiction produced by a comparison of one set of writings with another render such a conception unlikely. Then what to do? We concentrate not on all writings of a given period but on some sets of kindred writings to ask about the Judaism that forms the foundation and the premise of that set of writings. That is, once we recognize the diverse character of various bodies of Judaic writings, we take up a single body of what appear on the surface to be closely congruent documents and read them. It follows, in its method, ours is a documentary approach to the study of (a) Judaism. For we insist that each piece of writing or set of cognate writings tells us about the Judaism to which it wishes to attest. We reject the notion that all writings inform us about one and the same Judaism, because we see too vast a diversity, too complex a range of disagreement, among the various writings to allow all to speak to a single religious tradition, even to find the lowest common denominator for their supposedly common address.

Then what? Once we abandon the idea that all (acceptable, canonical) writings speak of one and the same Judaism, one that is cumulative, traditional, and paramount, then a new possibility comes to the fore. It is that each writing that speaks for a single, coherent community of Jews will tell us about its religious system – its Judaism – and, further, take its place in the arena of comparison and contrast with other such Judaic religious systems. We no longer treat all Judaisms as exemplary of one Judaism nor assign priority to one over another, nor, yet, treat one Judaism as in any way related to, influenced by, or dependent upon another Judaism, whether of the prior or of the same age. We may compare and contrast Judaisms (the system of the New Testament with that of the Mishnah, for example), and temporal considerations – the one comes prior to and influences the other, for example – no longer govern the making of comparisons.

And that observation brings us back to the task of this book and the question we here propose to answer. Once we have defined our interest as not a single Judaism supposedly covering everybody but the Christians (there are no other candidates for exclusion!), then, it follows, we take to heart the Christians' insistence that they formed (an) Israel or a part of Israel, so their writings too have to be read alongside those of all other Judaic groups that saw themselves as (an) Israel or as part of Israel. But that changes the very framing of the question, what is the role of Judaism in the New Testament? It becomes, what does the New Testament look like when we understand it as the statement of a Judaism, that is, the religious world-view, way of life, and theory of "Israel" of a group of Jews whose writings we possess?

THE JUDAISM OF THE NEW TESTAMENT

Hence the proper title of this book should be "*the* Judaism *of* the New Testament," since we regard the New Testament as the documentary statement of a community of faithful practitioners of (a) Judaism, comparable to the documentary statements – in other terms to be sure – of other communities of faithful practitioners of other Judaisms. We take seriously the insistence of diverse social groups of Jews that they formed (an) "Israel," the (sole remnant of the) people whom God loved for their acceptance of the Torah at Sinai. Each such group, distinguishing itself from others of Israel (the people), set forth the Torah as it understood the Torah, and all groups defined for themselves an urgent question and a self-evidently valid answer that, for the respective groups, formed their Judaism. How do these broadly recognized facts concerning Judaisms in ancient times change matters so far as earliest Christianity's greatest literary evidence is concerned? In the setting of the diversity of social groups and their viewpoints in ancient Israel, we therefore cannot treat the New Testament as a foreign body, asking about how an alien religion played its part in the formation of that body. We rather see a variety of Judaic religious groups as equally representative Judaisms, all of them heirs to the same Scripture, every one of them insisting on the unique truth it alone possessed.

We propose here to spell out the implications for the reading of the New Testament of the now widespread recognition of the diversity of Judaisms in ancient times, before, during, and after the first century. While many discussions of Judaism and the New Testament recognize the profoundly Israelite character of the New Testament, so far as we know, none has recast matters in the way we do here. That is, if we really think that there were many Judaisms and no one orthodox Judaism, and if we truly maintain that the Jews comprised a diverse group with more points of diversity than uniformity, then how should we think, also, about the New Testament in its original context: writings by Jews for Jews who formed a very special "Israel?" Hence the title we might have used, the Judaism of the New Testament, meaning, a systematic reading of the New Testament as a document meant to set forth a Judaism, a Judaic system (language we explain presently). That is, by comparison to the Judaisms of other writings valued by groups of Judaic faithful in the same time and place, how do these writings comprise a Judaism?

If that title would have puzzled more readers than it would have beckoned, our intent will hardly present a surprise to the many people who see earliest Christianity in the framework just now outlined. We propose to explain not so much why but how the New Testament should be read as documents of the Judaism they champion, among other Judaisms of antiquity, and in insisting upon the multiplicity of Judaisms at that time and upon the integral place of the communities of Christian believers among those Judaisms, we replicate the very perspectives of the documents and their authors themselves. For they held that they formed Israel, and, in our categories, theirs was a Judaism (that is, the Torah). Hence to speak of the Judaism in the New Testament frames matters in a way that violates the native category of that document, since it treats as distinct entities – Judaism, the New Testament community of faithful – what those who composed the books assumed belonged together. We do not suggest ours is the sole or the best possible reading of the New Testament's Judaism, but we do offer an account of the New Testament in the context of Judaisms that takes account of how, in general, people today understand the character of Judaism in ancient times.

What happens when we carry out a shift in perspective, changing the refraction of our spectacles in favor of one that affords greater precision of vision? We hope that the familiar will become clearer and more distinct, that what can have produced confusion will now turn out to clarify and explain. The facts will persist, but they will serve a different purpose. Our argument here depends upon a single premise: a fresh way of asking about Judaism in the New Testament will prove illuminating, a shift of perspective both providing provocation for fresh thought on familiar subjects and also deeper understanding of enduring problems. Once we ask how the New Testament serves as documents of various Judaisms, writings valued by communities that saw themselves as uniquely (even exclusively) Israel, as much as the library found at Qumran is generally taken to represent a free-standing Judaic structure and system, the remnant of Israel, our reading of the foundation-documents of Christianity is going to yield dimensions of meaning that we should otherwise have missed. And yet the fundamental proposition of this reading of Judaism in the New Testament's practice and belief accords entirely with the givens of every writer in the New Testament.

FROM ONE UNIVERSAL JUDAISM UNIVERSALLY ATTESTED FOR A GIVEN AGE TO A SINGULAR JUDAISM ATTESTED BY A COHERENT CANON

It follows that here we approach a classic problem – how to understand the New Testament in the setting of Judaism – by shifting the frame of reference from a period of time to a specific document. That is, it is commonplace to portray a single, universal, traditional Judaism described out of diverse evidence for a given era. But, recognizing no single, universal, cumulative Judaism everywhere paramount, we also differentiate among accounts of diverse groups, preserved in their canonical writings. And we ask ourselves, how do we understand the New Testament's Christianity if we recognize no single, universal traditional Judaism, from which Christianity supposedly took its leave, but rather diverse Judaisms, of which those set forth in the New Testament count as several among a greater number? So we undertake to understand the New Testament's religious system (indifferent to whether we call it Judaism or Christianity) as Judaisms among Judaisms. That is what happens when we recognize the facts of diversity and no longer assume a uniformity of faith to which all documents attest, hence the move from a period of time to a specific document and the religious system of the group that values that document.

Like all simple ideas, this one finds its provocation in an ambitious and systematic statement of a quite wrong conception. Specifically, we owe the idea for this book to Professor E. P. Sanders, Duke University, who, in his *Judaism. 63 BCE–66 CE Practice and Belief,*[1] has given us a single, unitary, cumulative, traditional "Judaism." That, specifically, explains why our title mimics his. We agree that to describe a Judaism, focus rests upon belief and practice, the latter without the former standing for orthopraxy (of which more below, pp. 19–41), the former without the latter contradicting the practiced and social character of religions. In place of his dates, 63–66, we introduce *in the New Testament.* After *Judaism,* we could have substituted for *in the New Testament* such alternative systems as *in*

10

the Mishnah or *in the Dead Sea Library at Qumran* or *in the Talmud* or *in* any other body of Judaic writings closely associated with a particular social entity of Israel. For we concur that belief and practice form the organizing categories, though, as we make clear, we add a third, which is, theory of the social order or "Israel." But for reasons now spelled out, Sanders clearly errs by claiming to tell us anything consequential about a single common-denominator Judaism, to which every document of any value attests. That is, Sanders speaks of a homogeneous Judaism in a particular period, covering all Jews everywhere and drawing upon all documents that are supposed to tell us about that period. That Judaism is cumulative, the product of centuries of agglutination; it is uniform; it is geographically and socially distributive and normative; all Jews adhered to this Judaism, whatever the special traits they further imputed to that same Judaism. Sanders thus matches a single, unitary Judaism against that single, unitary Christianity that took its leave of said Judaism and defined itself by contrast and opposition to it.

Let us dwell on a single example of the definition of a single Judaism out of all the sources, read all together, that of E. P. Sanders, to which reference has already been made. Sanders thinks that any and every source, whoever wrote it, without regard to its time or place or venue, tells us about one and the same Judaism. The only way to see everything all together and all at once is to rise high above the evidence, so high that we no longer see the lines of rivers, the height of mountains, the undulations of plains – any of the details of the earth's true configuration. This conflation of all sources yields a fabricated Judaism. The result of this Judaic equivalent of a "harmony of the Gospels" is more often than not a dreary progress through pointless information.

This fabrication of a single Judaism is supposed to tell us something that pertains equally to all: the Judaism that forms the basis for all the sources, the common denominator among them all. If we know a book or an artifact is "Jewish," then we are supposed automatically to know various other facts about said book or artifact. But the upshot is either too general to mean much (for example, monotheism) or too abstract to form an intelligible statement. Let me be specific. How Philo will have understood the Dead Sea Scrolls, or the authors of apocalyptic writings will have understood those of the Mishnah-passages Sanders admits to his account of Judaism from 63 BC to 66 AD, we are never told. Each of these distinctive documents gets to speak whenever Sanders wants it to; none is ever brought into relationship

11

– comparison and contrast – with any other. The homogenization of Philo, the Mishnah, the Dead Sea Scrolls, Ben Sira, apocryphal and pseudepigraphic writings, the results of archaeology, and on and on and on turns out to yield generalizations about a religion that none of those responsible for the evidence at hand will have recognized: lifeless, dull, hopelessly abstract, lacking all social relevance. After a while, readers come to realize, it hardly matters, the results reaching so stratospheric a level of generalization that all precise vision of real people practicing a vivid religion is lost.

To understand what goes into Sanders' picture of Judaism, let us now provide a reasonable sample (pp. 103–4), representative of the whole, namely the opening paragraphs of his discussion, chapter seven, entitled "Sacrifices:"

The Bible does not offer a single, clearly presented list of sacrifices. The legal books (Exodus, Leviticus, Numbers and Deuteronomy), we know now, incorporate various sources from different periods, and priestly practice evidently varied from time to time. There are three principal sources of information about sacrifices in the first century: Josephus, Philo and the Mishnah. On most points they agree among themselves and with Leviticus and Numbers; consequently the main outline of sacrifices is not in dispute. Josephus, in our judgment, is the best source. He knew what the common practice of the priesthood of his day was: he had learned it in school, as a boy he had watched and assisted, and as an adult he had worked in the temple. It is important for evaluating his evidence to note that his description of the sacrifices sometimes disagrees with Leviticus or goes beyond it. This is not an instance in which he is simply summarizing what is written in the Bible: he is almost certainly depending on what he had learned as a priest.

Though the Mishnah is often right with regard to pre-70 temple practice, many of the discussions are from the second century: the rabbis continued to debate rules of sacrifice long after living memory of how it had been done had vanished. Consequently, in reading the Mishnah one is sometimes reading second-century theory. Occasionally this can be seen clearly. For example, there is a debate about whether or not the priest who sacrificed an animal could keep its hide if for any reason the animal was made invalid (e.g. by touching something impure) after it was sacrificed but before it was flayed. The mishnah on this topic opens with an anonymous opinion, according to which the priest did not get the hide. R. Hanina the Prefect of the Priests disagreed: "Never have we seen a hide taken out to the place of burning"; that is, the priests always kept the hides. R. Akiba (early second century) accepted this and was of the view that the priests could keep the hides of invalid sacrifices. "The Sages," however, ruled the other way (*Zevahim* 12.4). R. Hanina the Prefect of the Priests apparently worked in the temple before 70, but survived its destruction and became part of the rabbinic movement. Akiba died *c.* 135; 'the sages' of this passage are probably his contemporaries or possibly the rabbis of the next generation. Here we see that second-century rabbis were quite willing to vote against actual practice in discussing the behavior of the priests and the rules they followed. The problem with using the Mishnah is that there is very seldom this sort of reference to pre-70 practice that allows us to make critical distinctions: not only are we often reading second-century discussions, we may be learning only second-century theory.

Philo had visited the temple, and some of his statements about it (e.g. the guards) seem to be based on personal knowledge. But his discussion of the sacrifices is "bookish", and at some important points it reveals that he is passing on information derived from the Greek translation of the Hebrew Bible (the Septuagint), not from observation. The following description basically follows the Hebrew Bible and Josephus, but it sometimes incorporates details from other sources.

One may make the following distinctions among sacrifices:

With regard to what was offered: meal, wine, birds (doves or pigeons) and quadrupeds (sheep, goats and cattle).

With regard to who provided the sacrifice: the community or an individual.

With regard to the purpose of the sacrifice: worship of and communion with God, glorification of him, thanksgiving, purification, atonement for sin, and feasting.

With regard to the disposition of the sacrifice: it was either burned or eaten. The priests got most of the food that sacrifices provided, though one of the categories of sacrifice provided food for the person who brought it and his family and friends. The Passover lambs were also eaten by the worshippers.

Sacrifices were conceived as meals, or, better, banquets. The full and ideal sacrificial offering consisted of meat, cereal, oil and wine. (Numbers 14:1–10, *Ant.* 3.233f.; the menu was sometimes reduced: see below).

Now let us ask ourselves, what, exactly, does Sanders wish to tell his readers about the sacrifices in this account of *Judaism. Practice and Belief*? He starts in the middle of things. He assumes we know what he means by "sacrifices," why they are important, what they meant, so all we require is details. He will deal with Josephus, Philo, the Mishnah, and Leviticus and Numbers. Does he then tell us the distinctive viewpoint of each? Not at all. All he wants us to know is the facts common to them all. Hence his procedure is not one of description, analysis, and interpretation of documents, but a conflation of the information contained in each that he deems usable. Since that is his principal concern, he discusses "sacrifice" by telling us why the Mishnah's information is useless, except when it is usable. But Sanders never suggests to his readers what the Mishnah's discussion of sacrifice wishes to find out, nor how its ideas on the subject may prove religiously engaging. It is just a rule book, so it has no ideas on the subject – so Sanders; that is not our view. Philo is then set forth. Here too we are told why he tells us nothing, but not what he tells us. Then there follows the facts, the indented "with regard to" paragraphs.

Sanders did not have to tell us all about how Leviticus, Numbers, Philo, and Josephus and the Mishnah concur, then about how we may ignore or must cite the several documents respectively, if his sole intent was to tell us the facts of the "with regard to . . ." paragraphs. And how he knows how "sacrifices were conceived," who conceived them in this way, and what sense the words made ("worship of and communion with God, glorification of him, thanksgiving, purification, atonement for sin, and feasting"), and to whom they made sense, and how other Judaisms, besides the Judaism portrayed by Philo, Josephus, the Mishnah, and so on and so forth, viewed sacrifices, or the Temple as it was – none of this is set forth. The conflation has its own purpose, which the following outline of the remainder of the chapter reveals: community sacrifices; individual sacrifices ("Neither Josephus, Philo, nor other first-century Jews thought that burnt offerings provided God with food"), a family at the temple, an example; the daily temple routine. In this mass of information on a subject, one question is lost: what it all meant. Sanders really does suppose that he is telling us how things were, what people did, and, in his stress on common-denominator Judaism, he finds it entirely reasonable to bypass all questions of analysis and interpretation and so forgets to tell us what it all meant. His language, "worship of and communion with God, glorification of him, thanksgiving, purification, atonement for sin, and feasting" – that Protestant formulation begs every question and answers none.

But this common-denominator Judaism yields little that is more than simply banal, for "common theology," e.g. "The history of Israel in general, and of our period in particular, shows that Jews believed that the one God of the universe had given them his law and that they were to obey it" (p. 240). No one, obviously, can disagree, but what applies to everyone equally, in a nation so riven with division and rich in diversity, also cannot make much of a difference. That is to say, knowing that they all were monotheists or valued the Hebrew Scriptures (but which passages he does not identify, how he read them he does not say) does not tell us more than previously we knew about the religion of those diverse people. Sanders knows what people thought, because anything any Jew wrote tells us what "Jews" or most Jews or people in general thought. He proceeds to cite as evidence of what "Jews" thought opinions of Philo and Josephus, the Dead Sea Scrolls, rabbinic literature, and so on and so forth. The generality of scholarship understands that the Dead Sea Scrolls represent their writers, Philo speaks for Philo, Josephus says what he thinks, and the Mishnah is whatever it is and is not whatever it is not. No one, to our knowledge, until Sanders has come to the judgment that anything any Jew thought has to have been in the mind of all the other Jews.

But it is only with that premise that we can understand the connections Sanders makes and the conclusions about large, general topics that he reaches. Let us skim through his treatment of graven images, which captures the flavor of the whole (pp. 244–7):

> Comments by Philo and Josephus show how Jews could interpret other objects symbolically and thus make physical depictions acceptable, so that they were not seen as transgressions of one of the Ten Commandments, but as symbols of the glory of the God who gave them.

There follows a reference to *War* 5:214. Then Sanders proceeds: "Josephus, as did Philo, found astral and other symbolism in many other things. . . ." Some paragraphs later, in the same context, we have:

> The sun was personified and worshipped. . . . The most imporant

15

instance was when Josiah . . . instituted a reform of worship . . . [now with reference to 2 Kings 23:4f.]. This is usually regarded as having been a decisive rejection of other deities, but elements derived from sun worship continued. Subsequently Ezekiel attacked those who turned "their backs to the Temple of the Lord . . ." (Ezekiel 8:16). According to the Mishnah, at one point during the feast of Booths priests "turned their faces to the west," recalling that their predecessors had faced east and worshipped the sun and proclaimed that "our eyes are turned toward the Lord" (Sukkah 5:4). Despite this, the practice that Ezekiel condemned was continued by some. Josephus wrote that the Essenes "are particularly reverent towards the divinity. . . ."

This is continued with a citation of the Qumran *Temple Scroll* and then the Tosefta:

That the Essenes really offered prayer to the sun is made more probable by a passage in the Qumran Temple Scroll. . . .
Above we noted the floor of the synagogue at Hammath that had as its main decoration the signs of the zodiac in a circle. . . . This synagogue floor, with its blatant pagan decoration, was built at the time when rabbinic Judaism was strong in Galilee – after the redaction and publication of the Mishnah, during the years when the material in the Tosefta and the Palestinian Talmud was being produced and edited. According to the Tosefta, Rabbi Judah, who flourished in the middle of the second century, said that "If anyone says a blessing over the sun – this is a heterodox practice" (T. Berakhot 6[7].6). In the light of the floor, it seems he was opposing contemporary practice.

And so on and on he goes, introducing in the paragraph that follows references to Christian symbols (John 1:9, 15:1); the issue of whether "one God" meant there were no other supernatural beings (yielding a citation to Paul who was a Pharisee, with reference to Philippians 3:2–6).

Here matters emerge otherwise. If not cumulative, ubiquitous ("normative"), and characteristic of everyone in general but no one in particular, then what? For our part, in place of Sanders' dates, we substitute the name of the document, promising also to describe Judaism, but this time the Judaism portrayed by a coherent set of documents, which speak for a well-defined, self-defined social group or Israel. From all Jews everywhere involved in one and the same

Judaism, to which a mass of conflicting documents are supposed to attest, then, we make an important move. It is to that particular group to which a single coherent body of official, public writings speaks: the Torah, or Judaism, of an Israel that values, in addition to the Torah of Sinai, further authoritative writings. Nothing is cumulative and historical, all things are discrete and systemic.

What makes this group distinctive in context, and what are the stakes involved in its Judaism? When we speak of the practice and belief of this Judaism, these questions, to be addressed to every Judaism, take over. And, when they do, instead of a lowest common-denominator Judaism to which anyone will have subscribed but no one will have attached much consequence ("Sure, so what?"), we come up with a Judaic system that is profoundly crafted to speak for a particular and unique perspective, like the Judaism of the Dead Sea library at Qumran, like the Judaism of the Mishnah and the Talmud, and like the other Judaisms portrayed in documents that speak for well-delineated groups of Jews, or, in the native categories, like the Torah as set forth by this Israel or that Israel. Since Sanders proposes to describe Judaism in New Testament times, we find it appropriate to respond to his description with our description, moving, as is clear, from a single Judaism to many Judaisms, a single period to which many documents attest to a single Judaic system portrayed in its own, but only in its own, canon.

If we turn to documents, does that mean we conceive a Judaism to correspond to a book, so that as we wish to speak of the New Testament's Judaism, so we should proceed to the Judaism of Philo or of Josephus or of the composite Enoch-writings? The answer is negative, for we distinguish a book that speaks for an individual from one that makes a statement on behalf of a clearly delineated community. Religion is not individual, private, and philosophical (although some religious writings are) but public and social. That is why we do not confuse a book with a religion. When a book enjoys the sponsorship of a community and clearly speaks to and for that community, then the book affords evidence for the description of a religious system, in our setting, a Judaism.

In choosing the New Testament as our base document for the study of a Judaism, with the Mishnah occasionally offered for purpose of comparison and contrast, it is because both sets of writings clearly speak for a community and define matters as that community in particular wishes to see them. We propose as another candidate for this approach to the study of (a) Judaism any document that clearly speaks to its distinctive social setting, hence the Elephantine papyri, the Dead Sea Scrolls, and the Talmud of Babylonia, but not the compositions of Philo or Josephus, which speak for individuals and set forth their distinctive perspective, a philosophy, perhaps, but not a Judaism – a religious system of the social order of (an) Israel.

2

NO ORTHODOX, TRADITIONAL JUDAISM?

The Issue of the Mishnah, the Judaism of orthopraxy

A RELIGIOUS SYSTEM: NOT A BOOK BUT A COMMUNITY REPRESENTED BY A BOOK

Religions find definition to begin with not in doctrine let alone in a book or rite but in social entities, e.g. communities of faithful. These are the groups that give social consequence to doctrine; they accord to beliefs the required, palpable context; hence they frame the plausibility of rite. It is no accident that, when Christianity wishes to invoke a sanctifying myth for its social entity, called "the church," it appeals to the basic and generative symbol, "the mystical body of Christ," just as Islam does to "the Nation of Islam," that is, the social entity that embodies true submission to God, and just as (a) Judaism does to (its) "Israel," meaning, the mythic entity portrayed by Scripture's supernatural history, beginning with Abraham and Sarah and forming an enchanted family of their descendants. It follows, therefore, that the first task in describing a religion is to identify the group of the faithful, and then to describe the faith of the faithful – their practice and their belief. Finally, where the description yields contrasts between literary evidence on practice and belief and the evidence of common practice, the task further involves interpreting the points of difference between what the books of the faith say and what the practitioners of the faith do.

So religions are public, social, and shared; they are what people do together when they conceive that they form a social entity singled out by God, a church, the mystical body of Christ; a holy people, that is "Israel" (with all that the name entails); the Nation of Islam. Beginning with the facts of the society formed by the faithful, however, immediately presents its particular complexity. For if we examine the communities of the faithful of Judaism, whether now or in antiquity, we are struck by the diversity of those communities and their faiths, all of them calling themselves "Israel" and their faiths "the Torah."[1] The question that demands an answer, therefore, is not why anyone should have imagined there ever was a single, uniform, homogeneous Judaism, but how so many people have taken for granted that there was? That point of insistence, defying the evidence of diversity, requires definitions to be crafted to fit the evidence, hence a lowest common-denominator Judaism, or a Judaism made up of shared practices mostly unaffected by points of disagreement, and similar ungainly solutions. We must wonder, therefore, why anyone should take the trouble to explain away simple and obvious facts, rather than conceiving matters in the light of them.

The conception of a single Judaism, or Christianity, or Hinduism, or Buddhism, enjoys credence as a labor-saving device, an argument for a theological position, and a medium of historical explanation. As a labor-saving device, the conception that all of the diverse religious groups that deem themselves Judaic or Christian or Hindu or Buddhist may be classified as one thing makes differentiation unnecessary. But who really conceives that Catholics and Mormons, Methodists and Russian Orthodox Christians form one religion for any descriptive, this-worldly purpose other than a census in a Muslim or Judaic state? And when we treat as homogeneous (perhaps at some profound and inaccessible level) data violently differentiated through history we turn out to understand nothing of the facts of the faith. Serbian and Croatian or Ulster and Irish Republican Christians surely are not best understood when we explain to ourselves that they form part of a single Christian religion. The same is self-evidently true for Judaism, with its Reform and Orthodox groups, with its integrationist and its segregationist ones. Islam presents the world with two enormous and distinct communities, which recently fought a long war; there too, defining what people have in common turns out to obscure all the interesting problems and to settle not the simplest one. The notion of a single Judaism or Christianity or Islam is convenient in a reductionist context, but that context never encompasses the real life of a lived religious community.

True, theological contexts welcome, indeed require, the fabrication of a single religion out of the data of conflicting, if kindred religions. For one example, the claim that there is only one Judaism often masks polemic claims that only one is authentic. The insistence of Israeli

Judaism under political auspices (itself a complex social phenomenon and hardly a single, uniform religious world) that the sole Judaism conforms to a single pattern of belief and behavior serves in practice only to exclude Reform and Conservative Judaisms, forming a political way of making the theological statement that "we are right and you are wrong, because ours is the only Judaism." For another example, the conception of a single Christianity, deriving from the Founder, finds convenient the fabrication of a single Judaism, against which the Founder formulated his faith; then we emerge with the new and the true, the old and the false, each readily defined. Here too a theological argument, *mutatis mutandis*, is founded upon the insistence of a single Judaism. The purpose shifts, the polemical charge remains the same.

That same theological insistence upon a single Judaism out of which a single and alien Christianity emerged forms a principal medium of historical, as against theological and supernatural, explanation for Christianity. In this secular mode, rejecting as beyond consideration a theological reading of matters, Christianity came into being within the body of Judaism, as a this-worldly medium of protest, or as a secular mode of improvement, a superior religion superseding an inferior one – public policy stated in religious language but retaining its essentially secular character. The superiority that is alleged for this Christianity against Judaism then derives from the flaws imputed to the prior religion. Since the (single, uniform) new religion so markedly transcended the (single, uniform) old religion, we explain the advent of the new by appeal to the inferior qualities of the old; and, in the nature of things, a complex and diverse set of religious systems, all of them passing among their faithful for Judaism, hardly serves the requirement of argument in such a context; diversity by its nature makes the appeal to comparison and contrast too complex to serve – this Judaism had this bad trait, but that one demonstrably did not, so why should the new religion have surpassed every Judaism when it improved upon only one of them?

When faced with the simple and familiar fact that documents held authoritative by one group of Jews and records characteristic of another group scarcely intersect, each set of writings dealing with topics unique to itself and scarcely addressed by any other, people have invented a variety of explanations. First, where difference is blatant, one group may be deemed heretical, all other groups conforming. Second, where documents scarcely intersect, it is argued that unstated points of common agreement are to be imputed even where not articulated. That proposition finds itself alleged more than it is argued, and evidence by definition proves sparse. And, third, most commonly, a single common-denominator Judaism is imputed to all Jews, whatever special beliefs or practices may have characterized some of them.

This third approach, moreover, shades over into the allegation of a single Judaism defined solely by (some, few) common rites, e.g. circumcision, dietary rules, the Sabbath. Orthodox Judaism gives way to the orthoprax kind: the claim that while Jews manifestly differed in matters of belief – the sole point on which all evidence concerning Jews' religious affairs concurs – they all practiced the same law. Judaism then forms an orthopraxy, a religion defined not at all by what people say but only by what they do. Every argument on behalf of a single ubiquitous, authoritative, official, normative, classical, Orthodox Judaism (whether or not alleged to have been the same as today's Orthodox Judaism) in the end will tell us about the minima of action, e.g. dietary laws, Sabbath, circumcision, that all Jews practiced and that therefore define that one Judaism that is alleged to have flourished somewhere behind all the evidence of particularity and conflict.

The allegation of a single, uniform orthoprax Judaism presents a problem to the perspective just now set forth and therefore requires extended attention. If we conceive that while there was no single Orthodox Judaism, yet there was an orthopraxy, then the earliest Christians, beyond Pentecost (for Peter's Church) or at least after Paul's great reformation, find no place in the context of any Judaism. This is because, as a matter of fact, for most of them the orthoprax Judaism of dietary laws, circumcision, and the Sabbath lost all meaning when Heaven itself permitted Christians to eat formerly forbidden food, on the one side, and when Paul's churches abandoned circumcision, on the other. But the issue vastly transcends the problem and argument of this book and is therefore to be addressed in its own terms: can we describe if not a single Judaism then at least a single and uniform, universally practiced Judaic law?

NO SINGLE JUDAISM BUT A SINGLE AND UNIFORM JUDAIC LAW? THE ALLEGATION OF ORTHOPRAXY EXAMINED

The allegation of orthopraxy in support of the conception of a single Judaism takes the form of the insistence that, whatever the diversity of local beliefs, a single, ubiquitous law, practiced by all ("loyal") Jews but no one else, serves to validate the use of the singular "Judaism" in place of the plural "Judaisms." But the evidence that does not support a single Judaism also does not sustain the conception of a uniform law of Judaism.

The reason is simple. Apart from the scriptural law codes, in antiquity no single system of law governed all Jews everywhere. So we cannot describe "Jewish law" as one encompassing system. The Scripture's several codes of course made their impact on the diverse systems of law that governed various groups of Jews, or Jewish communities in various places. But that impact never proved uniform. In consequence, in no way may we speak of "Jewish law," meaning a single legal code or even a common set of encompassing rules everywhere held authoritative by Jewry. The relationship between the legal system of one distinct group of Jews to that governing some other proves various.[2]

Certain practices, to be sure, characterized all – so far as we now know.[3] But these, too, do not validate the premise that such a thing as "Jewish law" operated, even in the points in common, pretty much everywhere. The fact that Jews ordinarily observed certain taboos, for example, concerning the Sabbath day and forbidden foods, hardly changes the picture. On the basis of the prohibition of pork and the observance of a common calendar one can hardly describe a common law of Jewry, hence "Jewish law." Such evidence as we have of diverse Jews' laws points in the opposite direction. What these sets of laws shared in common in part derives from the Scripture all revered. What turns up in a number of contexts in further measure proves so general or so fragmentary as to yield no trace of a single, systematic and comprehensive law common among Jews.

An example of the latter – something too general to make much difference – is the marriage contract. It is a fact that marriage contracts occur in the Jewish community records of Elephantine, in the fragments found from the time of Bar Kokhba, and in the setting of Mishnaic law. But in detail the contracts that have been found scarcely intersect.[4] The Mishnah's rules governing the scribal preparation of such contracts hardly dictated to the authorities of fifth-century BC Elephantine[5] or second-century CE Palestine how to do their work. So it is misleading to speak of "the halakhah," meaning a single system of law operative among all Jews.[6] It is still more confusing to treat as fragments of a single legal system all of the bits and pieces of information deriving from various and sundry communities, scattered throughout the territories of the Near and Middle East, and dated over a span of hundreds of years.

Once more, the documentary approach to the description of a Judaism makes its mark. Each of these several systems of law applying to diverse Jewish groups or communities emerges from its distinct historical setting, addresses its own social entity, and tells us, usually only in bits and pieces of detailed information, about itself alone. Whether whole or fragmentary, systems of Jewish law do not coalesce into one ideal system. That is why we may indeed propose to describe any of several legal systems governing one or more groups of Jews. It is possible to trace development of systems of halakhah characteristic of communities of Jews. To begin with, however, an account of the development of such systems will compare wholes, that is, one system to another system.

True, one might seek the lowest common denominator among all of the systems of law followed by Jewish groups. That then would be deemed "the halakhah," or "Jewish law." But details shared among a variety of Judaisms make sense only in their respective contexts. Each on its own matters in the system in which it makes its appearance and plays its role. So if we wish to consider the development of "the halakhah," we have first to decide whose halakhah, among a variety of candidates, we propose to describe and to analyze. Among a range of choices subject to documentation a choice is to be made. Systematic studies of the halakhah of the Jews in Alexandria,[7] the Jews in Elephantine,[8] the Jews in the Essene community of Qumran,[9] and, of course, the Jews who stand behind the law now presented in the Mishnah and its successor documents[10] all present appropriate foci of inquiry. Among these and other systems of law produced by Jews, the one of greatest importance is that first written down in the Mishnah, c. 200 CE.

A JUDAIC SYSTEM THAT MAKES ITS STATEMENT THROUGH LAW: THE MISHNAH AND THE ISSUE OF A CUMULATIVE TRADITION OF ORTHOPRAXY

Definitions of a uniform, ubiquitous orthoprax Judaism always appeal to the Mishnah as the writing down of that Judaism's common practices, and any consideration of orthopraxy therefore requires us to address that document. But our perspective upon it – not a historical one at all – will allow us to raise questions directly relevant to the description of the Judaism of any documentary statement, inclusive of the New Testament. The specific issue at hand requires us to use a Hebrew word, *halakhah*, meaning normative law. We are asked to maintain that while theologies conflicted in Judaism, a single *halakhah* prevailed, and the Mishnah represents its best statement.

The Mishnah is an encompassing law code brought to closure in *c.* 200 CE under the sponsorship of Judah the Patriarch, ethnic ruler of the Jewish communities of the Land of Israel ("Palestine"). Laid forth in six divisions, the laws of the Mishnah take up the sanctity of the land and its use in accord with God's law ("Seeds" or agriculture), the differentiation and passage of sacred time and its impact upon the cult and the village ("Appointed Times"), the sacred aspects of the relationship between woman and man ("Women" or family law), civil law ("Damages"), the conduct of the cult in appropriate regularity and order ("Holy Things"), and the protection of food prepared under the rules of cultic taboos from contamination ("Purities"). The laws of the document throughout lay stress upon the sanctification of Israel's life in the natural world through conformity to the rules governed by the supernatural world. So the Mishnah's halakhah presents a very particular construction, one proposing to form Israel into a holy community in accord with God's holy law, revealed in the Torah given to Moses at Mount Sinai.

In the Mishnah we see how a group of jurisprudents drew together a rich heritage of legal and moral traditions and facts, and made of them a single system. From Scripture onward, no other composition compares in size, comprehensive treatment of a vast variety of topics, balance, proportion, and cogency. We can demonstrate that many laws in the Mishnah vastly antedate the formation of that document, and, it follows, the Mishnah's writers drew upon a corpus of data with antecedents in remote antiquity. Since the definition of an orthoprax Judaism makes much of that fact, we shall address it. First, let us rapidly review the various types of evidence for the antiquity of numerous facts utilized by the Mishnah's framers in the construction of their system.

Some legal facts in the Mishnah, as in other law codes of its place and age, derive from remote antiquity. Categories of law and investment, for instance, prove continuous with Akkadian and even Sumerian ones. To cite a single instance, there are the sorts of investment classified as *nikhse melug* or *nikhse son barzel* (M. Yebamot 7:1–2), investments in which the investor shares in the loss or the profit, on the one side, or in which the investor is guaranteed the return of the capital without regard to the actual course of the investment transaction, on the other. (The former would correspond to common stock, the latter to preferred or even to a government bond, a gilt, in British parlance.) It has been shown that the linguistic and legal datum of Mishnah's rules goes back to Assyrian law.[11] Other important continuities in the common law of the ancient Near East have emerged in a broad diversity of research, on Elephantine law for instance.[12] The issue therefore cannot focus upon whether or not the Mishnah in diverse details draws upon established rules of jurisprudence. It assuredly does.

Yet another mode of demonstrating that facts in the Mishnah's system derive from a period substantially prior to that in which the Mishnah reached closure carries us to the data provided by documents redacted long before the Mishnah. For one example, details of rules in the law codes found in the library of the Essene community of Qumran intersect with details of rules in the Mishnah. More interesting still, accounts of aspects of Israelite life take for granted that issues lively in the Mishnah came under debate long before the closure of the Mishnah. The Gospels' accounts of Jesus' encounter with the Pharisees, among others, encompass rules of law, or topics dealt with, important to the Mishnah.[13] It is, for instance, not merely the datum that a writ of divorce severs the tie between wife and husband. The matter of grounds for divorce proves important to sages whose names occur in the Mishnah, and one position of one of these sages turns out to accord with that imputed to Jesus.[14] It follows that not only isolated facts but critical matters of jurisprudential philosophy came to the surface long before the closure of the Mishnah.

That fact yields one incontrovertible result. The Mishnah's rules have to come into juxtaposition, wherever possible, with the rules that occur in prior law codes, whether Israelite or otherwise. That is the case even though it presently appears that only a small proportion of all of the rules in the Mishnah fall within the frame of prior documents, remote or proximate. For every rule we can parallel in an earlier composition, the Mishnah gives us dozens of rules that in topic, logic, or even mere detail bear no comparison to anything now known in a prior composition, from Sumerian and Akkadian to Essene and Christian writers alike. (The sole exception, the Hebrew Scripture's law codes, comes under analysis presently.) Details of the law, wherever possible, still must stand in comparison with equivalent details in earlier documents, whether narrative or legislative. In that way we gain perspective on what, in the Mishnah, has come into the framers' hands from an earlier period. At stake in such perspective is insight into the mind of the Mishnah's framers and the character of their system. We see what they have made out of available materials. What do we learn from the occurrence of facts more than two millennia old by the time of the Mishnah, or of issues important two centuries earlier? We review the resources selected by those who contributed to the traditions brought to closure in the Mishnah.

For the authors of the Mishnah in using available, sometimes very ancient, materials, reshaped whatever came into their hands. The document upon close reading proves systematic and orderly, purposive and well composed.[15] It is no mere scrapbook of legal facts, arranged for purposes of reference. It is a document in which the critical problematic at the center always exercises influence over the peripheral facts, dictating how they are chosen, arranged, utilized. So even though some facts in the document prove very old indeed, on that basis we understand no more than we did before we knew that some facts come from ancient times. True halakhah as the Mishnah presents law derives from diverse sources, from remote antiquity onward. But the halakhah as it emerges whole and complete in the Mishnah, in particular, that is, the system, the structure, the proportions and composition, the topical program and the logical and syllogistic whole – these derive from the imagination and wit of the final two generations, in the second century CE, of the authors of the Mishnah.

A simple exercise will show that, whatever the antiquity of rules viewed discretely, the meaning and proportionate importance of rules taken all together derive from the perspective and encompassing theory of the authors of the Mishnah themselves. That is what will show that the history of halakhah as the Mishnah presents the halakhah can be traced, whole and cogent, only within the data of the Mishnah itself: systemically, not episodically. The desired exercise brings us to the relationship of the Mishnah to Scripture. For, as noted just now, that is the one substantial source to which the authors of the Mishnah did make reference. Accordingly, to demonstrate the antiquity of more than discrete and minor details of law of the Mishnah, we turn to Scripture. There, it is clear, we can find out whether the Mishnah constitutes merely a repository of ancient halakhah.

Indeed, proof that there was not merely law characteristic of a given group, but the halakhah, shared by all Israel, should derive solely from the Scripture common to all Israel everywhere. How so? The theory of a single, continuous halakhah rests upon the simple fact that all Israel by definition acknowledged the authority of Scripture, its law and theology. It must follow that, in diverse ways and within discrete exegetical processes, every group now known to us drew its basic legal propositions from Scripture and therefore contributes evidence on the unilinear formation of a single law, based upon a single source, common to all Israel, that is, the halakhah.

SCRIPTURE AND (A) JUDAISM: THE CASE OF THE MISHNAH

In examining the notion of *the* halakhah, as distinct from the theory, argued here, that diverse systems of halakhah governed diverse communities of Judaism, we turn now to the critical issue. It does not concern whether a given rule derives from exegesis of Scripture. That issue, by itself, leads to no deep insight. Rather we want to know how the several systems now known to us define their respective relationships to Scripture. That is to say, we ask about the nature of scriptural authority, the use of Scripture's facts in a code, or system, of law. The answer to the question settles an important issue. If two (or more) systems of law governing groups of Israelites turn out to respond to, to draw upon, Scripture's rules in much the same way, then these discrete systems merge at their roots, in a generative and definitive aspect of their structure. In consequence, we may conclude the two (or more) systems do form part of a single common law, once more, the halakhah. But if two or more systems of law approach Scripture each in its own way and for its own purposes, then we have to analyze each system on its own terms and not as part of, and contributory to, the halakhah.

For the present purpose it will suffice to demonstrate one modest fact. The authors of the Mishnah read Scripture, as they read much else, in terms of the system and structure they proposed to construct. That statement will not surprise New Testament learning, deeply experienced as it is in the systematic reading of the Old Testament in the light of the New. And the characterization of the Mishnah's authors' utilization of Scripture will hardly present cause for astonishment. It is the simple fact that the Mishnah's sages' goals and conceptions told them what, in Scripture, they would borrow, what they would expand and articulate, what they would acknowledge but neglect, and what they would simply ignore. That fact shows that law in the Mishnah, even though shared here and there with other codes, and even though intersecting with still other systems, constitutes a distinct and autonomous system of law, a halakhah on its own. So, to review, the Mishnah then does not absorb and merely portray in its own way established rules of law out of a single, continuous, and cogent legal system, the halakhah. Why not? Because, as we shall now see, the Mishnah's authors turn out to have taken from Scripture what they chose in accord with the criterion of the one thing they wished to accomplish. This was the construction of their system of law with its distinctive traits of topical and logical composition: their halakhah, not *the* halakhah.

In order to show the pre-eminence, in the encounter with Scripture's laws, of the perspective and purpose of the authors of the Mishnah, we simply review the Mishnah's tractates and ask how, overall, we may characterize their relationships to Scripture. Were these wholly dependent, wholly autonomous, or somewhere in between? That is, at the foundations in fact and generative problematic of a given tractate we may discover nothing more than facts and interests of Scripture's law. The tractate's authors may articulate the data of Scripture. Or when we reach the bedrock of a tractate, the point at which the articulation of the structure of the tractate rests, we may find no point of contact with facts, let alone interests, of Scripture's laws. And, third, we may discover facts shared by Scripture but developed in ways distinctive to the purposes of the framers of the Mishnah tractate at hand. These three relationships, in theory, encompass all possibilities. Let us turn to the facts.[16]

First, there are tractates which simply repeat in their own words precisely what Scripture has to say, and at best serve to amplify and complete the basic ideas of Scripture. For example, all of the cultic tractates of the Second Division, the one on Appointed Times, which tell what one is supposed to do in the Temple on the various special days of the year, and the bulk of the cultic tractates of the Fifth Division, which deals with Holy Things, simply restate facts of Scripture. For another example, all of those tractates of the Sixth Division, on Purities, which specify sources of uncleanness, depend completely on information supplied by Scripture. Every important statement in Niddah, on menstrual uncleanness, and the most fundamental notions of Zabim, on the uncleanness of the person with flux referred to in Leviticus 15, as well as every detail in Negaim, on the uncleanness of the person or house suffering the uncleanness described at Leviticus 13 and 14 – all of these tractates serve only to restate the basic facts of Scripture and to complement those facts with other important ones.

There are, second, tractates which take up facts of Scripture but work them out in a way in which those scriptural facts could not have led us to predict. A supposition concerning what is important about the facts, utterly remote from the supposition of Scripture, will explain why the Mishnah tractates under discussion say the original things they say in confronting those scripturally provided facts. For one example, Scripture takes for granted that the red cow will be burned in a state of uncleanness, because it is burned outside the camp, meaning the Temple. The priestly writers could not have imagined that a state of cultic cleanness was to be attained outside of the cult. The absolute datum of tractate Parah, by contrast, is that cultic cleanness not only can be attained outside of the "tent of meeting," but that the red cow was to be burned in a state of cleanness exceeding even that cultic cleanness required in the Temple itself. The problematic which generates the intellectual agendum of Parah, therefore, is how to work out the conduct of the rite of burning the cow in relationship to the Temple: is it to be done in exactly the same way, or in exactly the opposite way? This mode of contrastive and analogical thinking helps us to understand the generative problematic of such tractates as Erubin and Besah, to mention only two.

And, third, there are, predictably, many tractates which either take up problems in no way suggested by Scripture, or begin from facts at best merely relevant to facts of Scripture. In the former category are Tohorot, on the cleanness of foods, with its companion, Uqsin; Demai, on doubtfully tithed produce; Tamid, on the conduct of the daily whole-offering; Baba Batra, on rules of real estate transactions and certain other commercial and property relationships, and so on. In the latter category are Ohalot, which spins out its strange problems with the theory that a tent and a utensil are to be compared to one another(!); Kelim, on the susceptibility to uncleanness of various sorts of utensils; Miqvaot, on the sorts of water which effect purification from uncleanness; and many others. These tractates draw on facts of Scripture. But the problems confronted in these tractates in no way respond to problems important to Scripture. What we have here is a prior program of inquiry, which will make ample provision for facts of Scripture in an inquiry initially generated essentially outside of the framework of Scripture.

Some tractates merely repeat what we find in Scripture. Some are totally independent of Scripture. Some fall in between. Scripture confronts the framers of the Mishnah as revelation, not merely as a source of facts. But the framers of the Mishnah had their own world with which to deal. They made statements in the framework and fellowship of their own age and generation. They were bound, therefore, to come to Scripture with a set of questions generated elsewhere than in Scripture. They brought their own ideas about what was going to be important in Scripture. This is perfectly natural.

The philosophers of the Mishnah conceded to Scripture the highest authority. At the same time what they chose to hear, within the authoritative statements of Scripture, in the end formed a statement of its own. To state matters simply: all of Scripture is authoritative. But only some of Scripture is relevant. And what happened is that the framers and philosophers of the tradition of the Mishnah came to Scripture when they had reason to. That is to say, they brought to Scripture a program of questions and inquiries framed essentially among themselves. So they were highly selective. Their program itself constituted a statement upon the meaning of Scripture. As they and their apologists of one sort hastened to add, their program consisted of a statement of and not only upon the meaning of Scripture.

The authority of Scripture therefore for the Mishnah is simply stated. Scripture provides indisputable facts. It is wholly authoritative – once we have made our choice of which part of Scripture we shall read. Scripture generated important and authoritative structures of the community, including disciplinary and doctrinal statements, decisions, and interpretations – once people had determined which part of Scripture to ask to provide those statements and decisions. Community structures envisaged by the Mishnah were wholly based on Scripture – when Scripture had anything to lay down. But Scripture is not wholly and exhaustively expressed in those structures which the Mishnah does borrow. Scripture has dictated the character of formative structures of the Mishnah. But the Mishnah's system is not the result of the dictation of close exegesis of Scripture, except after the fact.

AN EXAMPLE OF A DOCUMENTARY STATEMENT OF A JUDAIC SYSTEM: THE MISHNAH'S JUDAISM

The documentary representation of a Judaism requires that we commence within the category-formation of the documents, even though our work of interpretation will lead us far beyond, as our own category-formation takes over to impart meaning to our data. The Mishnah's categories follow the lines of the divisions and tractates – that by definition! – and the main points may be summarized in this way.

The Division of Agriculture treats two topics: first, producing crops in accord with the scriptural rules on the subject; second, paying the required offerings and tithes to the priests, Levites, and poor. The principal point of the division is that the Land is holy, because God has a claim both on it and upon what it produces. God's claim must be honored by setting aside a portion of the produce for those for whom God has designated it. God's ownership must be acknowledged by observing the rules God has laid down for use of the Land.

The Mishnaic Division of Appointed Times forms a system in which the advent of a holy day, like the Sabbath of creation, sanctifies the life of the Israelite village through imposing on the village rules modeled on those of the Temple. The purpose of the system, therefore, is to bring into alignment the moment of sanctification of the village and the life of the home with the moment of sanctification of the Temple on those same occasions of appointed times. The underlying and generative theory of the system is that the village is the mirror-image of the Temple. If things are done in one way in the Temple, they will be done in the opposite way in the village. Together the village and the Temple on the occasion of the holy day form a single continuum, a completed creation, thus awaiting sanctification.

The village is made like the Temple in that on appointed times one may not freely cross the lines distinguishing the village from the rest of the world, just as one may not freely cross the lines distinguishing the Temple from the world. But the village is a mirror-image of the Temple. The boundary lines prevent free entry into the Temple, so they restrict free egress from the village. On the holy day what one may do in the Temple is precisely what one may not do in the village. So the advent of the holy day affects the village by bringing it into sacred symmetry so as to effect a system of opposites; each is holy, in a way precisely the opposite of the other. Because of the underlying conception of perfection attained through the union of opposites, the village is not represented as conforming to the model of the cult, but as constituting its antithesis.

The world thus regains perfection when on the holy day Heaven and earth are united, the whole completed and done: the Heaven, the earth, and all their hosts. This moment of perfection renders the events of ordinary time, of "history," essentially irrelevant. For what really matters in time is that moment in which sacred time intervenes and effects the perfection formed of the union of Heaven and earth, of Temple, in the model of the former, and Israel, its complement. It is not a return to a perfect time but a recovery of perfect being, a fulfillment of creation, which explains the essentially ahistorical character of the Mishnah's Division on Appointed Times. Sanctification constitutes an ontological category and is effected by the creator. The halakhah of the division works itself out through the comparison, in the context of sacred time, of the spatial life of the Temple to the spatial life of the village, with activities and restrictions to be specified for each, upon the common occasion of the Sabbath or festival. The Mishnah's purpose therefore is to correlate the sanctity of the Temple, as defined by the holy day, with the restrictions of space and of action which make the life of the village different and holy, as defined by the holy day.

The Mishnaic system of Women defines the position of women in the social economy of Israel's supernatural and natural reality. That position acquires definition wholly in relationship to men, who impart form to the Israelite social economy. It is effected through both supernatural and natural, this-worldly action. What man and woman do on earth provokes a response in Heaven, and the correspondences are perfect. So the position of women is defined and secured both in Heaven and here on earth, and that position is always and invariably relative to men.

The principal interest for the Mishnah is the point at which a woman becomes, and ceases to be, holy to a particular man, that is, enters and leaves the marital union. These transfers of women are the dangerous and disorderly points in the relationship of woman to man and, therefore, as we said, to society as well. The division and its system delineate the natural and supernatural character of the woman's role in the social economy framed by man: the beginning, end, and middle of the relationship. The Mishnaic system of Women thus focuses upon the two crucial stages in the transfer of women and of property from one domain to another, the leaving of the father's house in the formation of a marriage, and the return to the father's house at its dissolution through divorce or the husband's death. There is yet a third point of interest, though, as is clear, it is much less important than these first two stages: the duration of the marriage. Finally, included within the division and at a few points relevant to women in particular are rules of vows and of the special vow to be a Nazir. The former are included because, in the scriptural treatment of the theme, the rights of the father or husband to annul the vows of a daughter or wife form the central problematic. The latter is included for no very clear reason except that it is a species of which the vow is the genus.

There is in the Division of Women a clearly defined and neatly conceived system of laws, not about women in general, but concerning what is important about women to the framers of the Mishnah. This is the transfer of woman and property from one domain, the father's, to another, the husband's, and back. The whole constitutes a significant part of the Mishnah's encompassing system of sanctification, for the reason that Heaven confirms what men do on earth. A correctly prepared writ of divorce on earth changes the status of the woman to whom it is given, so that in Heaven she is available for sanctification to some other man, while, without that same writ, in Heaven's view, should she go to some other man, she would be liable to be put to death. The earthly deed and the Heavenly perspective correlate. That is indeed very much part of the larger system, which says the same thing over and over again.

The Division of Damages comprises two subsystems, which fit together in a logical way. One part presents rules for the normal conduct of civil society. These cover commerce, trade, real estate, and other matters of everyday intercourse, as well as mishaps, such as damages by chattels and persons, fraud, overcharge, interest, and the like, in that same context of everyday social life. The other part describes the institutions governing the normal conduct of civil society, that is, courts of administration, and the penalties at the disposal of the government for the enforcement of the law. The two subjects form a single tight and systematic dissertation on the nature of Israelite society and its economic, social, and political relationships, as the Mishnah envisages them. The main point is that the task of society is to maintain perfect stasis, to preserve the prevailing situation, and to secure the stability of all relationships. To this end, in the interchanges of buying and selling, giving and taking, borrowing and lending, it is important that there be an essential equality of interchange. No party in the end should have more than what he had at the outset, and none should be the victim of a sizeable shift in fortune and circumstance. All parties' rights to, and in, this stable and unchanging economy of society are to be preserved. When the condition of a person is violated, so far as possible the law will secure the restoration of the antecedent status.

The goal of the system of civil law is the recovery of the prevailing order and balance, the preservation of the established wholeness of the social economy. This idea is powerfully expressed in the organization of the three Babas, which treat first abnormal and then normal transactions. The framers deal with damages done by chattels and by human beings, thefts, and other sorts of malfeasance against the property of others. The Babas in both aspects pay closest attention to how the property and person of the injured party so far as possible are restored to their prior condition, that is, a state of normality. So attention to torts focuses upon penalties paid by the malefactor to the victim, rather than upon penalties inflicted by the court on the malefactor for what he has done. When speaking of damages, the Mishnah thus takes as its principal concern the restoration of the fortune of victims of assault or robbery. Then the framers take up the complementary and corresponding set of topics, the regulation of normal transactions. When we rapidly survey the kinds of transactions of special interest, we see from the topics selected for discussion what we have already uncovered in the deepest structure of organization and articulation of the basic theme.

The character and interests of the Division of Damages present probative evidence of the larger program of the philosophers of the Mishnah. Their intention is to create nothing less than a full-scale Israelite government, subject to the administration of sages. This government is fully supplied with a constitution and by-laws (Sanhedrin, Makkot). It makes provision for a court system and procedures, as well as a full set of laws governing civil society. This government, moreover, mediates between its own community and the outside ("pagan") world. Through its system of laws it expresses its judgment of the others and at the same time defines, protects, and defends its own society and social frontiers. It even makes provision for procedures of remission, to expiate its own errors (Horayot).

The (then nonexistent) Israelite government imagined by the second-century philosophers centers upon the (then nonexistent) Temple, and the (then forbidden) city, Jerusalem. For the Temple is one principal focus. There the highest court is in session; there the high priest reigns. The penalties for law infringement are of four kinds: sacrifice in the Temple to atone for the sinful aspect of a misdeed, compensation, physical punishment, and death. The basic conception of punishment, moreover, is that unintentional infringement of the rules of society, whether "religious" or otherwise, is not penalized but rather expiated through an offering in the Temple. If a member of the people of Israel intentionally infringes against the law, to be sure, that one must be removed from society and is put to death. And if there is a claim of one member of the people against another, that must be righted, so that the prior, prevailing status may be restored. So offerings in the Temple are given up to appease Heaven and restore a whole bond between Heaven and Israel, specifically on those occasions on which without malice or ill will an Israelite has disturbed the relationship. Israelite civil society without a Temple is not stable or normal, and is not to be imagined. And the Mishnah is above all an act of imagination in defiance of reality.

The plan for the government involves a clear-cut philosophy of society, a philosophy which defines the purpose of the government and ensures that its task is not merely to perpetuate its own power. What the Israelite government, within the Mishnaic fantasy, is supposed to do is to preserve that state of perfection which, within the same fantasy, the society to begin with everywhere attains and expresses. This is in at least five aspects. First of all, one of the ongoing principles of the law, expressed in one tractate after another, is that people are to follow and maintain the prevailing practice of their locale. Second, the purpose of civil penalties, as we have noted, is to restore the injured party to his prior condition, so far as this is possible, rather than merely to penalize the aggressor. Third, there is the conception of true value, meaning that a given object has an intrinsic worth, which, in the course of a transaction, must be paid. In this way the seller does not leave the transaction any richer than when he entered it, or the buyer any poorer (parallel to penalties for damages). Fourth, there can be no usury, a biblical prohibition adopted and vastly enriched in the Mishnaic thought, for money ("coins") is what it is. Any pretense that it has become more than what it was violates, in its way, the conception of true value. Fifth, when real estate is divided, it must be done with full attention to the rights of all concerned, so that, once more, one party does not gain at the expense of the other. In these and many other aspects the law expresses its obsession with the perfect stasis of Israelite society. Its paramount purpose is in preserving and ensuring that that perfection of the division of this world is kept inviolate or restored to its true status when violated.

The Division of Holy Things presents a system of sacrifice and sanctuary: matters concerning the praxis of the altar and maintenance of the sanctuary. The system of the cult of the Jerusalem Temple, seen as an ordinary and everyday affair, takes as its premise the maintenance of a continuing and routine operation. That is why special rules for the cult, both in respect to the altar and in regard to the maintenance of the buildings, personnel, and even the holy city, will be elsewhere – in Appointed Times and Agriculture. But from the perspective of Holy Things, those divisions intersect by supplying special rules and raising extraordinary (Agriculture: land-bound; Appointed Times: time-bound) considerations for that theme which Holy Things claims to set forth in its most general and unexceptional way: the cult as something permanent and everyday. The order of Holy Things thus in a concrete way maps out the cosmology of the sanctuary and its sacrificial system, that is, the world of the Temple, which had been the cosmic center of Israelite life. A later saying states matters as follows:

> Just as the navel is found at the center of a human being, so the Land of Israel is found at the center of the world . . . and it is the foundation of the world. Jerusalem is at the center of the Land of Israel, the Temple is at the center of Jerusalem, the Holy of Holies is at the center of the Temple, the Ark is at the center of the Holy of Holies, and the Foundation Stone is in front of the Ark, which spot is the foundation of the world.
>
> (Tanhuma Qedoshim 10)

The Division of Purities presents a very simple system of three principal parts: sources of uncleanness, objects and substances susceptible to uncleanness, and modes of purification from uncleanness. So it tells the story of what makes a given sort of object unclean and what makes it clean. Viewed as a whole, the Division of Purities treats the interplay of persons, food, and liquids. Dry inanimate objects or food are not susceptible to uncleanness. What is wet is susceptible. So liquids activate the system. What is unclean, moreover, emerges from uncleanness through the operation of liquids, specifically, through immersion in fit water of requisite volume and in natural condition. Liquids thus deactivate the system. Thus, water in its natural condition is what concludes the process by removing uncleanness. Water in its unnatural condition, that is, deliberately affected by human agency, is what imparts susceptibility to uncleanness to begin with. The uncleanness of persons, furthermore, is signified by body liquids or flux in the case of the menstruating woman and the Zab. Corpse uncleanness is conceived to be a kind of effluent, a viscous gas, which flows like liquid. Utensils for their part receive uncleanness when they form receptacles able to contain liquid. In sum, we have a system in which the invisible flow of fluid-like substances or powers serve to put food, drink, and receptacles into the status of uncleanness and to remove those things from that status. Whether or not we call the system "metaphysical," it certainly has no material base but is conditioned upon highly abstract notions. Thus in material terms, the effect of liquid is upon food, drink, utensils, and man. The consequence has to do with who may eat and drink what food and liquid, and what food and drink may be consumed in which pots and pans. These loci are specified by tractates on utensils (Kelim) and on food and drink.

The human being is ambivalent. Persons fall in the middle, between sources and loci of uncleanness, because they are both. They serve as sources of uncleanness. They also become unclean. The Zab, the menstruating woman, the woman after childbirth, the Tebul Yom, and the person afflicted with nega – all are sources of uncleanness. But being unclean, they fall within the system's loci, its program of consequences. So they make other things unclean and are subject to penalties because they are unclean. Unambiguous sources of uncleanness never also constitute loci affected by uncleanness. They always are unclean and can never become clean: the corpse, the dead creeping thing, and things like them. Inanimate sources of uncleanness and inanimate objects are affected by uncleanness. Systemically unique, man and liquids have the capacity to inaugurate the processes of uncleanness (as sources) and also are subject to those same processes (as objects of uncleanness). The Division of Purities, which presents the basically simple system just now described, is not only the oldest in the Mishnah, it also is the largest and contains by far the most complex laws and ideas.

The halakhic system presented by the Mishnah consists of a coherent logic and topic, a cogent world-view, and comprehensive way of living. It is a world-view which speaks of transcendent things, a way of life in response to the supernatural meaning of what is done, a heightened and deepened perception of the sanctification of Israel in deed and in deliberation. Sanctification means two things: first, it distinguishes Israel in all its dimensions from the world in all its ways; second, it establishes the stability, order, regularity, predictability, and reliability of Israel at moments and in contexts of danger. Danger means instability, disorder, irregularity, uncertainty, and betrayal. Each topic of the system as a whole takes up a critical and indispensable moment or context of social being. Through what is said in regard to each of the Mishnah's principal topics, what the halakhic system as a whole wishes to declare is fully expressed. Yet if the parts severally and jointly give the message of the whole, the whole cannot exist without all of the parts, so well joined and carefully crafted are they all.

ORTHOPRAXY OR A JUDAISM?

We see that the Mishnah makes its statements through halakhah, but the system of the Mishnah vastly transcends the details of the law, and its theology imparts to the laws the position, order, and meaning that the laws have in the system. Not a single law speaks only of deeds, and every one of them makes its contribution to the formation and representation of a vast Judaic system. Take, for example, the matter of tithing and the giving of agricultural offerings, with which, as we shall see, Jesus is presented as being impatient. In his system these represented mere practice, orthopraxy indeed. But in the system of the Mishnah they formed part of a larger statement about political economy. Israel, as tenant on God's Holy Land, maintains the property in the ways God requires, keeping the rules which mark the Land and its crops as holy. Next, the hour at which the sanctification of the Land comes to form a critical mass, namely, in the ripened crops, is the moment ponderous with danger and heightened holiness. Israel's will so affects the crops as to mark a part of them as holy, the rest of them as available for common use. The human will is determinative in the process of sanctification. So the moment at which tithing is required marks the point at which God responds to the human will – "thy will be done," indeed!

What happens in the Land at certain times, at "appointed times," marks off spaces of the Land as holy in yet another way. The center of the Land and the focus of its sanctification is the Temple. There the produce of the Land is received and given back to God, the one who created and sanctified the Land. At these unusual moments of sanctification, the inhabitants of the Land in their social being in villages enter a state of spatial sanctification. That is to say, the village boundaries mark off holy space. This is expressed in two ways. First, the Temple itself observes and expresses the special, recurring holy time. Second, the villages of the Land are brought into alignment with the Temple, forming a complement and completion to the Temple's sacred being. The advent of the appointed times precipitates a spatial reordering of the Land, so that the boundaries of the sacred are matched and mirrored in village and in Temple. At the heightened holiness marked by these moments of appointed times, therefore, the occasion for an effective sanctification is worked out. Like the harvest, the advent of an appointed time such as a pilgrim festival is also a sacred season and is made to express that regular, orderly, and predictable sort of sanctification for Israel which the system as a whole seeks.

The counterpart of the Divisions of Agriculture and Appointed Times are Holy Things and Purities, dealing with the everyday and the ordinary, as against the special moments of harvest, on the one side, and special time or season, on the other. The Temple, the locus of sanctification, is conducted in a wholly routine and trustworthy, punctilious manner (Holy Things). The one thing which may unsettle matters is the intention and will of the human actor. This is subjected to carefully prescribed limitations and remedies. The Division of Holy Things generates its companion, the one on cultic cleanness, Purities. A system of cleanness, taking into account what imparts uncleanness and how this is done, what is subject to uncleanness, and how that state is overcome, is fully expressed, once more, in response to the participation of the human will. Without the wish and act of a human being, the system does not function. It is inert. Sources of uncleanness, which come naturally and not by volition, and modes of purification, which work naturally and not by human intervention, remain inert until human will has imparted susceptibility to uncleanness, that is, introduced into the system food and drink, bed, pot, chair, and pan, which to begin with form the focus of the system. The movement from sanctification to uncleanness takes place when human will and work precipitate it.

The middle divisions, the third and fourth, on Women and Damages, finally, take their place in the structure of the whole by showing the congruence, within the larger framework of regularity and order, of human concerns of family and farm, politics and workaday transactions among ordinary people. For without attending to these matters, the Mishnah's system would not encompass what, at its foundations, it is meant to comprehend and order. So what is at issue is fully cogent with the rest. In the case of Women, attention focuses upon the point of disorder marked by the transfer of that disordering anomaly, woman, from the regular status provided by one man, to the equally trustworthy status provided by another. That is the point at which the Mishnah's interests are aroused: once more, predictably, the moment of disorder. In the case of Damages, there are two important concerns. First, there is the paramount interest in preventing, so far as possible, the disorderly rise of one person and fall of another, and in sustaining the status quo of the economy of Israel, the holy society in stasis. Second, there is the necessary concomitant in the provision of a system of political institutions to carry out the laws which preserve the balance and steady state of persons. So the systemic statement comes to expression in law, but it is hardly a system of orthopraxy, not at all.

3

ANALYZING A JUDAISM

How and why?

DEFINING A JUDAISM AND ITS COMPONENTS: WHAT IS TO BE DONE?

Turning from the negative to the positive side of the argument, we ask: what changes when we see a coherent set of writings associated with the Hebrew Scriptures or Old Testament, identified with a social entity, as a statement of a Judaic religious system? To grasp the answer to that question, we have rapidly to survey the components of a religious system and to ask about the point of systemic analysis, or, in simpler language, the purpose of reading documents in their social context as the statement of a Judaism. As has already been suggested, there are three necessary components of a religious system of the social order: an account of the social group at hand, a statement of the way of life that characterizes that group (in details perhaps shared with kindred groups), and an explicit formulation of the world-view that animates the group. These three – way of life, world-view, theory of the social entity – together set forth who does what and why, the ethics, ethnos, and ethnic entity at hand. In the case of a Judaism, as distinct from a religious system situated within a different setting, a Judaic theory of the social order will always call its social entity "Israel," invariably will appeal to the Torah, and inevitably will link the main propositions of the theory to the Torah, whether through explicit, verbal exegesis, or through gestures or actions or rites that mirror or mimic those of the Torah, or through other media of cultural continuity.

Taking up a coherent body of writings valued by a group of like-minded people, we begin with the question that takes priority: who are we? That is, the group's definition of itself as a social entity has to produce a well-considered statement, or the matters of world-view and way of life lose all social specificity; then a book will by itself set forth a religious theory of the social order, but, as we have noted, a book is not a religion, it is only that which records a religion. What makes the group noteworthy always begins with the way in which it marks out its own limits, on the one side, and also discerns the links among its adherents, on the other. To explain what I mean is simple. A group that emerges along the lines of the givens, within the natural limits of the group's life, will identify itself by boundaries of family or territory or appeal to a myth of familial or territorial origin. Thus, to take one example, in Joshua Israel is made up of families attached to given pieces of territory. But a Judaism, later on, will comprise individuals, not necessarily entire families, and the Judaic systems put forth by the Christians and the rabbis of the Mishnah, to name two striking cases among many, explicitly declare that the community of the faithful (Christ's followers, the sages' disciples) abandon the natural family in favor of a supernatural one; they may even leave the natural location, e.g. native village, in favor of a supernatural one. So there is no social given for a Judaic statement of the social order. To the contrary, that which others receive as a given is here accepted as a gift. The theory of the social order will commonly take up the natural limits of the social group, familial or territorial, and rework them in an unusual way.

The way of life of a Judaism finds its critical task in mediating between a way of living deemed natural and broadly accepted and the special traits of the distinct social entity, that is, in defining "we" as against "they" (we being differentiated internally, they being the undifferentiated other). In the case of a Judaism, nearly all Jews are assumed to have obeyed laws of the Torah. A Judaism will teach which laws bear emphasis, which may be ignored, which ones are to be kept in a special way, different from the way of others, and which ones are kept in the ordinary way and therefore not deemed systemically indicative. No one eats pork, but if everyone is the same on that score, then the group will not have found definition in such a datum. But these are details. When we speak of the way of life of a group, we do not mean mainly the details of the everyday world, even those governing who marries whom or how offspring enter the community. We mean, what exactly are people supposed to do with their lives by reason of their adherence to the group? Analyzing a systemic document, we will want to know how the writers define the ideal activity, what it is that people are supposed to deem their highest public priority for everyday engagement. In the case of the Mishnah, for example, the study of the Torah is one such activity, while in the case of the Talmud, it is the only one. But the Mishnah's definition of its way of life encompasses and even privileges study of the Torah without identifying that activity as the norm – the goal of the public, corporate community in its everyday life.

The world-view answers the question, why, with a clear statement of systemic teleology, the goal of the system. That teleology may draw upon the scriptural ones, therefore exhibiting points in common with other systemic teleologies. But, as before, what is shared will prove systemically inert and not indicative, and what is special will serve as a key to defining the group. To take two obvious examples, no Jew in antiquity will have found implausible the conception of God as bearing the traits of man, since Scripture is explicit on that score. What makes the Christian doctrine of incarnation systemically special is the unique status accorded to the Incarnation of Jesus Christ, the only man to whom the category "incarnation" applied. And, again, every-one in antiquity found the Messiah-theme quite familiar. But while some systems laid heavy emphasis on that theme, formulating their teleologies in terms of eschatology and identifying the Messiah as the teleological crux, others found the theme of negligible systemic inter-est. The Talmud's system and that of the Gospels represent the former, the Mishnah's, the latter type. Here too, therefore, the systemic analysis must identify what is at the center and the heart of the system, not merely classifying data within the three categories now in hand, but sorting out the data to indicate relative priority, on the one side, and systemic neutrality, on the other.

WHAT IS AT STAKE AND WHAT IS TO BE GAINED?

The critical issue of systemic analysis concerns not the analysis of the parts but the cogency of the whole: how the parts hold together and make a single statement, each in its own context. For, in the end, if we claim that a religious system of the social order makes a statement concerning a group, then it is the coherence of the group that is the subject of the statement, and how each of the systemic components contributes its portion of the larger statement becomes the generative question of analysis of the details. A system will then prove to repeat itself, saying some few things in a great many ways, and the repetitive quality of the statement will attest to the presence of the system to begin with. The work of systemic analysis then involves the explana-tion of the system's power to say the same thing about everything, the description, analysis, and interpretation of the system's conception of self-evident connection. The system will select this to juxtapose with that, and why the juxtaposition is self-evident, while another juxtaposition will be deemed jarring or even implausible, forms the task of analysis. The upshot is, systemic description of a religious system entails the exegesis of exegesis.

Imprecise at best, the systemic analysis clearly has to commence at the outer limits of the system (just as we said when taking up the components of the system and insisting on the priority of its theory of the social entity). Standing back, we look at the group that stands behind the documents and ask ourselves, what problems must this group address, and what considerations do we imagine confronted the members of the group every day? The answer to that question will form our initial hypothesis for systemic analysis. A social group will face certain tasks to sustain itself; its context may well define those tasks – malign or benign, few or numerous, closely akin or quite alien, for instance. If the context is one of malignity, then the social group will require high walls of self-esteem; if the group forms a negligible part of the larger world in which it finds itself, then the group will have to take measures to ensure its stability and demographic continuity; if the larger setting is marked off by low, porous boundaries, then the group will have to raise the walls high and thicken them too. From our perspective, the task becomes one of correlating the contents of the systemic statement with the circumstance to which the system, overall, addresses itself.

That correlation will yield a paramount and urgent question that the system simply must address, a question that, in small ways and in acute angles, finds an answer in the details of the system. The urgent question identified, we have to articulate what we conceive to form the system's self-evidently valid answer, the answer that is repeated everywhere and in masses of details. These two – urgent question, self-evidently valid answer – form the systemic center, set forth its statement, impart cogency to its details, make the system coherent and comprehensible to its participants and to onlookers as well. Obviously, when we insist upon a coherent question and answer that infuse the whole, we may well take the path of reductionism, alleging that many complex things are few and simple. A heavy component of subjectivity burdens analysis, and matters of judgment produce lively debate. But the case is there to be made, and it is the analytical process that forms the centerpiece of learning: how do we make sense of what is before us?

A RELIGIOUS READING OF RELIGION

The presently more familiar approach to the study of ancient Judaism seeks a different set of correlations, temporal ones. At stake in the reading of the Judaic system of the Dead Sea library commonly are answers to three questions: who are the people who wrote these books, what happened to them, and how do they relate to the ongoing history of the Jews or even of Judaism? These are questions of history and context, and the answers serve a historical goal, which is to explain the specific data at hand not in their own terms, as accounts of a religious community, but in terms supplied by historical study of the people, Israel, viewed as an encompassing entity and an ongoing one. But the authors of the Dead Sea documents viewed themselves as Israel, that is the key to their existence, and when we ignore the premise of their writing and substitute the premise of our interest in them, we close ourselves off from the possibility of hearing what they are saying. The same is to be said when we turn to the Gospels, where our principal questions concern who Jesus really was and what he really said, as distinct from who the Gospels say he was and what they say he said. In substituting a superior truth, the historical one, for the claims of a supernatural character, we ignore the religion of the documents in favor of their (allegedly) historical detritus.

What then matters to us concerns not what the documents say, but what they do not say but may well contain nonetheless: not their statements about Jesus Christ, God Incarnate, but their facts about a man, Jesus, to whom people assigned some diverse sayings, and about whom they told stories of an uneven, and mostly unhistorical, character. The historical reading, with its interest in long-term traditions of a cumulative and unitary character, finds difficult the religious dimension of the systemic writings of a religious community. But an "Israel" that is merely an episode in the Jews' continuous, cumulative this-worldly progress through time bears testimony to a merely adventitious fact: Jews lived here and did this, rather than living there and doing that. That "Israel" may differ in some detail from other Israels, but the distinctions make little difference, and the points in common predominate.

Within that perspective, we perceive not difference from other groups but the sameness of all groups. And when we cannot account for difference, we also cannot explain it effectively – hence the fabrication of a single Judaism, whether the one of the common denominator, or the one of orthopraxy, such as we considered in

Chapter Two. The flaw lies not in the trivialization of the differences between one group and another – even of the fact that one group values as authoritative and part of the Torah what another group dismisses as inconsequential. The flaw lies in the difficulty of getting at the religious character of self-evidently religious writings when our hermeneutics comes to us from secular history. We turn out not to care very much about those matters that, on the very surface of things, the community and its writers found deeply engaging. They had in mind to write down and hand on their encounter with God in the Torah, reducing to words the religious world they conceived and proposed to embody. What does it mean in the here and now to be "Israel," the people whom God calls into being at Sinai through the Torah? That is the question that all Judaic religious systems answer.

It is not a historical question, except so far as time and change, context and circumstance, contribute to the shaping of the answer (as they always do, but mostly after the fact). It is a religious question, answered in the context of the historical here and now, a general question dealt with in the specificities of time and circumstance. A religious reading of religion commences with the certainty that the facts of religion possess their own autonomy and do not stand at the bar of historical judgment at all. Whether or not the facts of religion constitute also this-worldly facts of history is monumentally irrelevant to the world of religion, even though the faithful will naturally take for granted that the use of the past tense refers to facts of time and circumstance.

DO WE EVER KNOW WHAT WE CANNOT SHOW? THE QUESTION OF WHAT IS TO BE TAKEN FOR GRANTED

Since we stress what differentiates one set of Judaic systemic writings from another, we must ask ourselves whether we accord sufficient appreciation to what these writings possess in common but do not articulate with emphasis, that is, the shared premise of various Judaisms. Should we not take into account in our process of systemic analysis not only what the documents say, but what they take for granted? When we answer that question affirmatively, as we obviously must, we find ourselves confronted with a considerable issue, recently subject to much debate, on how we know what is taken for granted. For our part, we insist upon evidence on behalf of allegations, denying that we possess historical knowledge a priori or know things that we cannot show. At the same time, we underscore our conviction that when we read a document, our principal task is to discern what the document does not say in so many words but clearly deems not only true but also important.

Let us ask the question of premise and inference in simple, general terms: if I know this, what else do I know? If an author tells me this, what else does he tell me about what he is thinking or how he knows what he knows and how he thinks he knows it? Can I move back from the text to the intellectual context the text presupposes? Everybody understands that the definitive documents of a religion expose something, but contain everything. So it is the task of learning to explore the premises, presuppositions, and processes of imagination and of critical thought that yield in the end the statements that we find on the surface of the writings. But the work has to be done systematically and not episodically, in a thorough way and not through episode, anecdote, and example. That defines the task of the systemic analysis of a Judaism: we address an entire canon with the question: precisely what are the premises demonstrably present throughout, the generative presuppositions not in general but in all their rich specificity?

These observations carry us to a contemporary debate bearing heavy implications for the study of a Judaic system, the one on whether a single Judaism can be shown to be implicit in diverse documents. A simple challenge precipitates the discussion: "one must press behind the contents of the Mishnah and attempt to discover what the contents of the Mishnah presuppose . . ." (E. P. Sanders).[1] Sanders correctly insists that we know more about the religion of a piece of writing than what the document tells us in so many words. We may gain access to what the document presupposes. But what we mean by "presupposition" has to be clarified. And the sort of "presupposition" that contributes to our understanding of the givens of a document and the system it sets forth requires a clear definition. Sanders insists that there is a single Judaism, which produces many variations, but which holds all the documentary evidence together. But the result of such an effort yields a Judaism of such banality and platitudinous character that, knowing what he thinks we know about the whole, we understand better neither the whole nor any one of the parts.

In fact, the Judaism beyond the texts is the Judaism that the texts take for granted outside of themselves. If we understand the position represented by Sanders, that is what is at stake in his formulation of the question. He has asked the right question in the right way, but he expects answers that the texts cannot give, and that is for a simple reason: a gross error of simple logic. It is this: what the text takes for granted is the text and its writers' viewpoint, not the world beyond the text and the attitudes of those for whom the text cannot claim to speak. If the text expresses its distinctive viewpoint about matters particular to its writers, what makes us think that it is an objective witness to matters that (we think) are not particular to its writers? The sum of the parts cannot exceed that of the whole; bias in detail will be magnified into bias in general. There is a substantial difference between presuppositions concerning the world *beyond*, which simply project outward what is within, and presuppositions concerning the world *behind*, the premise that the text itself contains and that it reliably exhibits for our close inspection. A text is expert testimony only about its own perspective, encompassing all manner of facts shaped within the said perspective. What we cannot show we do not know, and merely because a document takes for granted people do one thing and not some other, that does not mean we know how people really were doing things. All we know is how the text's authors imagined, or wanted, things to be done. In the world of difference between fantasy and social facts lies the distinction between "beyond" the texts and "behind" the texts.

IS THERE A SINGLE JUDAISM BEHIND THE MULTIPLICITY OF DOCUMENTS? THE DEBATE WITH E. P. SANDERS

What Sanders wishes to find is the Judaism that encompasses all Judaisms, but that excludes Christianity, that is, the single viewpoint that characterizes all of the diverse systems that distinctive sets of writings put forward, except for the one important system. So when he speaks of "presuppositions," he has in mind an account of what everybody knows but no one (necessarily) makes explicit. That is why "beyond" rather than "behind" is the right word for what he wishes to investigate.[2]

Sanders' principal criticism of our approach to the study of formative Judaism is that we have no imagination. What he means by presupposition and what we mean are simply not the same thing. We mean, working back from the words people use and the sense they convey to what (may) lie behind, that is, the premises of a given statement or conception. He means, working outward from what they say to what else they ought to have said. The study of presuppositions is not an act of undisciplined imagination, but a careful, step-by-step review of solid evidence read in the light of a set of crafted questions. Let us turn to the entire passage, italicizing the sentences that we find astounding (pp. 414–15):

> We have seen that, for details, we must have recourse to rabbinic literature, especially to the passages that we can attribute to the earliest layer. Early rabbinic literature, however, is largely legal; one can derive from it general theological beliefs, such as that charity is important, but nothing like the rich substance that the Dead Sea Scrolls provide for the Essenes. If all we had from Qumran were the *Community Rule,* without its concluding hymn, the evidence would be analogous to what the Mishnah tells us about the Pharisees: the Dead Sea sect would look like a religion in which nothing mattered but rules. *Neusner, in fact, has proposed that this was true of the early rabbis. This shows a lack of imagination and a failure to consider the accident of survival. If we had a collection of private Pharisaic prayers, we would find them as deeply devotional as are the hymns from Qumran.* Since they did not survive, it will be important to reconsider the main themes of the Eighteen Benedictions, which probably show something of Pharisaic piety.
>
> The accident of survival poses a further problem. If the earliest rabbinic literature tells us too little about Pharisaic theology and piety, it tells us too much about their legal interpretation; that is, too much to be adequately covered in the present chapter. The required stratification is, in the first place, very difficult to achieve. The earliest rabbinic document, the Mishnah, is usually dated *c.* 200–220 CE. Much of the material is anonymous, while other passages are attributed to named sages. Of the attributed material, the bulk is second-century rather than first (even assuming that all attributions are accurate). Separating the possibly first-century material from later passages in the Mishnah and other rabbinic sources is slow, difficult work, and categorizing it is almost equally hard. Neusner spent three volumes at the second task, but he mis-categorized the passages, and the entire job needs to be done again. We have attempted to do it for Purity (see n. 5), but the analysis of rabbinic legal debates is not really our métier, and we wanted to do just enough of it to see whether or not Neusner's passages support his conclusions. They do not.

Sanders knows that if we had a collection of private Pharisaic prayers, we would find them as deeply devotional as are the hymns from Qumran. We have no imagination, because, if we did, we would know that fact that Sanders knows. Not only so, but we also have no confidence in our capacity to make up evidence that does not exist, which accounts for our "failure to consider the accident of survival."

We do not know what that collection would say, and neither does Sanders, because at this time we have no such collection. So while what he says "stands to reason," or "is obvious," it is hardly very solid ground on which to base any conclusions whatsoever: what we cannot show, we do not know. Still, for not knowing what we cannot show, we should not accuse our academic adversaries of a "lack of imagination." True, we do not make things up as we go along; Sanders does – proudly says so, and in so many words. He knows what has not survived, which is why "the accident of survival" is a consideration. We simply describe what we have and draw conclusions based on what we do know. We do not regard that characteristic of our scholarship as a vice but as a virtue. Scholarship in general regards certainty about what absent evidence says as bizarre, and conclusions based on imagination as fiction.

THE JUDAISM BEHIND THE TEXTS

Clearly, in our reading of the documents of a Judaism, such as those of Christianity that will concern us in the next four chapters, our systemic analysis requires us to ask about what is taken for granted. Now, when we ask about "the Judaism behind the texts in this case of the New Testament," we refer to a variety of specific matters. All of them concern the premises or presuppositions of a document and of important statements within that document. We want to know what someone must take for granted as fact in order to make an allegation of some consequence within a legal or theological writing. Taking as our given what is alleged in a document, we ask, in order to take that position, what do we have to have known as fact? What must we have taken for granted as a principle? What set of issues or large-scale questions – fundamental issues that seem to us to pop up everywhere – has to have preoccupied us, so as to lead us to identify a given problem for solution, a given possibility awaiting testing?

These statements left unsaid but ubiquitously assumed may be of three kinds, from the obvious, conventional, unsurprising, unexceptional, uninteresting, routine, and systemically inert to the highly suggestive, provocative, and systemically generative.

First, a statement in a text may presuppose a religious norm of belief or behavior (halakhah or *aggadah*, in the native categories). For one example, if a rule concerns itself with when the Shema is to be recited, the rule presupposes a prayer, the Shema – and so throughout. Such a presupposition clearly is to be acknowledged, but ordinarily, the fact that is taken for granted will not stand behind an exegetical initiative or intellectual problem to which a document pays substantial attention.

Second, a statement in a text may presuppose knowledge of a prior, authoritative text. For instance, rules in the Mishnah take for granted uncited texts of Scripture, nearly the whole of tractate Yoma providing a particularly fine instance, since the very order and structure of that tractate prove incomprehensible without a verse-by-verse review of Leviticus chapter 16. Many passages in the Gospels presuppose a deep knowledge of prophetic books. Knowing that the framers of a document had access to a prior holy book by itself does not help us to understand what the framers of that document learned from the earlier one; they will have selected what they found relevant or important, ignoring what they found routine; we cannot simply assign to the later authorship complete acquiescence in all that a prior set of writers handed on, merely because the later authorship took cognizance of what the earlier one had to say. It is one thing to acknowledge, it is another to make use of, to respond to, a received truth.

Third, a concrete statement in a text may rest upon a prior conception of a more abstract character, much as applied mathematics rests upon theoretical mathematics, or technology upon the principles of engineering and physics. And this set of premises and presuppositions does lead us deep into the foundations of thought of a given, important, and systematic writing. In the main, what we want to know here concerns the active and generative premises of documents: the things the writers had to know in order to define the problems they wished to solve. We seek the key to the exegesis of the law that the framers of the Mishnah put forth, the exegesis of Scripture that they systematically provided. When we can say not only what they said but also what they took for granted, if we can explain their principles of organization and the bases for their identification of the problems they wished to solve, then, but only then, do we enter into that vast Judaic system and structure that their various writings put forth in bits and pieces and only adumbrated in its entirety.

Accordingly, this project focuses upon the third category of presuppositions, stipulating that the first two require no more than routine inquiry. That is to say, we all know that the sages of the writings deemed the Scriptures of ancient Israel, which they knew as the written part of the Torah, to be authoritative; they took for granted the facticity and authority of every line of that writing, to be sure picking and choosing, among available truths, those that required emphasis and even development. That simple fact permits us to take for granted, without laboring to prove the obvious, that the Judaism not articulated in the literature encompassed the way of life and world-view and conception of Israel that, in broad outlines, Scripture set forth. But that fact standing on its own is trivial. It allows for everything but the main thing: what characterized the specific, distinctive character of the Judaic system set forth in writings, and, it goes without saying, how the particular point of view of those writings dictated the ways in which Scripture's teachings and rules gained entry into, and a place for themselves in, the structure and system of the Judaism of the dual Torah.

Prior to a vast number of rulings, generating the problems that require those rulings, a few fundamental conceptions or principles, never articulated, await identification. And, once identified, these several conceptions or principles demand a labor of composition: how does the generative problematic that precipitates the issues of one tractate, or forms the datum of that tractate's inquiry, fit together with the generative problematic of some other tractate and its sustained exegesis of the law? Once we know what stands behind the law, we have to ask, what holds together the several fundamental principles, all of them of enormous weight and vast capacity for specification in numerous detailed cases? Before we know how to define this Judaism, we have to show that a coherent metaphysics underpins the detailed physics, a cogent principle the concrete cases, a proportioned, balanced, harmonious statement the many, derivative and distinct cases of which the law and theology of Judaism are comprised.

What documents tell us that bears consequence for the definition of their Judaism in particular – not merely what was likely to be common to all Judaism, e.g. a sacred calendar, a record of generations' encounter with God and the like – then requires specification, and the third of the three types of presuppositions or premises points toward the definition of what is at stake and under study here. That is, specifically, the deeper, implicit affirmations of documents: what they know that stands behind what they say, the metaphysics behind the physics (to resort to the metaphor just now introduced). For a close reading of both law and lore, halakhah and *aggadah*, yields a glimpse at a vast structure of implicit conceptions, those to which Sanders makes reference in his correct prescription of what is to be done: "one must press behind the contents of the Mishnah and attempt to discover what the contents of the Mishnah presuppose," as Sanders says.

It remains to explain that, when we refer to "generative premises," we mean to exclude a variety of other givens that strike us as demonstrably present but systemically inert. There are many facts our documents know and acknowledge but leave in the background; there are others, that is, premises and presuppositions, that generate numerous specific problems, indeed that turn out, upon close examination of the details of documents, to stand behind numerous concrete inquiries. The former are systemically inert, the latter, systemically provocative and formative. Such premises as the sanctity of Israel and the Land of Israel, the election of Israel, the authority of the Torah (however defined), and the like in these writings prove systemic givens, assumed but rarely made the focus of exegetical thought.

Not only so: a very long list of platitudes and banalities can readily be constructed and every item on the list shown to be present throughout the documents under study here; but those platitudes and banalities make no contribution to the shaping of our documents and the formulation of their system. Therefore, having proven that the sun rises in the east, from those systemically inert givens, we should know no more about matters than we did beforehand. True, to those in search of "Judaism," as distinct from the diverse Judaic systems to which our evidence attests, that finding – God is one, God gave the Torah, Israel is God's chosen people, and the like – bears enormous consequence. But that God is one in no way accounts for the system's specific qualities and concerns, any more than does the fact that the laws of gravity operate.

What makes a Judaic system important is what marks that system as entire and imparts to that system its integrity: what makes it different from other systems, what holds that system together. Defining that single, encompassing "Judaism" into which genus all species, all Judaisms, fit helps us understand nothing at all about the various Judaisms. But all we really have in hand are the artifacts of Judaisms. As the prologue has already argued, efforts to find that one Judaism that holds together all Judaisms yields suffocating banalities and useless platitudes: we do not understand anything in particular any better than we did before we had thought up such generalities. So by "generative premises," we mean, the premises that counted: those that provoked the framers of a document's ideas to do their work, that made urgent the questions they address, that imparted self-evidence to the answers they set forth.

THE CONTEXT OF ALL JUDAISMS

The premise of our study of Judaisms (or other classes of religion) demands articulation. It is that we deal with religion, and that the artifacts of religion – the books people write, the communities they organize, the rites they practice, the wars they fight – take place as expressions of, or memorials to, the encounter with God. Religion is the this-worldly record of the meeting with the supernatural. The records of religion then are to be compared to the notes that record music. The notes are not the music, but they may serve to allow us to re-present the music, to realize once again what has one time taken place. When we take up what we conceive to constitute the critical center of various Judaisms, with our stress on the Christian Judaism set forth in the New Testament writings, our task is to identify what we conceive to form the center and the heart of the religious moment recorded and also replicated in the writings of the religious community, but also in the rites of the community, in the everyday life and affairs of that community, in the reconsideration of the entire history of the world and of Israel in the world (for a Judaism) that must take place by that community.

We do not mean to define that Judaism that is prior, and common, to all Judaisms when we specify what we conceive to define the context in religious experience that forms the foundation of all Judaic constructions. That is a conception that, as amply explained now, we do not hold but find incommensurate. Rather, we state what we conceive every Judaism takes up as its critical and generative concern. It is the question: how does God intersect with the world of nature and humanity? and that question finds as its self-evident answer, through the life of Israel, the people God has called into being as the cradle of his love, the object of his yearning. Before there can arise a conception of God Incarnate, there must be a prior given, that God cares for creation and wishes to walk on earth, as at Eden, in Israel.

The context of all Judaisms then finds its definition in the urgent questions: how does humanity know God? what are the terms of God's entry into the world? with their self-evident answer: through God's self-manifestation to Israel. For one Judaism, this conception comes to expression in so many words: God entered the world on account of Israel, and God departed from the world because of Israel's actions; the center of God's presence was the Temple in its time, but the presence abandoned the Temple in due course:

Fathers according to Rabbi Nathan XXXIV:VIII.1

A There were ten descents that the Presence of God made into the world.

B One into the Garden of Eden, as it says, *And they heard the sound of God walking in the garden* (Genesis 3:5).

C One in the generation of the tower of Babylon, as it is said, *And the Lord came down to see the city and the tower* (Genesis 11:5)

D One in Sodom: *I shall now go down and see whether it is in accord with the cry that has come to me* (Genesis 18:21).

E One in Egypt: *I shall go down and save them from the hand of the Egyptians* (Exodus 3:8).

F One at the sea: *He bowed the s also and came down* (2 Samuel 22:10).

G One at Sinai: *And the Lord came down onto Mount Sinai* (Exodus 19:20).

H One in the pillar of cloud: *And the Lord came down in a pillar* (Numbers 11:25).

I One in the Temple: *This gate will be closed and will not be open for the Lord, God of Israel, has come in through it* (Ezekiel 44:2).

J And one is destined to take place in the time of Gog and Magog: *And his feet shall stand that day on the mount of Olives* (Zechariah 14:4).

XXXIV:IX.1

A In ten upward stages the Presence of God departed, from one place to the next: from the ark cover to the cherub, from the cherub to the threshold of the temple-building; from the threshold of the temple to the two cherubim; from the two cherubim to the roof of the sanctuary; from the roof of the sanctuary to the wall of the temple court; from the wall of the temple court to the altar; from the altar to the city; from the city to the temple mount; from the temple mount to the wilderness.

B From the ark cover to the cherub: *And he rode upon a cherub and flew* (2 Samuel 22:11).

C From the cherub to the threshold of the temple-building: *And the glory of the Lord mounted up from the cherub to the threshold of the house* (Ezekiel 10:45).

D From the threshold of the temple to the two cherubim: *And the glory of the Lord went forth from off the threshold of the house and stood over the cherubim* (Ezekiel 10:18).

E From the two cherubim to the roof of the sanctuary: *It is better to dwell in a corner of the housetop* (Proverbs 21:9).

F From the roof of the sanctuary to the wall of the temple court: *And behold the Lord stood beside a wall made by a plumbline* (Amos 7:7).

G From the wall of the temple court to the altar: *I saw the Lord standing beside the altar* (Amos 9:1).

H From the altar to the city: *Hark, the Lord cries to the city* (Micah 6:9).

I From the city to the Temple mount: *And the glory of the Lord went up from the midst of the city and stood upon the mountain* (Ezekiel 11:23).

J From the temple mount to the wilderness: *It is better to dwell in a desert land* (Proverbs 21:19).

K And then to on high: *I will go and return to my place* (Hosea 5:15).

Here we see an entirely supernatural issue in the matter of who and what is Israel. When we speak of Jesus Christ, God Incarnate, we invoke a category that is no more "biographical" or historical than when we speak of Israel, we invoke a category that is ethnic. In both cases, as we shall now see, we find ourselves engaged in a profound inquiry, one wholly congruent with ancient Israel's deepest yearning, into how God and humanity meet. Israel or Christ, Torah or Christ – both formulations serve, each its own Judaism.

4

THEORY OF THE SOCIAL ENTITY

Who and what is "Israel" in the Judaism of St Paul?

THE URGENT QUESTION

For the earliest followers of Rabbi Joshua of Nazareth, that is Jesus Christ, the Master's teachings represented truths of the Torah, and the Master was comparable to Moses. But then, as gentiles received that same Torah – as happened very soon – the question of how these gentiles entered Israel had to find an answer. What accorded priority to a Christian theory of Israel? Two familiar reasons present themselves. First, the Christians early on undertook to convert gentiles to the Torah, so the status of their converts within Israel required attention. But other Judaisms converted gentiles, without the comparable result of obsessive concern with defining Israel. Perhaps the birth of children within the new community precipitated a crisis in family relationships, as the matter of circumcision, which St Paul regarded as no longer required for entry into Israel, played itself out for native-born Israelites as well. But why dropping that rite should have caused more critical problems than ceasing to practice others that early Christians no longer valued hardly proves obvious. They wished to distinguish themselves, and one indicative rite would serve as well as some other. We find ourselves confused by details which do not bear self-evident sense and meaning. Why should the matter of Israel have imposed itself on all else?

To answer that question, we have to identify what we conceive to have formed the soul of the earliest Christian moment. What strikes us as critical, the single most important religious experience that animated Christian Judaism, is the person of Jesus Christ, God Incarnate. That religious encounter, and that alone, formed the heart and defined the center of Christianity, and to that point all else was subordinated. Christian Judaism built upon the conviction among this sector of Israel that God had taken human form and walked among them, had been crucified, raised from the dead, and enthroned on high. These Israelites formed their community in the confidence that they knew God and had access to God even now. That religious event precipitated deep thinking on the subsidiary truths implicit in the same encounter with the living God in the here and now. It required rereading the Torah in the light of this newest revelation. If, then, we try to imagine ourselves within the small, beleaguered community of Christians, a handful here, a handful there, and ask ourselves how they will have formulated the critical issues of their shared life, what is the result? It is the obvious recognition that, for this Israel, a source of knowledge of God, what God wants of us, how we are to know and love and serve God, has become accessible to us beyond the limits of the knowledge of God Israel has possessed from Sinai, in the Torah.

Now the urgent question that permeated the life of the community emerges with slight ambiguity: if Christ, then what of the Torah? That is a question we shall enter in Chapter Seven when we take up the world-view of this Judaism, set forth in the Letter to the Hebrews, but a brief preview will place much else into context. If we know God through Christ, do we require the knowledge afforded by the Torah? We have now – so the Christians maintained in reflecting upon knowledge of God – another, better way of knowing God, not through the record of the past, true and accurate though that account was held to be, but through what our own eyes have seen and our own ears have heard: no longer through a dirty mirror but in the clear light of day. And that must mean, the recorded experience that had alone afforded access now takes second place to the direct encounter; the Torah registered its truths, but a better way to truth had opened up: God himself had walked among us, so the Christians maintained. It goes without saying that the way of life of Israel has also to undergo re-examination in the light of this new self-manifestation of God, besides that set forth in the Torah, and in our reading in Chapter Six of the Gospel of Matthew's portrait of the Torah of Christ we shall find illumination when we read the parts in the light of this central conception, that a new Moses has walked among us bringing torah, divine instruction, as an aspect of God's self-manifestation.

And that brings us to the question, what was the impact upon the definition of Israel? For the place of the Torah in the sanctification of

Israel was explicit from Sinai forward. If Israel is Israel by reason of the Torah, which affords to Israel that distinctive knowledge of God and God's will that defines Israel's way of life and world-view, then how are we Israel, how do we need to remain Israel, within the Torah, when we have been given a better way than the Torah's to God? Here is a formidable question, one that vastly transcends the petty questions of how to convert gentiles, on the one side, and how to admit male children to the covenant, on the other. The question of the continuing status of the Torah among people who have themselves stood at Sinai and received in place of the Torah the Christ-Messiah – that question would continue to trouble people. But the reason derives not from detail; rather, here is the main point of the New Testament's system – so we propose – and the heart and soul of its Judaism. And the question of Christ and the Torah would then play itself out at every point: if the one, then why the other. And vice versa, if the Torah, then what need for Christ?

So the urgent question addressed by each component of the Christian Judaism set forth in the New Testament took up the effects of the encounter with God through Jesus Christ, God Incarnate, as these worked themselves through the received faith of Israel set forth in the Torah. As we see, the question framed as we have defined it proves inner-facing, directed to the internal life of the Christian community itself; it was not a question precipitated by a political crisis – how to relate to the other Jews; by concerns of church order – how to receive converts to Israel; or by the psychological crisis precipitated for born Israelites by the advent of children born to them in their new condition (if there was such a crisis of a psychological character at all). The urgent question emerged from the generative experience of Christianity, from the very starting-point of its life: the Incarnate God they had known and now knew and proposed to introduce to not only their own Israel but – in the pattern of the proselytizing people that the Israelites then were – to everybody else as well.

TORAH AND CHRIST, ISRAEL AND THE GENTILES

Now for a deep thinker about the inner structure of ideas such as St Paul's writings show him to have been, the issue of "Israel" presented the opportunity to reflect upon the twin problems of the relationship of the Torah and Christ in the knowledge of God, on the one side, and the relationship of the Torah and Christ in the recognition of who and what is Israel, on the other. The former has already been spelled out with sufficient clarity; the latter requires a bit of reflection still. As we noted, through the Torah Israel came into being; through entering the disciplines of the Torah, gentiles joined Israel. But both facts, as we said, depended upon the same prior claim: in the Torah we know God. Then if through Christ we know God, should we not place Christ above the Torah and assign him the post at the entry point of Israel? That second proposition flows from the first.

But does the very status of Israel now come under question, when gentiles through the encounter with God Incarnate may know and serve God without undertaking to accept the originally received Torah at all? The claim of the Torah to make God manifest now competed with the claim that in Jesus Christ God is made known, so if the one, then why the other? And what status are we to accord to the rest of Israel, that part of Israel that has not yet known God in that Incarnation that we have known?

These two questions define the parameters of the problem that Paul was to address in some of his most profound and important writing: the relationship of Christ and the Torah, on the one side, the relationship of the Christian (of gentile origin, but now within the framework of the knowledge of God that for Israel is afforded by the Torah) to Israel on the other. The nascent Christian Judaism would remain well within the framework defined by other Judaic systems, all of them privileging the Hebrew Scriptures as primary and authoritative, all of them according to Israel pride of place in the divine plan for humanity, and each of them, to be sure, also pointing to a source of revelation in addition to that of the Torah. Had Jesus not said, "I come not to destroy but to fulfill," we should have imputed that conviction to the Christian Judaism by reason of the structure and character of Paul's thinking about Israel.

For what Paul did was two things. First, he defined the character of Israel in such a way that gentiles could gain access to what remained the community and people that God had chosen and would always cherish. Israel would be set forth in such a way that gentiles could join, but Israel would remain what Scripture always contended it was meant to be: God's first love. Second, he worked out the relationship of Christ and the Torah in such a way that the Torah remained authoritative, but Christ became definitive.

Paul is never more himself than in Romans chapters 9–11, which is just where he frames the issue of Israel in a way which became classic for Christianity. Romans itself is the most mature of the genuinely Pauline letters, written to a community which he had not personally founded. His letter to Rome is, in effect, a fulsome introduction to his own thinking, and the main lines of Paul's argument seem reasonably clear. But the form of his argumentation, with its many references to Scripture and deductions from Scripture, strikes most readers as both foreign and convoluted. Why is a basically simple idea wrapped up in an esoteric package? As we shall see, that question will itself require refinement as we encounter Paul's thinking, but it will serve us well as we first approach our text.

PAUL'S ARGUMENT IN ROMANS 9–11

An observant student could sketch out a précis of Paul's thought in Romans 9–11 without reference to the Scripture he cites. The result would be a reasonable, self-contained address, which could be delivered succinctly (along the lines of the following paraphrase):

> Although I am distressed that my people have not accepted the gospel (9:1–5), their failure is not God's: it is just that he has, as always, chosen freely whom he wills (9:6–13). That might seem hard, but God is sovereign in the matter of choice (9:14–23), and he has simply decided to call both Jews and gentiles (9:24–33).[1]
>
> There is now no distinction between Jew and Greek in the matter of salvation: if you confess the Lord Jesus and believe God raised him from the dead, you will be saved (10:1–21, v. 9). Those who are believers must not, however, imagine that God has rejected his people. After all, there are some Jews who do believe in Jesus (11:1–10), and even those who do not believe have, in their lack of faith, provided an opportunity for gentiles (11:11–24). Once the fullness of the gentiles is accomplished, *all* Israel, including both Jews and gentiles, will be seen to be saved (11:25–36).

There are, of course, crucial facets within each of the statements in the above précis which remain to be explored, but they are subsidiary to the main lines of the argument. What becomes unmistakably clear, when we boil Paul's ornate speech down to its essentials, is that he is making a cogent case for a particular view of how God's saving activity in Christ Jesus is consistent with his election of Israel. Once it is clear that Israel is *elected*, not sovereign, so that divine choice is operative, rather than divine right, Paul's observations follow logically.

Paul's design at this point comports well with the purpose of his letter to the Romans as a whole, and makes sense within the Hellenistic environment in which he functioned. In a relatively recent book, Stanley Stowers has explained that the writing of letters, whether at the common level of incidental discourse, or with a refined standard of rhetoric, was conventional within the culture of the Mediterranean basin and is a natural context in which to understand much of the New Testament.[2] That convention also influenced ancient Judaism, which – despite the impression of an isolated phenomenon which some writers give – was itself a lively constituent within the cultural life of its time.[3] But Stowers is well within the scholarly consensus when he concludes that Judaism did not actively appropriate the convention and transmit it directly to Christianity.[4]

Specifically, Paul in Romans appears to be writing a "protreptic letter," by which Stowers means a work designed to convert the reader to Paul's set of teachings. Stowers is able on the basis of a comparison with Graeco-Roman convention to argue that the entire letter is designed to present Paul's gospel of salvation for gentiles, and to defend it against the charge that it means the loss of Israel's salvation.[5] The analysis of Romans according to its function within its most plausible social setting therefore helps us to resolve the main lines of its purpose. Indeed, the clarity of function which emerges from such an approach may appear curiously at odds with the convoluted character of Paul's argument.

PAUL'S USE OF SCRIPTURE IN ROMANS 9–11

Whenever an exegete discovers that his or her explanation of a text is dramatically more homogeneous than the text itself, it is time to consider the possibility that over-simplification has crept in. Even if Romans be a "protreptic letter," the involved argument from Scripture in chapters 9–11 is obviously the result of a dynamic not evidenced by the letter as a whole. Of course, Scripture does play a crucial role in Romans generally (as it does normally in Pauline thought), but the consistency of recourse to textual argument makes our chapters appear distinctive.[6]

Before we consider why Paul's form of argumentation in Romans 9–11 is exegetical in a way most of the letter is not, we must first appreciate how the simple, discursive case Paul makes is enhanced by means of reference to Scripture. At each major point in the argument, well known passages of Scripture are cited.

A crucial bridge is provided by narratives concerning Isaac. In Romans 9:7, Paul quotes Genesis 21:12, "After Isaac shall your seed be named." Now that reference may appear simply to be an instance of using a "proof-text," chosen pretty much at random from a much larger number of those that might have been cited. But the quotation comes at the climax of a story in which God tells Abraham to accede to Sarah's demand, and cast out Hagar and Ishmael, "for the son of this slave woman shall not inherit with my son Isaac" (Genesis 21:10).

The analogy with the situation Paul believes he addresses is striking. He spells the analogy out in Romans 9:8, "That is, these children of flesh are not children of God, but children of the promise are reckoned as the seed." Of course, that finding requires that Isaac correspond to the promise, and Paul makes out just that correspondence. In Romans 9:9, he quotes Genesis 18:14 (or perhaps v. 10): "At this time [next year] I will come, and Sarah will have a son." That verse, of course, is resonant, since it caps the story of God's visitation at Mamre: Sarah laughs (v. 12), and is blessed with Isaac, whose name means "he laughs," because it is God's joke in the end. In Paul's argument, the apparent frivolity of God's sovereign choice is a serious principle, attested in Scripture.

The pattern established in Romans 9:6–9 is followed consistently in the chapters we are concerned with. At first, Paul does not cite a specific Scripture in what follows, but he does invoke the general case of Rebecca and Isaac (9:10, 11). She conceived twins, and before they did anything, or were even born, Rebecca was told, "The greater will serve the lesser" (Romans 9:12 and Genesis 25:23). At issue, of course, is the rivalry between Esau and Jacob, which is a major motif of Genesis. Paul sums it all up with a quotation from Malachi: "I loved Jacob and hated Esau" (Romans 9:13 and Malachi 1:2, 3). That Paul can draw upon Malachi's appropriation of the motif in Genesis is especially compelling: he implicitly claims that his analogy has prophetic warrant. The fundamentals of his scriptural reasoning are drawn from the Torah, but the nature of his reasoning, he claims, is in line with that of the prophets.

Paul appears to have operated with the conventional categorization of the Hebrew Bible in Judaism. That categorization recognized divisions of the canon into the Torah (the Pentateuch), the Prophets (including the Former Prophets, from Joshua through 2 Kings, and the Latter Prophets, more familiarly considered prophetic in English), and the Writings (an essentially miscellaneous category). The coherence and consistency of the canon is simply one of Paul's assumptions.

It is indicative of the consistency of Pauline rhetoric that he now moves from Genesis to Exodus. That shift in scriptural foundation (at

9:14f.) corresponds precisely to the development of Paul's argument (see p. 62): having rejoiced in God's sovereign choice as the fulfillment of promise, Paul now defends God's sovereignty against the charge that it is unjust or arbitrary (9:14). God said to Moses, "I will have mercy on whom I have mercy, and I will show compassion to whom I will show compassion" (Exodus 33:19; Romans 9:15). In Exodus, God speaks of his mercy and compassion just as he is revealing his goodness to Moses; Paul's point is that God's choices are consistent with his just revelation to Moses.

In the statement to Moses in Exodus 33:19, the narrative setting connects the definition of God's people with his revelation of his name and glory (Exodus 33:12–23): what is at issue is the very nature of God and the nature of his people together. A particular case in Exodus of God deciding *not* to have mercy, as Paul says (9:18), is that of Pharaoh, of whom Scripture says, "For this purpose I have raised you up, that I might display my power over you, and that my name might be announced in all the earth" (Romans 9:17; Exodus 9:16).[7] God's "name" is at issue in both passages in Exodus which have been cited (33:19 and 9:16), and their association reflects Paul's almost midrashic logic (see pp. 68–71), in which Scripture is held in different places and contexts to address the same issues coherently.

The assumption of that coherence is carried over to the prophets: Isaiah (29:16; 45:9 in Romans 9:20) and Jeremiah (18:6 in Romans 9:21) are used to demonstrate that it is misguided for a vessel of punishment to answer back to its maker. Consideration of Isaiah 29:16 and 45:9 and Jeremiah 18:6 within their literary contexts shows that Paul is still attending carefully to the sense of the passages he cites. In all, the paramount issue is the fate of Israel, as determined by a sovereign God.

The next development of Paul's argument (at 9:24f.; again, cf. p. 62) corresponds to a shift in canonical focus. It is demonstrated by citing Hosea and Isaiah that we who are called by God are from both Jews and gentiles (9:24). First, Hosea shows – at least, to Paul's satisfaction – that gentiles are to be included among God's people (9:25, 26). Paul garbles the quotation from Hosea, drawing first from 2:23, and then from 1:10, and here is stretching to make a point. Hosea is contextually concerned with the restoration of Israel, not the inclusion of gentiles; Paul reads what he takes to be a general truth of Scripture into a passage in which that meaning has no literary place.

He returns to his usual, more acute interpretation in 9:27–9 when he cites passages from Isaiah by way of arguing that Jews as such are not chosen, but that a remnant from their ranks is to be saved (Isaiah

10:22; 28:22 and Isaiah 1:9). Moreover, he cites a curious and creative mixture of Isaiah 28:16 and 8:14 in Romans 9:33, in order to show that the principle of selecting from the elect places a stone of stumbling and a rock of offense in the midst of Israel (Romans 9:30–2).

Paul's exegetical method is never more complex than in Romans 9, and we need to pause for breath before proceeding further. Although the details of the Pauline execution may dazzle us (as they were no doubt intended to), the fact is that certain characteristic traits are plain. Paul argues from the Torah that, first, God operates by fulfilling promises (9:1–13), and that, second, those promises are kept for those chosen by God (9:14–23). He then purports to demonstrate from the Prophets that God has chosen his people from among Jews and gentiles (9:24–33). On the whole, but for two exceptions, Paul cites his passages with care and contextual sensitivity, which means that any reader will better appreciate the argument if he or she is familiar with the Scriptures of Israel.

The two exceptions to Paul's care and sensitivity are instructive. As we have seen, he reads gentiles into Hosea (Romans 9:25, 26), and splices together two verses of Isaiah (9:33). These are not mere lapses on Paul's part. To his mind, the entry of gentiles among the ranks of God's chosen, and the coming of Christ as a rock of offense to many in Israel, are facts of experience which co-exist with and interpret facts of Scripture. Paul's "text" is not merely Scripture, but his awareness, and others' awareness, that Jesus is God's son.[8]

Once these interpretative characteristics of Paul's argument are appreciated, Romans 10 and 11 may more briefly be summarized from the point of view of their reference to Scripture. In chapter 10, Paul makes his famous, daring assertion that, in Deuteronomy 30:11–14, when Moses refers to the nearness of the commandment, he means not any precise instruction, but the presence of Christ, who can neither be brought down from Heaven, nor brought up from the abyss, except by God's power (Romans 10:6–8).

How does Paul know that the Scriptures, properly understood, adduce Christ? He has just told us in v. 4, "Christ is the point of the law, for the righteousness of every believer."[9] By again citing Isaiah 28:16, in v. 11, Paul may betray his own awareness that he is invoking Christ, rather than deducing Christ, at this point. The other usages in chapter 10 – of Leviticus 18:5[10] in 10:5, of Joel 3:5 in 10:13, of Isaiah 52:7 in 10:15, of Isaiah 53:1 in 10:16, of Psalm 19:4[11] in 10:18, and of Isaiah 65:1, 2 in 10:20, 21 – fall within the more usual Pauline range, of texts which illustrate a coherent principle.

Chapter 11 may be surveyed even more summarily, because the usages of Scripture are all illustrative. There are no special invocations of Christ or of the motif of the inclusion of the gentiles. Until this point, the bulk of Paul's references have come from the Torah and the Latter Prophets. Now he brings balance to his case scripturally, by citing the instance of Elijah from the Former Prophets.[12] Again, attention to the contexts of the Scriptures Paul cites richly rewards itself. The assertion that God has not rejected his people in 11:2, drawn from 1 Samuel 12:22, comes in a context in which the prophet Samuel assures Israel that, despite their wickedness, God's choice is constant (1 Samuel 12:19–25). The close of that passage, however, does threaten, "But if you act wickedly, you shall be swept away, both you and your king" (1 Samuel 12:25). Wickedness does not revoke God's choice, but it does alter its scope.

In other words, the thought of the remnant, which has been an explicit part of the argument since 9:27, 28 (by means of the citation of Isaiah 10:22, 23), has remained with Paul throughout. For that reason, the reference to Elijah in 11:2b-5 (cf. 1 Kings 19:1–18, and vv. 10, 14, and 18 in particular) is apposite: there is a prophetic analogy for the circumstances Paul finds himself in, where only a radical minority has kept faith. Once it is established that the residue of the remnant can be deliberately hardened in their rebellion (cf. Deuteronomy 29:3[13] in 11:8 and Psalm 69:22, 23[14] in 11:9), there is no further need of scriptural warrant for what Paul argues.

He does, however, offer a final citation of Isaiah (59:20, 21 and 27:9) in 11:26, 27, by way of making his comprehensive assertion that "all Israel" – but a chastened, forgiven Israel, not a claimant as of right – is to be saved.[15] At this crucial moment, he must again splice Scriptures, not merely cite them, to achieve the dual stress on deliverance and forgiveness that is the apogee of his argument.

We may set out mentally, as it were side by side, two analyses of Romans 9–11. Followed along one track, the chapters instance protreptic discourse, in which Paul appeals to his readers to follow his way of thinking. He wishes to convince them that God's inclusion of believing gentiles with Jews who accept Jesus as Christ represents a fulfillment of the promise to Israel. Followed along the second track, the same chapters represent a carefully orchestrated argument from all the main sections of the Hebrew canon, cited in translation, which is designed to sweep readers up in the promise that all Israel – namely forgiven Jews and gentiles – are to be saved (11:26, 27).

It is obvious that the two tracks of analysis are complementary, and neither alone would adequately account for the chapters as a whole. But it is equally obvious that the chapters are crafted *as* a whole: the references to Scripture are not only keyed to major developments of the argument, they contribute those developments. It is not a matter of discursive thought merely being illustrated scripturally (although illustration is one function of Scripture in Romans). Rather, logic and interpretation here interpenetrate to a remarkable degree, and give Romans 9–11 a unique character within the Pauline corpus.[16] The questions therefore emerge: what is Paul doing here, which makes the chapters distinctive, and why does he do it? Answers are forthcoming, when the purpose of Paul's argument is appreciated.

THE PURPOSE OF PAUL IN ROMANS 9–11

We would quickly decide that we understood what Paul is doing within this text and why he is doing it, were we able to accept the suggestion – developed in much recent scholarship – that Paul is here providing his readers with a Midrash.[17] It has become conventional to observe that the noun "Midrash" is derived from the verbal form *darash* (to "seek" or to "search" in Hebrew), and therefore to infer that "Midrash" refers to any "searching out" of meaning on the basis of Scripture within Judaism. It is fairly obvious that, if one is willing to work with such a free-wheeling definition, Romans 9–11 is indeed "Midrash." But such a description obscures more than it discloses.

When the rabbis produced the documents known collectively as Midrashim, the formal aim was – on the whole – to produce commentaries on Scripture. But the "commentary" was not, as in modern usage, an attempt strictly (and historically) to explain the meaning of a given document. Rather, the sense which the rabbis explored in their Midrashim was the meaning of Scripture within their practice and liturgy and teaching, which were understood as of a piece with the Torah revealed to Moses on Sinai. That is, Midrash represents a synthesis of written text and rabbinic sensibility, in which both are accorded the status of revelation.

Jacob Neusner has written the most compelling, systematic account of the development and character of the Midrashim.[18] Among other things, he shows that a given Midrash may be composed of four distinct orders of interpretation:[19]

1 close exegesis, or discussion by each word or phrase of Scripture;

2   amplification of the meaning of a passage;
3   illustration of a particular theme by various passages;
4   anthological collection around a general topic.

The result of the compilations of varying readings, involving different categories of interpretation, was the eleven distinct Midrashim (on various books of the Bible) which emerged by the end of the sixth century.[20]

When one sets out the Midrashim systematically, and provides precise examples (as Neusner does), the distance from Paul's activity in Romans in striking. His focus is no single biblical book, so that the general form of Midrash is not at issue. The categories of exegesis and amplification, which Neusner shows were most prominent in the earliest Midrashim (of the second century CE) simply do not obtain in the case of Paul. It *might* be said – at a stretch – that the third and fourth categories do characterize Pauline interpretation. But the stretch is considerable, because Paul does not merely illustrate by means of Scripture (although illustration is among his techniques); he argues through it and with it towards a conclusion which Scripture itself does not draw, but – at best – is generally consistent with. And, of course, his overarching theme, of Jesus Christ's completion of the Torah, the Prophets, and the Writings, could never be described as rabbinic. For all those reasons, to style Paul's interpretation as "Midrash" is misleading.

Having called attention to the inadequacy of any direct identification of Paul's method with the rabbis', a certain analogy remains. Both proceed synthetically, and the synthesis moves in two directions at once. First, both take Scripture as a whole, as making a harmonious, common claim upon the mind.[21] Indeed, it should be pointed out that Paul specifies Torah first, and then the Prophets (by name) and the Writings more punctiliously than the rabbis do. It appears that Paul wishes to make the point of Scripture's unity, and also that he is making an inherently convoluted argument easier to follow than it would be if he were addressing genuine experts. Second, both Paul and the rabbis also synthesize Scripture with their own sensibilities and their grasp of what Scripture as a whole means.

The last point is perhaps best illustrated by how the rabbis represented in Leviticus Rabbah took the reference to Isaac in Genesis 21:12, which Paul in Romans 9:7–8 interpreted to mean that the "children of promise" were the true "children of God." Instead, in Leviticus Rabbah Abraham's seed is defined, without justification, as those who believe in the world to come.[22] What was for Paul obviously christological was for the rabbis (of a much later period) self-evidently a halakhah of eschatological belief. Just when rabbinic and Pauline interpretation seem analogous, they prove they are antipodal.

Paul has also been compared to the sectarians of Qumran and to Philo, in respect of his interpretation of Scripture. But the famous *Pesherim* of Qumran are designed to relate Scripture exactly to the history of the community, and Philo is concerned to comment systematically on Scripture, so as to elucidate its allegedly philosophical truth.[23] Both the *Pesherim* and the Philonic corpus represent different activities and settings from Paul's: his scriptural interpretation strictly serves the protreptic function of Romans. He shows no sustained interest in historicizing Scripture (as in the *Pesherim*) or in philosophizing with it (as in Philo). Paul is driven by other motives, which is why Romans 9–11 is neither Midrash, *Pesher*, nor philosophical commentary.

Paul is arguing with all the Christians of Rome, both Jews and gentiles, in an attempt to promote unity. It is true that Paul had no direct, personal acquaintance with the community at Rome; to that extent, there is an abstract quality about the letter to the Romans which sets it apart from other Pauline letters. Writing at a distance from a church known only at second hand, Paul approximates, more nearly than he ever does, to the presentation of his theology in a systematic fashion.[24]

Nonetheless, the central, social issue in the church at Rome was known to Paul: there had been disturbances involving Jews in the city, and probably Christians as well, that resulted in their being expelled in 49 CE under the Emperor Claudius.[25] Their gradual reintegration into a single church with gentiles, which is Paul's goal, could only be accomplished by means of conveying a coherent vision in which both Jews and gentiles had a place.

The letter to the Romans offers just such a vision, which is summed up under the slogan which appears here, and only here, within the Pauline corpus: salvation is for the Jew first, and then for the Greek (1:16; 2:9, 10; cf. 3:9, 29; 9:24; 10:12). Salvation is the possession of neither, but it is offered and granted to both as children of promise, provided it is accepted by means of a willingness to be forgiven.

His letter to the Galatians presents Paul in such heated controversy with Jews who were also Christians, and with those who demanded that the conditions of Judaism be fulfilled by all followers of Christ (whether Jew or gentile), that one might have expected Paul to have used the occasion of his letter to the Romans finally to argue that the gospel of Christ could rightly be severed from its Judaic roots. Yet having written to the Galatians *c.* 53 CE, Paul went on in his Corinthian correspondence (*c.* 55–6 CE) himself to appropriate scriptural stories of Israel's salvation directly for the Church (see, for example, 1 Corinthians 10:1–4), and even to put believing Christians in the role of teachers comparable to – if greater than! – Moses (cf. 2 Corinthians 3:7–18).[26]

Here, in Rome (*c.* 57 CE),[27] was a case in which Judaism had been weakened to the point that gentiles in the Church were tempted to imagine that the divine right of Israel had been usurped definitively by the non-Jewish Church (cf. Romans 11:13–24). Paul's response is unequivocal: the rejection of many in Israel does not give latecomers any special privilege. Indeed, the implication of the "remnant" is that the essential promise to Israel is confirmed, although the rebellion of some in Israel demonstrates that no one, Jewish or not, can presume upon God's gracious election. When Paul insists throughout Romans that salvation is for Jews first, and then for Greeks, the implication is that the same dynamics of redemption, initially worked out in the case of Israel, are now available to all humanity by means of Jesus Christ.

Romans 9–11 embody that leitmotif in the letter generally. The salvation effected in Christ is uniquely comprehended by means of Scripture, where "Scripture" refers to the canon of Israel. When Paul turns to his gentile readers alone in 11:13–24, he momentarily drops any reference to Scripture, and argues from an agricultural image.[28] His message is clear: however weak the Jewish component may appear, they are root and you are branch. And it is all Israel, root and branch, which God is determined to save. Paul's purpose, once identified, explains both the nature and the form of his argument.

FINDING A PLACE FOR GENTILES WITHIN ISRAEL

How, specifically, did Paul find a place for gentiles within Israel? The answer comes to us from his deep reflections in Romans on who and what is Israel. The conclusion he reached was, Israel forms an ethnic group, a family after the flesh. But there is another Israel, an Israel of the spirit, and to this other Israel, the other-than-ethnic one, gentiles could adhere, and, indeed by their faith in Christ, they joined that Israel after the spirit that found its definition in faith. Paul stressed the character of Israel after the flesh as a family, a family of a particular order, that is, all Jews descend from Abraham, Isaac, and Jacob, Sarah, Rebecca, Leah, and Rachel.

To see the context in which Paul pursued his thought, we first address choices made by other Judaisms, turning first to the Judaic system of the Mishnah. This system, recorded long after Paul's, took exactly the position that Paul would take: to be Israel is an act of supernatural faith; belonging to this Israel depends upon faith – what is believed, what is denied. A born-Israelite in context enjoys no advantages over an Israelite by choice, since in this context he or she by an act of disbelief may be denied a portion in the world to come. Now, curiously, Paul concurs on both points – an act of faith, which overcomes ethnic distinction between home-born and converts. But Paul has a second definition of Israel, the one after the flesh, not only the one after the spirit, which the Mishnah sets forth.

In contrast to Paul's distinction between Israel after the flesh and Israel after the spirit, another Judaism, that set forth in the Mishnah, recognized no such distinction. For the Mishnah, to be "Israel" is not to believe the wrong things. In the Mishnah "Israel" is a supernatural category, for Israel consists of all those who are born in Israel, *except for those who deny the principles of the faith.* The categories are defined in terms of belief: affirming a given doctrine, denying another. That fact bears in its wake the implication that Israel as a social entity, encompassing each of its members, is defined by reference to matters of correct doctrine. All "Israelites" – persons who hold the correct opinion – then constitute "Israel." Here is an "Israel" that, at first glance, is defined not in relationships but intransitively and intrinsically. What this means, therefore, is that Israel is not a social entity at all like other social entities but an entity that finds definition, as to genus and not species, elsewhere.

No passage of the Mishnah and related literature of Mishnah-amplification is more concrete and explicit than the one cited below on who is in and who is out. But the "in" is not within this world at all. It is who enters or has a share of the world to come. Then all those "Israelites" who constitute in themselves the social entity, the group, "Israel," form a supernatural, not merely a social entity – and no wonder all metaphors fail. Gentiles who enter Israel gain the world to come, not a place in a merely-this-worldly ethnic entity. The premise is that we speak only of Israel, and the result is the definition of Israel in terms we should not have anticipated at all: not Israel as against non-Israel, gentile, nor Israel as against non-Israel, the priest, but

Israel as against those who deny convictions now deemed – explicitly – indicatively and normatively to form the characteristics of "Israel"(ite). Here is an "Israel" that, at first glance, is defined not in relationships but intransitively and intrinsically – contrary to allegations just some pages ago. But that impression will soon shift, for Israel now invokes non-Israel, just as it did earlier, but for a different purpose and in a separate context. What this means, therefore, is that Israel is not a social entity at all like other social entities, for the purposes of present discourse, but an entity that finds definition, as to genus and not species, elsewhere. To state the result simply: in what follows, Israel is implicitly *sui generis*. The passage is sufficiently important to warrant recapitulation:

M. Sanhedrin 10:1

A   All Israelites have a share in the world to come,

B   as it is said, "your people also shall be all righteous, they shall inherit the land forever; the branch of my planting, the work of my hands, that I may be glorified" (Isaiah 60:21).

C   And these are the ones who have no portion in the world to come:

D   He who says, the resurrection of the dead is a teaching which does not derive from the Torah, and the Torah does not come from Heaven; and an Epicurean.

E   R. Aqiba says, "Also: He who reads in heretical books,

F   and he who whispers over a wound and says, 'I will put none of the diseases upon you which I have put on the Egyptians, for I am the Lord who heals you' " (Exodus 15:26).

G   Abba Saul says, "Also: He who pronounces the divine Name as it is spelled out."

Israel is defined inclusively: to be "Israel" is to have a share in the world to come. "Israel" then is a social entity that is made up of those who share a common conviction, and that "Israel" therefore bears an other-worldly destiny. Other social entities are not so defined within the Mishnah – and that by definition! – and it must follow that (an) "Israel" in the conception of the authorship of the Mishnah is *sui generis*, in that other social entities do not find their definition within the range of supernatural facts pertinent to "Israel;" an "Israel" is a social group that endows its individual members with life in the world to come; an "Israel"(ite) is one who enjoys the world to come. Excluded from this "Israel" are "Israel"(ite)s who within the established criteria of social identification exclude themselves. The power to define by relationships does not run out, however, since in this supernatural context of an Israel that is *sui generis* we still know who is "Israel" because we are told who is "not-Israel," namely specific non-believers or sinners. These are, as we should expect, persons who reject the stated belief.

M. Sanhedrin 10:2

A Three kings and four ordinary folk have no portion in the world to come.

B Three kings: Jeroboam, Ahab, and Manasseh.

C R. Judah says, "Manasseh has a portion in the world to come,

D since it is said, 'And he prayed to him and he was entreated of him and heard his supplication and brought him again to Jerusalem into his kingdom' " (2 Chronicles 33:13).

E They said to him, "To his kingdom he brought him back, but to the life of the world to come he did not bring him back."

F Four ordinary folk: Balaam, Doeg, Ahitophel, and Gehazi.

Not only persons, but also classes of Israelites are specified, in all cases contributing to the definition of (an) Israel. The excluded classes of Israelites bear in common a supernatural fault, which is that they have sinned against God. Everywhere, of course, Scripture provides the established facts, out of which we are to formulate doctrine.

We begin with those excluded from the world to come who are not Israel, namely, the generation of the flood, and the generation of the dispersion. This somewhat complicates matters, since we should have thought that at issue in enjoying the world to come would be only (an) "Israel." It should follow that gentiles of whatever sort hardly require specification; they all are alike. But the focus of what follows – classes of excluded Israelites, who have sinned against God – leads to the supposition that the specified gentiles are included because of their place in the biblical narrative. The implication is not that all other gentiles enjoy the world to come except for these, and the focus of definition remains on Israel, pure and simple.

Mishnah-tractate Sanhedrin 10:3A–CC

A   The generation of the flood has no share in the world to come,

B   and they shall not stand in the judgment,

C   since it is written, "My spirit shall not judge with man forever" (Genesis 6:3)

D   neither judgment nor spirit.

E   The generation of the dispersion has no share in the world to come,

F   since it is said, "So the Lord scattered them abroad from there upon the face of the whole earth" (Genesis 11:8).

G   "So the Lord scattered them abroad" – in this world,

H   "and the Lord scattered them from there" – in the world to come.

I   The men of Sodom have no portion in the world to come,

J   since it is said, "Now the men of Sodom were wicked and sinners against the Lord exceedingly" (Genesis 13:13).

K   "Wicked" – in this world,

L   "And sinners" – in the world to come.

M   But they will stand in judgment.

N   R. Nehemiah says, "Both these and those will not stand in judgment,

O   for it is said, 'Therefore the wicked shall not stand in judgment [108A], nor sinners in the congregation of the righteous' (Psalms. 1:5).

P   'Therefore the wicked shall not stand in judgment' – this refers to the generation of the flood.

Q   'Nor sinners in the congregation of the righteous' – this refers to the men of Sodom."

R   They said to him, "They will not stand in the congregation of the righteous, but they will stand in the congregation of the sinners."

S   The spies have no portion in the world to come,

T   as it is said, "Even those men who brought up an evil report of the land died by the plague before the Lord" (Numbers14:37).

U   "Died" – in this world.

V   "By the plague" – in the world to come.

W   "The generation of the wilderness has no portion in the world to come and will not stand in judgment,

X   for it is written, 'In this wilderness they shall be consumed and there they shall die' (Numbers 14:35)," the words of R. Aqiba.

Y   R. Eliezer says, "Concerning them it says, 'Gather my saints together to me, those that have made a covenant with me by sacrifice'" (Psalms 50:5).

Z   "The party of Korah is not destined to rise up,

AA for it is written, 'And the earth closed upon them' – in this world.

BB 'And they perished from among the assembly' – in the world to come," the words of R. Aqiba.

CC And R. Eliezer says, "Concerning them it says, 'The Lord kills and resurrects, brings down to Sheol and brings up again' "(1 Samuel 2:6).

The catalogue leaves us in no doubt that the candidates for inclusion or exclusion are presented by the biblical narrative. Hence there is no implicit assumption that all *gentiles* except those specified have a share in the world to come. That seems to us a proposition altogether beyond the imagination of our authorship. The main point is inescapable: "Israel" are those who have a portion in the world to come, and excluded from "Israel" are those whose actions, including acts of bad faith, deny them their portion. If Israel is to be divided, it is not between ethnic and religious components, but among religious components.

SUPERNATURAL, TRANSCENDENTAL ISRAEL

The consequent questions are, in turn: how has this supernatural social entity come into being, and how do outsiders gain a place within it? The answer to the first question defines matters for the second. And it is, Israel becomes Israel through the Torah. It must follow that an ethnic definition is set aside in favor of one that invokes faith, covenant, obedience. These may form a cover for ethnic chauvinism, unless gentiles may enter on equal terms with Israel. And that is made explicit. That Israel becomes Israel at Sinai through accepting the Torah is formulated in the following language:

Sifra to Ahare MOT CXCIV:II.1

A   "The Lord spoke to Moses saying, Speak to the Israelite people and say to them, I am the Lord your God."

B   R. Simeon b. Yohai says, "That is in line with what is said elsewhere: 'I am the Lord your God [who brought you out of the land of Egypt, out of the house of bondage]' (Exodus 20:2).

C   'Am I the Lord, whose sovereignty you took upon yourself in Egypt?'

D   They said to him, 'Indeed.'

E   'Indeed you have accepted my dominion.'

F   'They accepted my decrees: "You will have no other gods before me."

G   That is what is said here: 'I am the Lord your God,' meaning, 'Am I the one whose dominion you accepted at Sinai?'

H   They said to him, 'Indeed.'

I   'Indeed you have accepted my dominion.'

J   'They accepted my decrees: "You shall not copy the practices of the land of Egypt where you dwelt, or of the land of Canaan to which I am taking you; nor shall you follow their laws." ' "

But theories of divine origin of ethnic groups surely circulate broadly, so the claim that, because the Torah brings Israel into being, Israel therefore forms a supernatural social entity, not an ethnic group, need not be fully exposed in the statement just now given.

That gentiles belong on equal terms when they accept that same Torah that makes Israel the people of God changes the ethnic into the universal. In what follows we find the opposite of the view that "God is our God and not yours, God of our way of life and not yours." Rather, we find the conception that God should be your God, not only ours; when God becomes your God, you become part of us; and the way of life that we follow is not "ours," but the one that God demands of everyone. God's people comprises all who accept God's commandments; "we" are not "exclusive channels of divine grace," because God opens the way to everyone who wishes to accept that same grace that now we have. Proof that that forms not an ethnic but a purely religious formulation of matters derives from the status of the gentile who accepts the Torah, the covenant, the commandments. The gentile is transformed, no longer what he or she had been, but now become utterly a new creation.

Accepting the Torah makes an ordinary human being into an Israelite. Then the proselyte becomes fully an Israelite. That is not a matter of mere theory. We recall how critical to the formation of "Israel" is genealogy, with Israel defined as wholly the descendants of the same couple, Abraham and Sarah. It must follow that if the gentile enters Israel, it must be either as a second-class Israelite, the gentile possessing no physical genealogy at all, or as a first-class Israelite, the gentile deemed fully a child of Abraham and Sarah. That obviously is no matter of theory. Can the gentile's child marry a home-born Israelite? If so, then Israel is not ethnic at all; if not, then it is. And, as a matter of fact, the gentile's daughter may marry into the priesthood, if he studies the Torah and otherwise attains merit, like any other Israelite. It follows that the gentile is no longer a gentile upon entering Israel, and that can only mean, Israel forms not an ethnic category but a supernatural one. A concrete example suffices. Gentiles are not eligible to bring a sin offering, even if they inadvertently violate the religious duties that pertain to the children of Noah; but Israelites, including proselytes and slaves (purchased as gentiles and converted), do have to do so:

Sifra to Vayyiqra Dibura Dehobah

1 A ["And the Lord said to Moses, 'Say to the people of Israel, "If any one sins unwittingly in any of the things which the Lord has commanded not to be done, and does any one of them ..." ' " (Leviticus 4:1–12):]

B Israelites bring a sin-offering, but gentiles do not bring a sin-offering.

C It is not necessary to say that [they do not have to bring a sin-offering for inadvertently violating] religious duties that were not assigned to the children of Noah, but even for violating religious duties concerning which the children of Noah were commanded, they do not have to bring a sin-offering on that account.

2 A "Say to the people of Israel:" I know that the sin-offering is owing only from Israelites.

B How do I know that it is owing also from proselytes and bondmen?

C Scripture says, "If any one [sins unwittingly]."

It follows that the gentile stands on one side of the line, the convert or slave (one and the same thing) on the other, and there is no distinguishing converts from home-born Israelites. That is the force of the proof before us. One final point concludes the demonstration. The gentile not only enters first-class citizenship in Israel but a gentile who keeps the Torah is in the status of the high priest:

Sifra to Ahare MOT CXCIV:II

15 A   " ... by the pursuit of which man shall live:"

   B   R. Jeremiah says, "How do I know that even a gentile who keeps the Torah, lo, he is like the high priest?

   C   Scripture says, 'by the pursuit of which man shall live.'"

   D   And so he says, "'And this is the Torah of the priests, Levites, and Israelites,' is not what is said here, but rather, 'This is the Torah of the man, O Lord God'" (2 Samuel 7:19).

   E   And so he says, "'open the gates and let priests, Levites, and Israelites enter it' is not what is said, but rather, 'Open the gates and let the righteous nation, who keeps faith, enter it'" (Isaiah 26:2).

   F   And so he says, "'This is the gate of the Lord. Priests, Levites, and Israelites ...' is not what is said, but rather, 'the righteous shall enter into it'" (Psalms 118:20).

   G   And so he says, "'What is said is not, 'Rejoice, priests, Levites, and Israelites,' but rather, 'Rejoice, O righteous, in the Lord'" (Psalms 33:1).

   H   And so he says, "It is not, 'Do good, O Lord, to the priests, Levites, and Israelites,' but rather, 'Do good, O Lord, to the good, to the upright in heart'" (Psalms 125:4).

   I   "Thus, even a gentile who keeps the Torah, lo, he is like the high priest."

These statements, which exemplify a broad variety of formulations throughout the Rabbinic literature, suffice to demonstrate that Rabbinic Judaism in no way defined "Israel" in ethnic terms. One could not enter its Israel through ethnic–territorial assimilation, e.g. by marrying a Jew and following Jewish customs and ceremonies. One entered Israel only through an act that we must call religious conversion, but, when one did (or does), that person became fully and completely Israel, as though his or her ancestors had stood at Sinai.

The reason, of course, is that by accepting the Torah, the convert personally takes up a position at Sinai.

What is unthinkable in the Mishnah is taken for granted by Paul as fact. And that is hardly surprising. Just as the Mishnah's system makes no provision for the distinction between the ethnic and the religious, since such a distinction is, in the exact sense of the word, simply unthinkable, so the distinction between the promise and the flesh marks the point at which for Paul thought begins. It is systemically central.

THE IMPORTANCE OF ISRAEL IN PAUL'S JUDAISM

When Romans is read from the perspective of chapters 9–11, the entire letter proves to hinge on the issue of the true Israel. "Children of the flesh," marked out by circumcision, are not identifiable with Israel; being Israel is rather a matter of joining oneself to the children of promise (Romans 9:6–8). The salvation which God has effected in Christ Jesus is offered to all humanity, to whomever understands how rightly to appropriate it.

The letter is grounded in a conviction of the divine wrath which rightly hangs over us all; only the accomplishment of "the good" provides a means of vindication, "to the Jew first, and to the Greek" (Romans 2:10, within the larger section defined by 1:18–2:16). That supremely valuable "good" is accessible by means of a radical redefinition of how the promises of creation and of Abraham's election may be regarded as fulfilled. Paul conceives of a "circumcision of heart" which is spiritual, unlike the circumcision of flesh: that is what Judaism truly consists of for him (Romans 2:28–9).

To be circumcised in that spiritual fashion involves accepting God's just judgment in the recognition that "all people, Jews and Greeks, are under sin" (Romans 3:9). From that position, one might join oneself to Abraham as one's "forefather," and believe, just as he did, in a state of physical uncircumcision (Romans 4:1–5:2). The act of belief itself is what Abraham engenders, and the believer appropriates that act and brings it to true realization by believing in the Lord Jesus Christ.

For Paul, as for most Christians in his time, the moment of belief was closely associated with baptism, the moment when the "gift in grace," opened by faith, was given through Christ (Romans 5:15). At baptism, Christians are identified with Christ, who stood in relation to God as a beloved child to a father. The Synoptic Gospels highlight baptism as the opening of Jesus' public ministry, a single moment of communion with God which has permanent consequences. They address that moment by relating the baptism of Jesus at the hands of John the baptist (Matthew 3:13–17; Mark 1:9–11; Luke 3:21–2). Here Jesus is addressed unequivocally by God as "my son," and from that point the spirit which descends upon him governs his actions. The position of Jesus in baptism is paradigmatic for believers' baptism; they refer to God as "Abba, father," and are known by him as his children (see Galatians 4:4–6).

That moment was so creative in Paul's understanding, that Jesus in the context of baptism is compared to Adam, except that Christ's grace is even more powerful than the consequences of Adam's sin, and over-rides it (Romans 5:12–21). The grace of baptism is in Paul's conception an energy which transforms believers, so that sin need no longer reign in their body (Romans 6:12). The transformation is both moral, in the behavior of those who are no longer enslaved to sin (Romans 6:12–23), and existential, in the confidence that death no longer has dominion (Romans 6:1–11). The inner doubt which binds us to sin is broken (Romans 7), and the transformation of the world itself commences with the spirit which is released in baptism (Romans 8).

Paul concludes the first half of Romans with his ringing statement of certainty (Romans 8:38–9):

> For I am persuaded that neither death nor life, neither angels nor rulers, neither things present nor things to come, nor powers, neither height nor depth, nor any other created thing, will separate us from the love of God which is in Christ Jesus our Lord.

His conclusion is not simply a matter of effective rhetoric. Rather, it follows upon his analysis in what precedes in the letter: human beings generally have "all sinned and are lacking the glory of God" (Romans 3:23). That diagnosis of the human condition corresponds to Christ as the prognosis of believers. By means of baptism, they realize the promise of Abraham, and become his descendants (Romans 4:13–25). At the same moment, each person who is baptized overcomes the consequences of Adam's fault, in the grace and righteousness which is thereby released (Romans 5:17).

Paul is deliberately wrestling with sweeping issues in Romans. Romans 9–11 provide a precise and dynamic instrument for the understanding of God's offer of reconciliation in Christ: Scripture and

Christ together, the past experience of Israel and the present experience of the apostle, are held to be the two, complementary sources of a single revelation. Taken together, in a manner akin to longitude and latitude, a careful reading of Scripture and a critical reflection on the implications of faith in Christ are held to open a vision of a single, restored humanity.

The generative problematic that tells Paul what he wishes to know about "Israel" derives from the larger concerns of the Christian system Paul proposes to work out. That problematic was framed in the need, in general, to explain the difference, as to salvific condition, between those who believed, and those who did not believe, in Christ. But it focused, specifically, upon the matter of "Israel," and how those who believed in Christ but did not derive from "Israel" related to both those who believed and also derived from "Israel" and those who did not believe but derived from "Israel." Do the first-named have to keep the Torah? Are the non-believing Jews subject to justification? Since, had Paul been a "gentile" and not an "Israelite," the issue cannot have proved critical in the working out of an individual system (but only in the address to the world at large), we may take for granted that Paul's own Jewish origin made the question at hand important, if not critical. What transformed the matter from a chronic into an acute question – the matter of salvation through keeping the Torah – encompassed, also, the matter of who is "Israel."

For his part, Paul appeals, for his taxic indicator of "Israel," to a consideration we have not found commonplace at all, namely, circumcision. It is certainly implicit in the Torah, but the Mishnah's laws, we recall, accommodate as "Israel" persons who (for good and sufficient reasons) are not circumcised, and treat as "not-Israel" persons who are circumcised but otherwise do not qualify. So for the Mishnah's system circumcision forms a premise, not a presence, a datum, but not a decisive taxic indicator. One may be circumcised yet not enter the world to come. But Paul, by contrast, could call "Israel" all those who are circumcised, and "not-Israel" all those who are not circumcised – pure and simple. That has been shown clearly by Jonathan Z. Smith.[29] He states,

> The strongest and most persistent use of circumcision as a taxic indicator is found in Paul and the deutero-Pauline literature. Paul's self-description is framed in terms of the two most fundamental halakic definitions of the Jewish male: circumcision and birth from a Jewish mother. . . . "Circumcised" is consis-

tently used in the Pauline literature as a technical term for the Jew, "uncircumcised," for the gentile.

It must follow, as I said, that for Paul, "Israel" is "the circumcised nation," and an "Israel" is a circumcised male. The reason for the meaning attached to "Israel" is spelled out by Smith (p. 12):

> What is at issue . . . is the attempt to establish a new taxon: "where there cannot be Greek and Jew, circumcised and uncircumcised, barbarian and Scythian" (Colossians 3:11), "for neither circumcision counts for anything nor uncircumcision but a new creation" (Galatians 6:115).

It follows that, for Paul, the matter of "Israel" and its definition forms part of a larger project of reclassifying Christians in terms not defined by the received categories, now (as we recall from Chapter One) a third race, a new race, a new man, in a new story. Smith (p. 12) proceeds to make the matter entirely explicit within Paul's larger system:

> Paul's theological arguments with respect to circumcision have their own internal logic and situation: that in the case of Abraham, it was posterior to faith (Romans 4:9–12); that spiritual things are superior to physical things (Colossians 3:11–14); that the Christian is the "true circumcision" as opposed to the Jew (Philippians 3:3). . . . But these appear secondary to the fundamental taxonomic premise, the Christian is a member of a new taxon.

In this same context Paul's letter to the Romans presents a consistent picture. In Chapters 9 through 11 he presents his reflections on what and who is (an) "Israel." Having specified that the family of Abraham will inherit the world not through the law but through the righteousness of faith (Romans 4:13), Paul confronts "Israel" as family and redefines the matter in a way coherent with his larger program. Then the children of Abraham will be those who "believe in him that raised from the dead Jesus our Lord, who was put to death for our trespasses and raised for our justification" (Romans 4:24–5). For us the critical issue is whether or not Paul sees these children of Abraham as "Israel." The answer is in his address to

> my kinsmen by race. They are Israelites, and to them belong the sonship, the glory, the covenants, the giving of the law, the worship, and the promises; to them belong the patriarchs, and

of their race, according to the flesh, is the Christ. God who is over all be blessed for ever.

(Romans 9:3–4)

"Israel" then is the holy people, the people of God.

But Paul proceeds to invoke a fresh metaphor, "Israel" as olive tree, and so to reframe the doctrine of "Israel" in a radical way:

Not all who are descended from Israel belong to Israel, and not all are children of Abraham because they are his descendants . . . it is not the children of the flesh who are the children of God, but the children of the promise are reckoned as descendants.

(Romans 9:6–8)

Here we have an explicit definition of "Israel," now not after the flesh but after the promise. "Israel" then is no longer a family in the concrete sense in which, in earlier materials, we have seen the notion. "Israel after the flesh" who pursued righteousness which is based on law did not succeed in fulfilling that law because they did not pursue it through faith (Romans 9:31), and "gentiles who did not pursue righteousness have attained it, that is, righteousness through faith" (Romans 9:30). Now there is an "Israel" after the flesh but *also* "a remnant chosen by grace . . . the elect obtained it" (Romans 11:5–7), with the consequence that the fleshly "Israel" remains, but gentiles ("a wild olive shoot") have been grafted "to share the richness of the olive tree" (Romans 11:17). Do these constitute "Israel"? Yes and no. They share in the promise. They are "Israel" in the earlier definition of the children of Abraham. There remains an "Israel" after the flesh, which has its place as well. And that place remains with God: "As regards election they are beloved for the sake of their forefathers. For the gifts and the call of God are irrevocable" (Romans 11:28–9).

Paul's ethnic Jewishness, comparing, in the singular individual, Jew to Greek, contrasts with the formulation of Israel characteristic of the sages of Judaism. They know only "Israel," the supernatural entity, the holy people; individuals simply exemplify and embody Israel. Their comparison is never Jew to Greek, always Israel to Rome.

If they never compare Jew to Greek, it is because their Israel falls into a different category from that formed by Greek, Median, Aramaean, Samaritan, Egyptian, and the like. First of all, "Israel" in their Hebrew speaks of the individual Israelite or Jew only in the setting of Israel the people or nation or family, so it would be difficult for them to formulate "Jew vs Greek" in terms of the individuated

84

person. The category is collective, yielding language to cover individuals to be sure. Any contrast involving an individual and his or her personal identity is beyond the conception of sages. They think in terms of large-scale entities. But are these entities ethnic? By "ethnic" here is meant that group with which the individual identifies as a matter of genealogy and territorial identity, on the one side, or language and culture, on the other.

By that definition, "Israel" does not form an ethnic entity at all. Nor is their "Israel" made up of individual Israelites. Israel is a world-empire; Israelites are its citizens, alike in their citizenship. Israel then contrasts with other empires, Israelites with Romans (who may, ethnically, derive from elsewhere than Rome), but not other ethnic groups in context. While sages may treat their Israel as incomparable to any other social entity, a group that is unique in its group-ness and that forms a classification unto itself, when they do speak of Israel in a setting of contrasts, the contrast will be drawn to either "the nations," without differentiation, or the four empires, Persia, Media, Greece, Rome, with Israel as fifth and last in line. They may well contrast Israel with Rome and Iran, the two world-empires of their day. Their "Israel," therefore, accommodates no definition that would assign a merely ethnic classification, such that would treat "Israel" in this-worldly terms at all. And, as we shall see later on, the same is to be said for "Israel" as family. It is indeed a family, but like no other family on the face of the earth.

"Israel" as a detail expresses, also, the main point of Paul's system. For Paul's Judaic system, encompassing believing (former) gentiles but also retaining a systemic status for non-believing Jews, "Israel" forms an important component within a larger structure. Not only so, but, more to the point, "Israel" finds definition on account of the logical requirements of that encompassing framework. Indeed, we cannot imagine making sense of the remarkably complex metaphor introduced by Paul – the metaphor of the olive tree – without understanding the problem of thought that confronted him, and that he solved through, among other details, his thinking on "Israel." The notion of entering "Israel" through belief but not behavior ("works") in one detail expresses the main point of Paul's system, which concerns not who "Israel" is but what faith in Christ means and how that faith transforms humanity.

Without "Israel," Paul simply would have had no system. The generative question of his system required him to focus attention on the definition of the social entity, "Israel." Paul originated among Jews but addressed both Jews and gentiles, seeking to form the lot into a single social entity "in Christ Jesus." The social dimension of his system formed the generative question with which he proposed to contend. His is the most ethnic Judaic system we have considered, simply because the issue of "Israel" focuses his attention, and the issue of ethnicity defines the solution to the problem he finds himself required to work out.

THE IMPORTANCE OF ISRAEL IN THE ESSENE JUDAISM OF QUMRAN

The Essene Judaism's "Israel" proves so exclusive that most of the Jews of their day must be classified as mere gentiles, outsiders to their "Israel." The Essenes meant by "us" simply "Israel," or "the true Israel." The Essenes' movement probably originated in opposition to the Hasmoneans. They pursued their own system of purity, ethics, and initiation, followed their own calendar, and withdrew into their own communities, either within cities or in isolated sites such as Qumran. There they awaited a coming, apocalyptic war, when they, as "the sons of light," would triumph over "the sons of darkness:" not only the gentiles, but anyone not of their vision. Two documents from Qumran clearly set out a sectarian perspective. The *War Scroll* establishes the plan of a final, apocalyptic campaign battle against those who resist the Essenes, and the *Manual of Discipline* comprehensively regulates the conduct of life in the community until that time. The culmination of those efforts was to be complete control of Jerusalem and the Temple, where worship would be offered according to the Essene revelation, the correct understanding of the law of Moses. The *Zadokite Document*, found both at Qumran and in Egypt, attests the conviction of the Essenes that they alone possessed the correct and ultimately regulative understanding of the law of Moses (see especially 5:17–6:11). Their insistence upon a doctrine of two messiahs, one of Israel and one of Aaron, would suggest that it was particularly the Hasmoneans' arrogation of priestly and royal powers which alienated the Essenes.

The group organized itself as a replication of "all Israel," as they read about "Israel" in those passages of Scripture that impressed them. They structured their group – in Geza Vermes' language, "so that it corresponded faithfully to that of Israel itself, dividing it into priests and laity, the priests being described as the 'sons of Zadok' – Zadok was High Priest in David's time – and the laity grouped after the biblical model into twelve tribes."[30] This particular Israel then divided itself into units of thousands, hundreds, fifties, and tens. The *Manual of Discipline* further knows divisions within the larger group, specifically, "the men of holiness," "the men of perfect holiness," within a larger "Community." The corporate being of the community came to realization in common meals, prayers, and deliberations. Vermes says, "Perfectly obedient to each and every one of the laws of Moses and to all that was commanded by the prophets, they were to love one another and to share with one another their knowledge, powers, and possessions."[31]

In the Essene Judaic system set forth in writings in the Dead Sea library, we deal with an "Israel" that in its metaphorical thought about itself forms the counterpart to the holy Temple in Jerusalem, an "Israel" that, as a social group, constitutes the entirety of the "community of Israel" in the here and now. Vermes makes this matter explicit:

> The Council of the Community was to be the "Most Holy Dwelling of Aaron" where "without the flesh of holocausts and the fat of sacrifice," a "sweet fragrance" was to be sent up to God, and where prayer was to serve "as an acceptable fragrance of righteousness."[32]

It follows, as Vermes says, that "the Community [we should read: this 'Israel'] itself was to be the sacrifice offered to God in atonement for Israel's sins."[33]

The authorships of the documents preserved by the Essenes of Qumran define "Israel" not as a fictive entity possessing spiritual traits alone or mainly, but as a concrete social group, an entity in the here and now, that may be defined by traits of persons subject to the same sanctions and norms, sharing the same values and ideals. Builders of a community or a *polis*, and hence politicians, the authorships of the Essenes of Qumran conceived and described in law a political "Israel." Their "Israel" constitutes a political entity and society. The "Israel" of the Essenes is the "Israel" of history and eschatology and Scripture.

When the library of the Essenes of Qumran takes up the issue of who and what is (an) "Israel," as a matter of fact it turns to what, to the authorships at hand, is its central question. Indeed, we may say that if the generative problematic of the Mishnah is defined by the exegesis of sanctification in the here and now of "Israel"'s everyday reality, accounting for the excruciating detail to which the Mishnah subjects its audience, the precipitating issue of the Essene system revealed in the library of Qumran is defined by the exegesis in detail of "us" as "Israel." And that issue holds together the principal documents and comes to expression even in a variety of fragments.

If, therefore, we ask whether "Israel" is critical to the Essenes of Qumran as it is for the Christian Judaism formulated by Paul, a simple fact answers our question. Were we to remove "Israel" in general and in detail from the topical program at hand, we should lose, if not the entirety of the library, then nearly the whole of some documents, and the larger part of many of them. The Essene library of Qumran constitutes a vast collection of writings about "Israel," its definition and conduct, history and destiny. The reason for the systemic importance among the Essenes of Qumran of "Israel," furthermore, derives from the meanings imputed to that category. The library stands for a social group that conceives of itself as "Israel," and that wishes, in these documents, to spell out what that "Israel" is and must do. The system as a whole forms an exercise in the definition of "Israel" as against that "non-Israel" composed not of gentiles but of erring (former) Israelites. The saving remnant is all that is left: "Israel."

From Paul the Judaism that became Christianity learned to distinguish the ethnic from the religious. For Paul and the sages (whose continuators produced the Mishnah) derived from the Pharisees, the former claiming that spiritual genealogy in so many words, the latter through a variety of no-less-explicit formulations. Both derived from the tradition of Gamaliel, thence from Hillel, his grandfather. Both understood that to enter the covenant God made with Israel an act of conversion had to take place. Both wanted gentiles to come to the worship of the God who had revealed the Torah at Sinai. Both inherited the distinction between "circumcision in the flesh" and "circumcision in the heart" (Paul in Romans 2:29), since Deuteronomy 30:6 makes the distinction explicit. It follows that, in distinguishing the children of the flesh from the children of the promise, Paul certainly drew upon an ancient and authoritative perspective of the Torah.

ISRAEL AND THE LAST ADAM

Our interest in placing Paul's Israel into the context of other Judaisms' Israels requires that we turn from the matter of Israel to the issue of anthropology: Paul's conception of what it means to be a human being. As we have seen, that is the focal interest of Romans. Who is the model for humanity? For every Christian the answer is self-evident: Christ, God Incarnate. For Paul, Christ is the counterpart to Adam, the Adam to restore Eden, the one who did not sin and did not fall but who now restores humanity to its right relationship with God. For "our sages of blessed memory," it is holy Israel that does precisely the same thing.[34]

Now what if Israel is not treated as a family or an ethnic group, a natural, as distinct from a supernatural, community? In the Judaic system set forth by the sages who inherited the Mishnah and defined matters in the Talmud, Israel in Judaism is set forth as the counterpart to Adam, the Land of Israel to Eden, the fall of Adam to the expulsion of Israel from the Land. Whether or not Paul contemplated these paradigms when he formulated his Christology is not at issue; that the sages appealed to Scripture's models in framing their doctrine of Israel is self-evident. And we grasp Paul's Judaism as a Judaism in a common model, but with its own systemic center and message.

"Israel" for the sages' Judaism forms the counterpart and opposite of Adam. Humanity knows two stories, one of Adam in Eden, and the other of Israel in the Land of Israel. These form counterparts. But they also mirror one another, for the Torah intervenes. Let us start with the comparison of Adam in Eden and Israel in the Land of Israel, demonstrating that Israel's history in the Land is comparable to Adam's history in Eden:

Genesis Rabbah XIX:IX

2 A R. Abbahu in the name of R. Yosé bar Haninah: "It is written, 'But they are like a man [Adam], they have transgressed the covenant' (Hosea 6:7).

   B 'They are like a man,' specifically, like the first man. [We shall now compare the story of the first man in Eden with the story of Israel in its land.]

   C 'In the case of the first man, I brought him into the garden of Eden, I commanded him, he violated my commandment, I judged him to be sent away and driven out, but I mourned for him, saying "How . . ."' [which begins the book of Lamentations, hence stands for a lament, but which, as we just saw, also is written with the consonants that also yield, 'Where are you'].

   D 'I brought him into the garden of Eden,' as it is written,

'And the Lord God took the man and put him into the garden of Eden' (Genesis 2:15).

E 'I commanded him,' as it is written, 'And the Lord God commanded . . .' (Genesis 2:16).

F 'And he violated my commandment,' as it is written, 'Did you eat from the tree concerning which I commanded you' (Genesis 3:11).

G 'I judged him to be sent away,' as it is written, 'And the Lord God sent him from the garden of Eden' (Genesis 3:23).

H 'And I judged him to be driven out.' 'And he drove out the man' (Genesis 3:24).

I 'But I mourned for him, saying, "How . . .".' 'And he said to him, "Where are you"' (Genesis 3:9), and the word for 'where are you' is written, 'How. . . .'

J 'So too in the case of his descendants, [God continues to speak,] I brought them into the Land of Israel, I commanded them, they violated my commandment, I judged them to be sent out and driven away but I mourned for them, saying, "How . . . ."'

K 'I brought them into the Land of Israel.' 'And I brought you into the land of Carmel' (Jeremiah 2:7).

L 'I commanded them.' 'And you, command the children of Israel' (Exodus 27:20). 'Command the children of Israel' (Leviticus 24:2).

M 'They violated my commandment.' 'And all Israel have violated your Torah' (Daniel 9:11).

N 'I judged them to be sent out.' 'Send them away, out of my sight and let them go forth' (Jeremiah 15:1).

O ' . . . and driven away.' 'From my house I shall drive them' (Hosea 9:15).

P 'But I mourned for them, saying, "How . . . ."' 'How has the city sat solitary, that was full of people'" (Lamentations 1:1).

But there is an important difference between Adam and Israel. Israel and Adam are counterparts, but opposites; what Adam did not succeed in accomplishing, Israel realized in abundance: obedience to the Torah.

Genesis Rabbah XXIV:V

2 A Said R. Yudah, "The first man [Adam] was worthy to have the Torah given through him. What is the verse of Scripture that so indicates? 'This is the book of the generations of man' (Genesis 5:1). ["This book can be given over to man."]

B Said the Holy One, blessed be he, 'He is the creation of my hands, and should I not give it to him?' Then he reversed himself and said, 'I gave him no more than six commandments to follow, and he did not stand by them, so how can I now give him six hundred thirteen commandments, two hundred forty-eight commandments of things to do and three hundred sixty-five commandments of things not to do?'

C 'And he said to man,' meaning, 'not-to-man' [reading the L before the consonants for 'man,' read as 'to man,' as though it bore the negative]. 'To man I shall not give it. And to whom shall I give it? To his children.' 'This is the book that belongs to the children of man' " (Genesis 5:1).

3 A Said R. Jacob of Kefar Hanan, "The first man was worthy to produce the twelve tribes. What is the verse of Scripture that so indicates? 'This is the book of man.'

B The word 'this' in Hebrew has consonants with the numerical value of twelve (Z and H).

C Said the Holy One, blessed be he, 'He is the creation of my hands, and should I not give it to him?' Then he reversed himself and said, 'Two sons I gave him, and one of them went and killed his fellow. How shall I then give him twelve?'

D 'And he said to man,' (Job 28:27) meaning, 'not-to-man' [reading the L before the consonants for man as though it bore the negative]. To man I shall not give it. And to whom shall I give it? To his children: 'This is the book that belongs to the children of man' " (Genesis 5:1).

It follows that Adam and Israel are comparable but not wholly alike. They are the same and not the same. The reason is that Israel has the Torah, which presents Israel with the possibility of escaping from the situation of guilt and alienation from God in which Adam is trapped. True, Israel's history in the land is the counterpart of Adam's history in Eden; with the destruction of Jerusalem in 586, Israel was driven out of Eden. But Israel can come back.

Lamentations Rabbati IV.I.1

A   R. Abbahu in the name of R. Yosé bar Haninah commenced [discourse by citing this verse]: " *'But they are like a man, they have transgressed the covenant. There they dealt treacherously against me'* (Hosea 6:7).

B   *They are like a man*, specifically, this refers to the first man [Adam]. [We shall now compare the story of the first man in Eden with the story of Israel in its land.]

C   Said the Holy One, blessed be He, 'In the case of the first man, I brought him into the garden of Eden, I commanded him, he violated my commandment, I judged him to be sent away and driven out, but I mourned for him, saying "How . . ."'[which begins the book of Lamentations, hence stands for a lament, but which also is written with the consonants that also yield, *Where are you?*].

D   *'I brought him into the garden of Eden'* as it is written, *And the Lord God took the man and put him into the garden of Eden* (Genesis 2:15).

E   *'I commanded him,'* as it is written, *And the Lord God commanded. . .* (Genesis 2:16).

F   *'And he violated my commandment,'* as it is written, *Did you eat from the tree concerning which I commanded you* (Genesis 3:11).

G   *'I judged him to be sent away,'* as it is written, *And the Lord God sent him from the garden of Eden* (Genesis 3:23).

H   *'And I judged him to be driven out.' And he drove out the man* (Genesis 3:24).

I   *'But I mourned for him, saying, How. . . .' And He said to him, Where are you* (Genesis 3:9), and the word for 'where are you' is written, *How. . . .*

J   'So too in the case of his descendants, [God continues to speak,] I brought them into the Land of Israel, I commanded them, they violated my commandment, I judged them to be sent out and driven away but I mourned for them, saying, *How. . . .'*

K 'I brought them into the Land of Israel:' 'And I brought you into the land of Carmel' (Jeremiah 2:7).

L 'I commanded them: ' 'And you, command the children of Israel' (Exodus 27:20). 'Command the children of Israel' (Leviticus 24:2).

M 'They violated my commandment:' 'And all Israel have violated your Torah' (Daniel 9:11).

N 'I judged them to be sent out:' 'Send them away, out of my sight and let them go forth' (Jeremiah 15:1).

O '. . . and driven away:' 'From my house I shall drive them' (Hosea 9:15).

P 'But I mourned for them, saying, How. . . .' How lonely sits the city [that was full of people! How like a widow has she become, she that was great among the nations! She that was a princess among the cities has become a vassal. She weeps bitterly in the night, tears on her cheeks, among all her lovers she has none to comfort her; all her friends have dealt treacherously with her, they have become her enemies]" (Lamentations 1:1–2).

These protracted abstracts state more eloquently than any words we can have formulated two propositions. First, Israel weighs in the balance, in the universal history of humanity, against Adam. Second, Scripture – cited throughout – says so in so many words.

The differences show us the points in common between the two Judaisms, Paul's and the sages'. The difference between the situation of Adam and the situation of Israel finds its definition in the Torah – the very point at which we commenced. Christ on the cross concludes the old Adam and in his resurrection commences the new. Here we find the Judaic counterpart to that enormous conception. It is the Torah that forms the antidote to Adam's sin. But then Israel has to regain the Land, that is, Eden, by that act of reconciliation with God that takes place through voluntary obedience to the covenant, the Torah, the commandments. Then Israel overcomes the situation of Adam; the Torah provides the occasion, but only Israel, the actuality. At this point, in this context, we have to ask ourselves how any aspect of this language speaks of an "ethnic identity." Forming the counterpart to Adam defines Israel in much the same way that the Last Adam is defined as counterpart and opposite to the first one, and the Last Adam is no more a this-worldly and secular figure than Israel is "ethnic." How the category "ethnic" fits into the present context is not at all clear. That "Israel is God's people" forms no more ethnic a statement than that Adam stands for humanity. Israel and Adam form species of the same genus, and what speciates them is the Torah.

WHAT IS AT STAKE IN THE ELECTION OF ISRAEL?

In what way does this "people" or "nation" relate to God, by whom – the Torah insists – this nation is known and elected, by whom this people is especially beloved? The Christian Judaism and that set forth by "our sages of blessed memory" could have concurred, and, in Paul, did concur, but for different reasons. God had chosen Israel not only to receive the Torah, which was God's first self-manifestation to humanity, but also to receive God Incarnate in the person of Jesus Christ. So Israel remained elect, by reason of the very choice God himself had made for his second and final revelation.

The concurrence between the two Judaic systems on the same proposition yields an important point of correspondence, between Israel and Christ. The social component of each Judaism spoke about the same religious realities, each in its own terms to be sure. That is to say, the sages' "Israel" and "the mystical body of Christ" would coincide in speaking about the same social component of the Judaic system of the social order set forth by each. When sages spoke of Israel in the context of election, they had in mind precisely what Christianity conceived the Church to comprise, broadly construed: the locus in this world for the presence of God. The people or nation, Israel, was not only a supernatural family, *sui generis*, it was a people or nation, also *sui generis*. For the peoplehood of Israel, what made the group distinctive and what imparted its existence with consequence such that God would care for that group above all others, found its definition in God's purpose in creating the world. Israel on its own bore no importance whatsoever. Israel within God's plan, living in accord with that plan, formed God's stake in this world.

The definition of "Israel" offered by the Judaism described here not only left no space for an ethnic Israel, it also comprehended the world of peoples and nations only under the aspect of Eternity, therefore defining Israel's peoplehood solely and uniquely by appeal to God's purpose. In the sense in which Rome was an empire, or Egypt a nation and people, Israel found no elements of a plausible definition; Israel's paradigmatic story set Israel as counterpart to Rome, defined Israel by appeal to its exodus from Egypt, always and only in conse- quence of God's intervention into human affairs, whether past, whether future: always present-tense in Israel's presence in this world. And this language, for the Christian faithful, surely resonates with the language that speaks of Jesus Christ as God Incarnate. God is no more incarnate in a human being like any other than God elects a nation by selection among nations of the same genus. Jesus Christ for Christianity – for Paul's Christianity – is unique and beyond all comparison to other human beings. Israel in our sages' Judaism is unique and defined in its own genus, not in the genus of (other) ethnic or national groups at all.

Sages say in so many words that Israel formed that locus in the world in which God's presence came to rest. In Torah-study Israel's sages prepare the way for prophecy. Israels, all together, form God's domain on earth. The vision of an "Israel" that takes shape around synagogues and schools carries us deep into this Judaism's understanding of Israel as God's (unique) people. That definition then forms part of a larger public conception of "Israel" within the metaphor of a God who takes up residence within a social group. Once more, abstracts from the authoritative writings, setting forth the sense of Scripture within the dual Torah of Sinai, come to the fore:

Genesis Rabbah XLII:III.2

A   "And it came to pass in the days of Ahaz" (Isaiah 7:1):

B   "The Aramaeans on the east and the Philistines on the west devour Israel with open mouth" (Isaiah 9:12):

C   The matter [of Israel's position] may be compared to the case of a king who handed over his son to a tutor, who hated the son. The tutor thought, "If I kill him now, I shall turn out to be liable to the death penalty before the king. So what I'll do is take away his wet-nurse, and he will die on his own."

D   So thought Ahaz, "If there are no kids, there will be no he-goats. If there are no he-goats, there will be no flock. If there is no flock, there will be no Shepherd, if there is no Shepherd, there will be no world."

E   So did Ahaz plan, "If there are no children, there will be no adults. If there are no adults, there will be no disciples. If there are no disciples, there will be no sages. If there are no sages, there will be no prophets. If there are no prophets, the Holy One, blessed be he, will not allow his presence to come to rest in the world." [Leviticus Rabbah: Torah. If there is no Torah, there will be no synagogues and schools. If there are no synagogues and schools, then the Holy One, blessed be he, will not allow his presence to come to rest in the world.]

F   That is in line with the following verse of Scripture: "Bind up the testimony, seal the Torah among my disciples" (Isaiah 8:16).

G   R. Huna in the name of R. Eleazar: "Why was he called Ahaz? Because he seized (*ahaz*) synagogues and schools."

Israel is the locus in which God's presence comes to realization in this world: Israel is then the Judaic counterpart to Christ. That is why we maintain, Paul's Christ is just as much comparable to any other human being as sages' Israel is comparable to other nations. True, Christ took human form as a human being, and so Israel takes human form as a family, people, or nation. But the human being who incarnates God and the holy family or people that affords to God's presence a place in which to come to rest in the world simply possess no comparable dimension whatsoever. God's presence in the world alone defines what is at stake in the life of the holy people.

To our sages, God is always God, everywhere God, uniquely God: creator of Heaven and earth. To our sages Adam and Eve, that is, all humanity, is created "in our image, after our likeness." Israel, within humanity, aspires to make a place for God within creation. God Incarnate and the language invented here for Ahaz represent the same definition of matters. Through Jesus Christ, God became a man and walked among us, so Paul, with all Christianity, affirms. Ahaz speaks for our sages' Israel:

If there are no children, there will be no adults. If there are no adults, there will be no disciples. If there are no disciples, there will be no sages. If there are no sages, there will be no prophets.If there are no prophets, the Holy One, blessed be he, will not allow his presence to come to rest in the world.

If Christianity's God Incarnate is to be distinguished from God's Presence coming to rest in the world, we do not know how to differentiate the sense of the one from the intent of the other. Incarnation and election address the same deeply scriptural aspiration: how we are to encounter, know, serve, and love God.

For those Christians for whom Jesus Christ represents God's entry into this world, God Incarnate, the conception of Israel will prove intelligible, comparable to, though different from, their own idea of how God enters the world. The sages' Judaism invoked the conception of Israel to explain God's relationship to the world. Specifically, God left the world in stages because of Adam's and Adam's descendants' actions, and God returned to the world in stages because of Abraham's and Abraham's descendants' actions. So, as we noted at the outset of this chapter, Israel forms the medium by which God comes down to earth.

5

PAUL'S COMPETITORS, JESUS' DISCIPLES, AND THE ISRAEL OF JESUS

We have seen that Paul's picture of a single, integrative people of God is developed in Romans by means of reference to the Scriptures of Israel and a clearly articulated, logical argument. His guiding principle, and at the same time the impetus of his position, is that "all Israel shall be saved" (Romans 11:26). The dominance of Paul's argument within the New Testament, attested by the number of letters included which were either written by Paul or later attributed to him, is a function of what the Church came to be. By social constitution and theological conviction, Christians as a whole gradually embraced the position of Paul, although in his own time he had been an isolated figure.

The communities which framed the canon of the New Testament, predominantly non-Jewish and widely represented in the Mediterranean basin, valued Paul as their apostle. He himself in fact had claimed that he had been appointed for the uncircumcised, just as Peter had been appointed for the circumcised (Galatians 2:7–8). The book of Acts, composed around 90 CE and looking back over the period of the most radical and rapid cultural shifts in all of Christian history, devotes its first half predominantly to the apostolate of Peter (Acts 1–12), and its second half predominantly to the apostolate of Paul (Acts 13–26). Acts' portrayal of harmony in the Church of the period (especially as compared to Paul's own attestation of serious conflict) is a good indication of the profound, social change which had altered the character of primitive Christianity and made it into a single Church striving for unity.

While Acts reflects the magnitude of the change which the movement underwent, its purpose is not to trace tension and disagreement within primitive Christianity. The theme of Acts is the coherence of Paul with Peter, and Peter's coherence with Jesus: the integrity of the single truth by which God would judge "the living and the dead." Peter speaks of that single, final truth (Acts 10:42) in the house of a Roman centurion, which he only visits after a special revelation. In daring to breach the boundary between Jews and non-Jews, Peter exemplified the point of Acts as a whole, just as he articulates its principal theme here. But Acts itself, together with the earliest letters of Paul, permit us to see clearly that there were competing views of God's Israel within primitive Christianity.

Paul's conception is the best attested, and therefore the most accessible. But his own testimony will show that his gospel of a single "Israel of God," including both the circumcised and the uncircumcised (so Galatians 6:15–16), made him both radical and unacceptable to many (if not most) other Christians in his time. Those who competed with Paul included the most influential leaders of the period: Peter, James, and Barnabas.

PAUL'S ABRAHAM: FATHER OF "THE ISRAEL OF GOD"

Before communicating to Christian communities in Rome, Paul wrote a letter to a group of churches in the northern part of Asia Minor (present-day Turkey) sometime around 53 CE.[1]

He was writing to communities in Galatia he himself had founded, where Christians were embroiled in a deep and (to his mind) destructive controversy. As Paul sees the matter (in chapter 2 of Galatians), he had established the practice of common fellowship at meals, including eucharistic meals, in churches which he founded. Such fellowship of course included Jews who became Christians, signaling their acceptance of Jesus' teaching by being baptized. But it also – and increasingly – saw the participation of non-Jews who had been baptized, but not circumcised. Paul won the agreement of Christian leaders in Jerusalem that circumcision should not be required of non-Jewish members of his church (Galatians 2:1–10).

The remarkable and early agreement that Jews and non-Jews could be included in the movement established a radical principle of inclusion. But it also brought about one of the greatest controversies within the early Church. Paul's version of events is the best available (in Galatians 2, as above, but seconded by Acts 15). At Antioch, Jews and non-Jews who had been baptized joined in meals of fellowship together. According to Paul, Peter and Barnabas fell in with the practice (Galatians 2:11–13). Peter – whom Paul also calls "Cephas," the

Aramaic word for the same thing, "rock" – was a founding apostle of the church in Jerusalem, whose nickname came from Jesus himself.[2] Barnabas, a Levite from Cyprus, was a prominent, loyal recruit in Jerusalem, who enjoyed the trust of the apostles and mediated relations between them and Paul.[3] Although Paul himself does not say Barnabas himself ate with gentiles (as Peter did), he evidently tolerated such practice.

Paul's policy of including gentiles with Jews in meals, as well as in baptism, needed the support of authorities such as Peter and Barnabas in order to prevail against the natural conservatism of those for whom such inclusion seemed a betrayal of the purity of Israel. When representatives of James arrived, James who was the brother of Jesus and the pre-eminent figure in the church in Jerusalem,[4] that natural conservatism reasserted itself. Peter "separated himself," along with the rest of the Jews, and even Barnabas (Galatians 2:12–13). Jews and gentiles again maintained distinct fellowship at meals, and Paul accuses the leadership of his own movement of hypocrisy (Galatians 2:13).

The radical quality of Paul's position needs to be appreciated, before his characteristic interpretation of Scripture may be understood. He was isolated from *every other Christian Jew* by his own account in Galatians 2:11–13: James, Peter, Barnabas, and "the rest of the Jews." His isolation required that he develop an alternative view of authority in order to justify his own practice. Within Galatians, Paul quickly articulates the distinctive approach to Scripture as authoritative which characterizes his writings as a whole.

He begins with the position of his readers at the time that they heard the preaching of the gospel of Jesus Christ: did you receive the spirit from "works of law" or from "hearing with faith" (Galatians 3:2)? The rhetoric of the question grounds Paul's readers in their own experience. They could not, as non-Jews, lay claim to have been obedient to the law, so that whatever enabled them to respond to the gospel must have been a matter of God's furnishing his spirit (Galatians 3:5). The experience of his readers at the time they heard the gospel is the explicit groundwork of Paul's approach to the Scripture.

Paul's letters as a whole were written for communities which had already received the message concerning Jesus Christ, and specifically for individuals who had already been baptized. (As we will see, the first three Gospels were written to help to prepare interested persons for baptism.) Given the nature of the literature of the New Testament, it is relatively rare to have a glimpse of what it was like for enthusiastic

100

hearers first to receive the gospel concerning Jesus. Here, however, Paul speaks of Jesus Christ as having been "placarded as crucified" before the eyes of the Galatians (3:1): evidently, the crucifixion was a vivid and dramatic moment in Paul's own preaching.

The drama was not merely decorative. Hearing with faith became the occasion on which the Galatians received the spirit, and God performed what Paul calls "powers" in their midst (Galatians 3:5). The nature of those wonders is not spelled out, but from what Paul says elsewhere, it is reasonable to suppose that he understands power as that which raised Jesus from the dead (2 Corinthians 13:4) and which enables the individual believer to overcome weakness (2 Corinthians 12:6–10). In other words, "power" is what people are endowed with when they receive spirit.

Paul does not refer to spirit or to power by way of argument; he simply assumes that they are part of the common experience of his audience. Christians during the primitive and early periods of the Church, for all their diversity, made a singular claim in regard to the spirit of God. That same spirit which moved over the face of the waters at the beginning of creation (Genesis 1:2), which animated prophets such as Isaiah (61:1), and which descended upon Jesus over the waters of his baptism (Mark 1:10), was claimed by Christians in their baptism. As Paul put it later in Galatians, because we are sons, God sent the spirit of his son into our hearts, crying, "Abba, father" (4:6). We feel what Jesus felt, as Paul says, and we call God "Abba," the Aramaic term used by Jesus.

To a large extent, the New Testament reflects divergences and controversies among communities of Christians who struggled with one another (and sometimes against one another) as their lives of faith developed. For that reason, in this volume we must trace distinctive (and sometimes contradictory) understandings of who the people of God are, and the distinctions are not only between Jews and Christians, but *among* Jews and Christians. But the underlying consensus among early Christians, that hearing the gospel of Jesus with faith endowed one with the spirit and its power, is what unified them and put them apart from other groups. Hellenistic philosophy during the period increasingly emphasized the rational nature of any genuine divinity, while Judaism offered both a reasonable and a traditional account of a single God and his ways. Christians' insistence upon their own consciousness of God's spirit made them seem rather like some of the esoteric movements of the Graeco-Roman world, which offered initiation into the secrets of a hidden realm. Unlike such movements, which could involve expensive rituals (as in the Mysteries) and expert training (as in Gnosticism), Christianity asserted that God made himself available personally after only a modest initiation. Baptism in Christian preaching held the key to God's spirit and the experience of divine power.

Paul therefore grounds his argument in what may be taken to be a matter of widespread agreement: belief in Jesus Christ endows one with spirit. But he spins the consensus in the interest of his polemical point (Galatians 3:3): "Are you so foolish that, having begun with spirit, you will now end with flesh?" The unexpressed assumption is that the observance of purity, such as the emissaries of James insist upon, is a matter of "flesh," not "spirit." Of course, just that presumption is what separates Paul from James, as well as Peter, Barnabas, and "the rest of the Jews." What Paul requires in order to sustain his polemic is some convincing demonstration that faith is on the side of spirit, and observance on the side of flesh.

Paul finds what he needs in Scripture, in the example of Abraham. He says that when believers hear with faith, they are "just as Abraham, who believed in God, and it was reckoned to him as righteousness" (Galatians 3:6). The characterization of Abraham is taken from Genesis (15:5–6), when Abraham is promised that his descendants shall be as the stars of the Heavens: his trust in what he is told makes him the father of faith, and in the course of the sacrifice which he subsequently offers, God seals his promise as the solemn covenant to give the land which would be called Israel (Genesis 15:7–21).

Paul understands the role of Abraham as the patriarch of Judaism, but he argues that Abraham's faith, not his obedience to the law, made him righteous in the sight of God (Galatians 3:7): "Know, therefore, that those who are of faith are sons of Abraham." Paul was capable of remarkable elaborations of that theme, in Galatians and elsewhere, but the essential simplicity of the thought must not be overlooked. Abraham, for Paul, embodied a principle of believing which was best fulfilled by means of faith in and through Jesus Christ. Descent from Abraham, therefore, was a matter of belief, not a matter of genealogy.

What follows in Galatians is an interpretative *tour de force* around that theme. Scripture itself is held to attest Paul's own view of Abraham. When Abraham is styled a blessing among the nations in Genesis 12:3, that is because gentiles who believe in Christ are blessed with Abraham's faith (Galatians 3:8–9, 11). Their blessing is their reception of the spirit in faith. Even at this point, then, Paul's interpretative argument is grounded in an appeal to the nature of Christian experience, especially in baptism.

But Paul's presentation of Abraham is designed to deny the strictures of James, as well as to legitimate his own point of view. "Works of law" did not occasion reception of the spirit; "hearing with faith" did (Galatians 3:2). That dichotomy between faith and law is also a theme within Paul's interpretation of Abraham. Scripture itself, as Paul reads it in Galatians 3:10–12, shows that law is quite different from faith. Deuteronomy (27:26) says that anyone is cursed who does not abide by everything that is written in the book of the law, while the prophet Habakkuk (2:4) insists that a righteous person shall live from faith. Law cannot be considered unconditional, because the same book of Deuteronomy (21:22–3) states that a person who is hanged is to be considered cursed: the very crucifixion which occasioned hearing with faith is condemned by the law! Viewed from the perspective of the law, the crucified Jesus is an outrage; viewed from the perspective of faith, he occasions our endowment with the spirit of God (Galatians 3:14).

The exact terms of the covenant with Abraham confirm the perspective of faith in Paul's interpretation. God directs his promises to Abraham's "seed," in the singular (Genesis 12:7 and elsewhere) as if a particular figure were in mind. That figure, Paul says without argument, is Christ (Galatians 3:16). The law cannot condition that covenantal promise; its function, when it came some 430 years after the promise, was only to deal with the interim until the seed should arrive to whom the promise was given (Galatians 3:15–22). It is promise which conditions law, rather than the reverse.

Judged from the point of view of the scriptural texts he cites, Paul's argument at various stages seems tenuous. Deuteronomy, after all, is not concerned to drive a wedge between faith and law; it is the book which includes the call to Israel to hear that the LORD is one, to love the LORD with all one's being, and on that basis to keep and teach the words of his command (6:4–9). Indeed, Jesus cited that passage, known as the *Shema Yisrael* (the "Hear, O Israel"), as the principal point of the law (see Mark 12:29–30). And the promise to the "seed" in Genesis 12:7 does *not* seem to be messianic in the original text or in the Septuagint;[5] the term appears to be a collective reference to Abraham's progeny, and is translated "descendants" in the Revised Standard Version.

But Paul's interpretation does not stand or fall by modern standards of exegesis. His use of Scripture is instrumental, because his point is more theological than exegetical (Galatians 3:26–9):

> For you are all sons of God through faith in Christ Jesus. For as many as were baptized into Christ, were clothed in Christ. There is neither Jew nor Greek, neither slave nor free, neither male nor female: for you are all one in Christ Jesus. And if you are of Christ, then you are Abraham's seed, heirs according to promise.

Once that is understood to be the central theme of Scripture, realized whenever one appropriates one's new identity in baptism, it becomes the purpose of interpretation to illustrate that theme.

For all that the documents of Israel's canon may vary, for all that their periods and perspectives differ, the documents attest a single truth on Paul's reading. What is said in the case of Abraham amounts to "the Scripture foreseeing that the gentiles would be righteous from faith" (Galatians 3:8). "Scripture" for Paul is what the documents finally mean, the ultimate significance in the light of which the interpretation of individual documents and passages unfolds. That is why it is natural for Paul to proceed from Christ to the passages at issue: the point of departure was the point at which one had arrived by means of baptism.

JAMES' JESUS: DAVIDIC SCION OF ISRAEL

The confrontation at Antioch which Paul recounts to his audience in Galatia did not turn out well for him at the time. His explanation of his own perspective is triumphant and ringing only in retrospect. Indeed, by the time he recollects his argument for the benefit of the Galatians, he seems so confident that one might overlook the fact that he was the loser in the battle with the representatives of James. But as he says himself, Peter, Barnabas, and "the rest of the Jews" separated from fellowship at meals with gentiles (Galatians 2:11–13).

The position of James is not directly represented, as is Paul's, by a writing of James himself; the epistle attributed to him in the New Testament is too derivative to serve as an adequate index of his position.[6] But the book of Acts does clearly reflect his perspective in regard to both circumcision and the issue of purity (Acts 15), the two principal matters of concern in Galatians. The account in Acts 15 is romanticized; one sees much less of the tension and controversy which Paul himself attests in Galatians 2. But once allowance has been made for the tendency in Acts to portray the ancient Church as a body at harmonious unity, the nature and force of James' position become clear.

The two issues in dispute, circumcision and purity, are dealt with in Acts 15 as if they were the agenda of a single meeting of leaders in Jerusalem. (Paul in Galatians 2 more accurately describes the meeting he had with the leaders as distinct from a later decision to return to the question of purity.) The first item on the agenda is settled by having Peter declare that, since God gave his holy spirit to gentiles who believed, no attempt should be made to add requirements such as circumcision to them (Acts 15:6–11). Paul could scarcely have said it better himself.[7]

The second item on the agenda is settled on James' authority, not Peter's, and the outcome is not in line with Paul's thought. James first confirms the position of Peter, but he states the position in a very different way: "Symeon[8] has related how God first visited the gentiles, to take a people in his name" (Acts 15:14). James' perspective here is not that all who believe are Israel (the Pauline definition), but that *in addition* to Israel God has established a people in his name. How the new people are to be regarded in relation to Israel is a question which is implicit in the statement, and James goes on to answer it.

The relationship between those taken from the gentiles and Israel is developed in two ways by James. The first method is the use of Scripture, while the second is a requirement of purity. The logic of them both inevitably involves a rejection of Paul's position (along the lines laid out in Galatians 2).

The use of Scripture, like the argument itself, is quite unlike Paul's. James claims that "with this [that is, his statement of Peter's position] the words of the prophets agree, just as it is written" (Acts 15:15), and he goes on to cite from the book of Amos. The passage cited will concern us in a moment; the *form* of James' interpretation is an immediate indication of a substantial difference from Paul. As James has it, there is actual agreement between "Symeon" and the words of the prophets, as two people might agree.[9] The continuity of Christian experience with Scripture is marked as a greater concern than within Paul's interpretation, and James expects that continuity to be verbal, a matter of agreeing with the prophets' *words*, not merely with possible ways of looking at what they mean.

The citation from Amos (9:11–12)[10] comports well with James' concern that the position of the Church agree with the principal vocabulary of the prophets (Acts 15:16–17):

After this I will come back and restore the tent of David which has fallen, and rebuild its ruins and set it up anew, that the rest of men may seek the Lord, and all the Gentiles upon whom my name is called . . .

In the argument of James as represented here, what the belief of gentiles achieves is not the redefinition of Israel (as in Paul's thought), but the *restoration* of the house of David. The argument is possible because Davidic genealogy of Jesus (and naturally of his brother James) is assumed.

An account of James' preaching in the Temple is given by Hegesippus, who wrote during the second century.[11] James there represents Jesus as the son of man who is to come from Heaven to judge the world.[12] Those who agree cry out, "Hosanna to the son of David!" Hegesippus shows that James' view of his brother came to be that, related as he was to David (as was the family generally), he was also a heavenly figure who was coming to judge the world.[13] When Acts and Hegesippus are taken together, they indicate that James contended Jesus was restoring the house of David because he was the agent of final judgment, and was being accepted as such by gentiles.

But on James' view, gentiles remain gentiles; they are not to be identified with Israel. His position was not anti-Pauline, at least not at first. His focus was on Jesus' role as the ultimate arbiter within the Davidic line, and there was never any question in his mind but that the Temple was the natural place to worship God and acknowledge Jesus.[14] Embracing the Temple as central meant for James, as it meant for everyone associated with worship there, maintaining the purity which it was understood that God required in his house.

Purity involved excluding gentiles from the interior courts of the Temple, where Israel was involved in sacrifice. A concern for the continuing validity of that exclusion is indicated by the way, according to Acts, Paul was treated at a later period when he came to Jerusalem. He was required by James to demonstrate by an act of sacrificial piety that his loyalty to the Temple continued, in order to contradict the rumor that Paul wished to deny the authority of Moses (see Acts 21:17–26).[15] The line of demarcation between Israel and non-Israel was no invention within the circle of James, but a natural result of seeing Jesus as the triumphant scion of the house of David.

Gentile belief in Jesus was therefore in James' understanding a vindication of his Davidic triumph, but it did not involve a fundamental change in the status of gentiles *vis-à-vis* Israel. That characterization of the gentiles, developed by means of the reference to Amos, enables James to proceed to his requirement of their recognition of purity. He first states that "I determine not to trouble those of the Gentiles who turn to God" (15:19) as if he were simply repeating the policy of Peter in regard to circumcision. (The implicit authority of that "I" contrasts sharply with the usual portrayal in Acts of apostolic decision as communal.) But he then continues that his determination is also "to write to them to abstain from the pollutions of the idols, and from fornication, and from what is strangled, and from blood" (15:20).

The rules set out by James are designed to separate believing gentiles from their ambient environment. They are to refrain from feasts in honor of the gods and from foods sacrificed to idols in the course of being butchered and sold. (The notional devotion of animals in the market to one god or another was a common practice in the Hellenistic world.) They are to observe stricter limits than usual on the type of sexual activity they might engage in, and with whom. They are to avoid the flesh of animals which had been strangled instead of bled, and they are not to consume blood itself. The proscription of blood, of course, was basic within Judaism.[16] And strangling an animal (as distinct from cutting its throat) increased the availability of blood in the meat. Such strictures are consistent with James' initial observation, that God had taken a people from the gentiles (15:14); they were to be similar to Israel in their distinction from the Hellenistic world at large.

The motive behind the rules is not separation in itself, however. James links them to the fact that the Mosaic legislation regarding purity is well and widely known (15:21): "For Moses from early generations has had those preaching him city by city, being read in the synagogues every Sabbath." Because the law is well known, James insists that believers, even gentile believers, are not to live in flagrant violation of it. As a result of James' insistence, the meeting in Jerusalem decides to send envoys and a letter to Antioch, in order to require gentiles to honor the prohibitions set out by James (Acts 15:22–35).

The same chapter of Leviticus which commands "love your neighbor as yourself" (19:18) also forbids blood to be eaten (19:26) and fornication (19:29, see also 18:6–30). The imperative to love and the imperative to remain pure are inextricably related in the Torah. The canonical (but secondly-hand) letter of James calls the commandment of love "the royal law" (James 2:8),[17] acknowledging that Jesus had accorded it privilege by citing it alongside the commandment to love

God as one of the two greatest commandments (see Mark 12:28–31). In Acts, James himself, while accepting that gentiles cannot be required to keep the whole law, insists that they should *acknowledge* its entirety – ethical and cultic – as Moses' constitution for Israel, by observing basic requirements concerning fornication and blood.

It is of interest that Leviticus forbids the eating of blood by sojourners as well as Israelites, and associates that prohibition with how animals are to be killed for the purpose of eating (17:10–13). Moreover, a principle of exclusivity in sacrifice is trenchantly maintained: anyone, whether of Israel or a sojourner dwelling among them, who offers a sacrifice which is not brought to the LORD's honor in the Temple is to be cut off from the people (17:8–9). In other words, the prohibitions of James, involving sacrifice, fornication, strangled meat produce, and blood, all derive easily from the very context in Leviticus from which the commandment to love is derived. They are elementary, and involve interest in what gentiles as well as Israelites do.[18]

James' prohibitions are designed to show that believing gentiles honor the law which is commonly read, without in any way changing their status as gentiles. Thereby, the tent of David is erected again in the midst of gentiles who show their awareness of the restoration by means of their respect for the Torah. The interpretation attributed to James involves an application of Davidic vocabulary to Jesus, as is consistent with the claim of Jesus' family to Davidic ancestry.[19] The transfer of Davidic promises to Jesus is accomplished within an acceptance of the terms of reference of the Scripture generally: to embrace David is to embrace Moses. There is no trace in James' interpretation of the Pauline gambit, setting one biblical principle (justification in the manner of Abraham) against another (obedience in the manner of Moses).[20] Where Paul divided the Scripture against itself in order to maintain the integrity of a single fellowship of Jews and gentiles, James insisted upon the integrity of Scripture, even at the cost of separating Christians from one another. In both cases, the interpretation of Scripture was also – at the same moment as the sacred text was apprehended – a matter of social policy.

PETER'S INTERPRETATION OF MOSES

Of all the disputants in the controversy at Antioch, Peter comes off the worst in Paul's account in Galatians 2. Not only is he said to go along with Paul, only then to side with James in separating from gentiles (Galatians 2:11–13), but Paul claims to have taken the occasion to deliver a diatribe on faith and works, using Peter's "hypocrisy" as his point of departure (Galatians 2:14–21). Indeed, it is difficult to see, on Paul's own accounting, why Paul ever left Antioch, which is just what Acts says that he did sometime after the envoys of James had visited (Acts 15:36–41).

Peter's position in the dispute is difficult to characterize, because Paul makes a caricature of it, and Acts virtually ignores it in favor of depicting James as the operative authority. But Peter is definitely associated in the New Testament with a style of interpretation which is distinct from Paul's and James'. It is a style of great nuance and resonance, but without the unequivocal finding of a Pauline new Israel or a Jacobean scion of David. Peter appears to have worked more in comparative terms than in an effort to legislate by interpretation, and the result is to set up an implicit analogy between the followers of Jesus and the Israel which followed Moses out of Egypt.

In the absence of direct evidence of the Petrine use of Scripture,[21] the best source for an example is the material in the Gospels which is attributed to Peter. From the second century, scholars of the Church pointed to Mark's Gospel especially as an interpretation of the teaching of Peter.[22] Peter in Mark appears frequently as the representative of the apostles, often in association with James and John, the sons of Zebedee. In one such passage, the influence of the Hebrew Bible, particularly in its portrayal of Moses in his role as the arbiter of Israel, is palpable.

In Mark 9:2–8, Jesus takes Peter, James, and John up a high mountain, and he is transformed before them. His clothing shines white; Moses and Elijah appear, speaking with him. Peter offers to make three booths, one for Jesus, one for Moses, and one for Elijah, but a cloud covers the scene, and a voice from the cloud says, "This is my beloved son, hear him." When the apostles are able to see again, only Jesus is there.

The reference to Moses and Elijah makes it plain that the Transfiguration requires a familiarity with the Hebrew Bible in order to be understood. Both of those prophetic figures were associated with revelation upon a mountain. Moses' mountain is called both Sinai and Horeb in the Pentateuch, following the designations of distinct, traditional sources. Elijah is placed on Horeb by the same tradition which knows Moses' mountain under that name (1 Kings 19).

But the Transfiguration resonates with a particular scene in the Pentateuch. In Exodus 24, Moses takes three followers with him up the mountain, as the particular representatives of an elite group (of seventy elders). Before they go up the mountain, Moses orders the preparation of a sacrifice at which the people as a whole accept the words of the LORD given to Moses as the covenant between them and the LORD (Exodus 24:3–8). Then comes the ascent of the mountain, and a vision of God (24:9–11). Moses is invited to ascend further, and a cloud of glory covered the mountain;[23] on the seventh day the LORD called to him, so that he could receive the tables of stone over the next forty days (Exodus 24:12–18).

The narrative structure of the Transfiguration is that of Moses' ascent of Sinai: the motifs of a single master, three disciples from a wider group, the sacred mountain, the cloud, the vision, the voice, are all shared. Just as the LORD called to Moses on the seventh day (Exodus 24:16), so Jesus took his three followers up his mountain "after six days" (Mark 9:2). The connection between the two passages is evident, but what does that connection suggest of the Petrine approach to Scripture?

Although the focus of the Transfiguration is on Jesus in his divinely disclosed identity as God's son, the identification is worked out within the general terms of reference of Moses and Elijah, and by means of particular motifs of the solemnization of the covenant in Exodus 24. The Transfiguration is so wedded to Scripture as the substance of what is revealed, it is difficult to draw the line between experience and interpretation. But that is exactly the point of the Transfiguration: neither experience alone nor interpretation alone will attest the truth of Jesus' identity. But together they furnish a vision of who precisely he is.

The vision of Jesus may be mediated to anyone who attends to the Transfiguration within its scriptural terms of reference. There is an allusion to the Transfiguration in 2 Peter (1:16–21) which is instructive. There, the vision is held to be the basis on which Peter made known the power of Jesus Christ, but then the passage goes on to say, "And we have more certain the prophetic word" (2 Peter 1:19). That is, once Jesus is correctly seen in prophetic terms, Scripture's prophecy finds its purpose, and whoever knows Scripture in that sense has access to the divine spirit of prophecy (2 Peter 1:20, 21). Both interpretation and experience are merely means to an end: the possession of spirit.

Finally, the Petrine approach to Scripture neither dissolves Moses in Jesus (the Pauline approach) nor corrals Jesus within Moses (the Jacobean approach). Although Peter's Transfiguration is not conceptually sophisticated, it is elegant: the prophetic covenant of Moses and the divine sonship of Jesus stand side by side, such that the one interprets the other. Of course, such a delicate balancing of two principles is problematic as an engine of social policy among believers; who can say in a given case whether the spirit of prophecy behind the Scripture agrees more with what the texts says or with what one experiences in the community of Jesus?

According to Acts 15, Peter concluded on the basis of God's gift of the spirit to gentiles that they could not be required to be circumcised (Acts 15:6–11). On the other hand, Paul shows in Galatians 2 that Peter was not willing to make a general principle for or against Mosaic requirements, and that he could change his mind when confronted with differing interpretations and practices. But his apparent ambivalence reflects a commitment to the *twin* loyalties of a single son and a single law, together mediating the same spirit. The Petrine compromise regards *as Israel* both the followers of Jesus and those who are loyal to Moses, and accepts the inevitability of tension between the two.

THE INTERPRETATIVE RESOLUTION OF "ISRAEL" IN THE SYNOPTIC GOSPELS

The three most influential approaches to Scripture within primitive Christianity (deriving from Paul, James, and Peter) were not simply theories of interpretation. Each came from within formative circles of the Church, and each was involved in how communities within its respective circle were ordered. Each was implicated in the preparation of catechumens for baptism within the traditions of a given circle. And each has left an indelible impression upon the character of the Church.

The Pauline approach is the most directly and fulsomely attested in the New Testament. Not only Paul's own letters, but writings from a later period in his name and style, together with Acts, represent the deep influence of a genuinely radical intellectual. Paul's claim that baptism made for a new Israel, after the manner of Abraham, but no longer subject to the Mosaic law, was in his own time a closely argued but controversial position. Only the growing number of gentile believers, as well as the destruction of the Temple and its consequences, would permit Pauline Christianity to become representative of the movement as a whole.

Once the tides of change moved in his favor, Paul arguably became the most influential intellectual in the history of the West. Even then, the fundamental challenge of his theology to *any* appeal to normative law within the social order of the Church has been difficult for many Christians to accept. The Reformation was (among other things) an attempt to assert that "grace" as conceived by Paul, rather than any law, was normative within the Church. The factionalism which ensued – between Roman Catholics and Protestants at first, and *among* both groups increasingly – is still characteristic of Christian history.

Just as Paul's influence grew unpredictably, James' influence declined precipitately from the time of the destruction of the Temple. The natural center of the movement in Jerusalem was given up to places such as Alexandria, Antioch, Corinth, Damascus, Ephesus, and Rome. The force of a genuinely Christian Judaism, extended to gentiles insofar as they would embrace some form of the law of Moses as symbolic of the whole, was certainly felt long after James was martyred. But demography as well as history was against his clear definition of the movement in unequivocally Mosaic terms.

In the stark contrast between Paul and James, Peter can seem an artless compromiser, agreeing now with one, now with another. But the twin emphasis of Peter upon Scripture and Jesus together, as providing the insight of the spirit, would prove to be a dominant influence in the formation of the Gospels. At the same time, the often unpredictable policy of early Christianity, sometimes siding with the traditions of Israel, sometimes with the new practices of believing communities, is explicable more easily on the basis of a Petrine approach than on the basis of a Pauline or a Jacobean approach.

Christians have typically believed that their inspiration comes both from Scripture and from their faithful practice, and that the single spirit – the spirit of God – unites them both. That emphasis upon a purely theological consistency, even at the expense of inevitable conflict in the social realm, is an inheritance of Petrine teaching. Any attempt to judge Christianity on the basis of social consistency alone will result in disappointment and confusion. The Church inevitably appears insufficiently radical or insufficiently conservative to secular historians, depending upon their bent. But that is because its identity lies in the dialectic between Scripture and practice, tradition and experience, a dialectic which it knows under the name of the spirit of God.

Once the distinctive character of each of the three major approaches is appreciated, it is fairly straightforward to understand the role of conflict within the early Church. But in order to make its claims about Jesus plausible, the Church required at least a common preparation for baptism, a standard for the practice of initiation. That standard is represented in the New Testament by what are known as the Synoptic Gospels (Matthew, Mark, and Luke). In that the first three Gospels emerged from the catechetical stage of the movement, when candidates were prepared for baptism, they provide the best indications of the governing concerns of the Church as it initiated new members.

The Synoptic Gospels

The first three Gospels are called "synoptic" in scholarly discussion because they may be viewed together when they are printed in columns. Unfortunately, their obviously literary relationship has caused scholars to presume that they were composed by scribes working in isolation who copied, one from another. A comparative approach,[24] served by an understanding of the development of tradition into documents both within early Judaism and early Christianity, has brought us to the point where deviations of one document from another, related document, are not assumed to be purely scribal changes. After all, the Gospels were not written by individual scholars for a learned public; the Synoptics rather represent how distinct communities, in contact with one another directly and indirectly, nurtured new members. Agreements and disagreements among the Synoptic Gospels provide a way to see how different communities of Christians pursued a common program of catechism, but in distinctive ways.

The story of the confession of Peter at Caesarea Philippi (Matthew 16:13–23; Mark 8:27–33; Luke 9:18–22) presents an example of Synoptic instruction in how to understand Jesus through the lens of the faith which is confessed at baptism. Jesus himself poses the question of his identity at the opening of the passage ("Who do people say I am?" in Mark), and the disciples reply with a startling range of biblically based answers, in which Jesus is identified in prophetic terms. He is said to be John the baptizer,[25] Elijah, or one of the prophets. In seeing Jesus in the Bible, and the Bible in Jesus, the disciples' response to Jesus' question immediately introduces us to a use of Scripture that is out of the ordinary. The prophets are not referred to as purely from the past, but are taken to be alive and effective in the ministry of Jesus.

The common element in these understandings is that they involve an approach to the Bible as a matter of experience. Jesus is seen in immediately prophetic terms; the prophets' activity lives on in the case of Jesus. Jesus was a catalyst both for his first followers and later within the memory of the Church; he set off a reaction between the Bible of the time and those who read the Bible. The experience of him was such that in the Synoptic Gospels biblical language and imagery became the vehicle of understanding and expressing what was happening in the case of Jesus. Jesus had taken his principal theme, the kingdom of God, from the Bible of his day (the Aramaic paraphrases know as the Targums). For him, however, the kingdom was not simply a promise contained in the Bible, but a reality that was changing the world. The principle that the Scripture refers to facts of experience was accepted by those who tried to understand Jesus as one of the prophets.

But Jesus in the Synoptic narrative is not content with a simple identification of himself with one of the prophets of old; he replies, "But who do you yourselves say I am?" The question is also a demand. The demand of Jesus is to use the measure of Scripture in a critical way, not only as a matter of experience. His disciples are to see him as importantly like John, Elijah, or another prophet, but also as crucially different.

By refusing to embrace any one prophetic designation in the story, Jesus presses Peter to use the title "Christ" or "Messiah," one of the most flexible terms in the Hebrew Bible.[26] It might refer, depending upon context, to a king in the line of David, to a high priest readied for his office, to a prophet commissioned to convey his message. The associations of the term with empowered anointing are evident, but Jesus then proceeds to relate the term to his own suffering. A criticism of the received understanding of Scripture is obvious here: it simply will not do to identify Jesus simply with the charisma of the prophets, with the might of kings, or with the dignity of priests. Jesus in the story insists on his difference from such figures.

His difference, his individuality, does not reside in his claim to be greater than an Elijah or any anticipated messiah. After all, Jesus did not expect to be taken up alive into Heaven, as was said of Elijah (see 2 Kings 2:9–12), and no one ever said that he actually ruled as the messiah of Israel. Jesus' distinctiveness is a matter of his suffering, which the story of Caesarea Philippi places alongside the prophetic and messianic designations as the key to Jesus' identity. The Synoptic Jesus insists not only that Scripture be seen as a matter of experience, but that the critical difference between present experience and the biblical testimony is as important for our understanding of God as the similarity between the two.

114

In a single word, there is an analogy between Jesus and the figures of the Hebrew Bible. He is experienced in terms of what they were, and yet he is also seen as different; and in that difference lies the meaning of his teaching and his action. Jesus liked to refer to Scripture as fulfilled in his ministry.[27] He called attention to both similarities and critical distinctions between what was said of God in Scripture and what he saw of God as a matter of experience. The promises to Israel might lead you to expect that the feast of the kingdom was to exclude those outside the nation, but Jesus anticipated that people would stream in from everywhere and that exclusions would be surprising (see Matthew 8:11, 12; Luke 13:28, 29, and the discussion on pp. 122–6). The analogy between Scripture and experience is rooted in the sensibility that a given biblical text is identifying and describing the God we experience. But under Jesus' approach there is no sense in which Scripture can be said to limit what God does and is about to do. In the Synoptic development of that approach, there is a stable analogy, not an identity, between Jesus and Scripture.

The experience of God as biblical is only the beginning, or the occasion, of the Bible's authority. Jesus refused to limit himself to the repetition of the biblical text: he was noted (and notorious) for departing from agreed norms in order to speak of God. Who else within his time and setting would compare the kingdom of the one, almighty God with a woman baking bread (Luke 13:20–1)? In addition to being experiential in reference to Scripture, Jesus was also critical. His critical perspective, of course, was not historical; rather, his creative adaptation of biblical language and imagery evidences an awareness that God in the text and God in experience do not entirely coincide. The Synoptics honor that awareness in their analogical presentation of Jesus and Scripture.

Because the God of the Bible is experienced, and yet – as experienced – may not be contained by the biblical text, the trademark of Jesus' instrumental use of Scripture is "fulfillment." By referring to Scripture as fulfilled, Jesus claimed to resolve the tension between the coincidence and the distance of the biblical God from his own experience. When, for example, Jesus says in the synagogue in Nazareth, "Today this Scripture has been fulfilled in your ears," he does not literally mean that he did everything referred to in the passage from Isaiah he has just read (see Luke 4:16–21). The simple facts are that Isaiah 61:1, 2 refers to things Jesus never did, such as releasing prisoners from jail, and that Jesus did things the text makes no mention of, such as declaring people free of impurity (see Matthew 8:2–4; Mark 1:40–5; Luke 5:12–16).

By means of their example, the Synoptic Gospels establish a thoroughly christological technique in the interpretation of Scripture as fulfilled. Christ, the guarantor of the kingdom, is the standard by which Scripture is experienced, corrected, and understood to have been fulfilled. There is here still no articulated theory of the relationship between Christ and Scripture; that would come later. But the Synoptics did insist that the catechesis of believers who sought baptism should include the christological technique of understanding the Scriptures.

Much as in the case of Peter's interpretation, the Synoptic approach is curiously indeterminate at the level of social policy. In order to predict whether a given element of the Hebrew Bible would be commended or set aside, one would need to know what image of Christ was being used as the standard of judgment. In the case of the Synoptic presentation of the discussion near Caesarea Philippi, a community which sought ethical guidance in following Jesus would not be told to be prophetic or priestly or royal, but to take on the burden of messianic suffering that Jesus alone instances (see Matthew 16:24–8; Mark 8:34–9:1; Luke 9:23–7). The finished product of interpretation is guided by Christ; the text of Scripture is necessary raw material, but raw material nonetheless. The Synoptics are not biased towards the position of a James or a Paul, because no principle of Scripture (such as the scion or David, or the faith of Abraham) is held up as the key to the texts as a whole. In that indeterminacy, there is even less predisposition toward any normative status of the Hebrew Bible than in Petrine interpretation, because Moses is not accorded the central position.

Synoptic hermeneutics are not a compromise, because they are the outcome of an evolution of technique. Nonetheless, they are open to the application of widely variant social policies, and that appears to have been part of the secret of their success. Because Antioch was the crucible where the great figures of primitive Christianity brought their differences to the most critical point, Antioch is best seen as the center where the Synoptic catechesis was first developed. It was then swiftly accepted (and adapted) in other major centers of what now indeed was a coherent Church with a certain standard of catechesis.

Among those who might have been responsible for the Synoptic breakthrough the most likely teacher is Barnabas. Unlike Paul, he remained near Antioch long after the famous confrontation, and his

116

remaining involved a dispute with Paul (see Acts 15:36–41). His position is most similar to Peter's, and yet the advance in the Synoptics at the level of technique of interpretation suggests that a new mind was at work. Finally, there is attributed to Barnabas an epistle (from the second century) which is centrally concerned with the relationship between Christ and the Scriptures and institutions of Judaism.[28] That would seem to be a continuation of his original contribution, the Synoptic hermeneutics of Scripture. Because those hermeneutics involve using Christ as the sole lens through which the whole of Israel's Scriptures are considered, the interpretative community itself becomes a new Israel, uniquely positioned to perceive and embrace the promises which have been vivified in the light of Christ.

MATTHEW, MARK, LUKE, AND JOHN

Once the Synoptic catechesis was accepted within communities, it was subjected to local developments. The result is the close relationship (and the striking differences) among Matthew, Mark, and Luke. Each of the Gospels, in turn, represents a distinctive application of the same basic technique of scriptural interpretation which was established in the Synoptic catechesis by Barnabas, and each presents its church as a new Israel in a fresh way.

Mark

Mark, the first of the Gospels to be written (c. 71 CE), was produced within the context of mounting persecution in Rome, and of increasing separation from synagogues. Its reference to Scripture is largely uninventive, determined by the tradition handed on to Rome. In the midst of immediately social concerns, the suspicion of civic authorities, and the growing antagonism of Judaic leaders, the relationship between Christ and Scripture was not a focal concern. The text of Mark does manifest an overt concern to distance itself culturally from Judaism. The famous remark about "the Pharisees and all the Jews," their obsession with washing all manner of produce and vessels as well as scrubbing their hands (Mark 7:3–4), seems nothing if not ironic and editorial. The Roman setting of Mark, especially in the period after the destruction of the Temple, makes the appeal to the oddity of Jewish custom seem at home. It is the sort of argument warranted by Cicero and Seneca.[29] Owing to its program of distinction from Judaism, Mark represents the Synoptic hermeneutic of Jesus' relation to

Israel's Scriptures quite straightforwardly, without much in the way of further refinement.

Matthew

Matthew – produced *c.* 80 CE in Damascus – cites Scripture more explicitly, and more insistently says it is fulfilled by Jesus, than does any other Gospel. The citation of passages verbatim is especially striking, and is somewhat reminiscent of the Essene technique of the Pesher.[30] But the Matthean application of Scripture to Christ is pictorial to the point that sometimes it is literalistic.

Perhaps the most famous distortion which results is the picture of Jesus riding into Jerusalem on *both* a donkey and its colt (Matthew 21:1–7). In the book of Zechariah (9:9), the messianic king is predicted to arrive "on a ass, on a colt the foal of an ass." Matthew is the only Synoptic Gospel which quotes the passage at length, in a Greek form, "on an ass *and* the foal of an ass" (italics added). In the interests of consistency, the Matthean Jesus is then described as sitting upon both of the animals.

Just as the application of Scripture to Jesus is more exact in Matthew than in any other document of the New Testament, so does Matthew embrace "Israel" as the designation of its own community. Only Matthew cites Micah 5:2 as a prediction of Jesus' birth in Bethlehem, and the citation includes the words, "from you shall come a ruler, who shall shepherd my people Israel" (Matthew 2:6). "Israel" here refers forward to all those who will be incorporated within the flock of Jesus during the course of the narrative, and is an alternative designation of "Church."[31]

Luke

The natural counterpart in Luke to Matthew's citation of Micah is the passage known as the song of Simeon (Luke 2:29–32), which is still used as a canticle at evensong in the liturgical churches of Christianity. The last of the Synoptics to be written (*c.* 90 CE) – and in Antioch – Luke's Gospel constitutes a suitable advance of the christological technique of interpretation pioneered by Barnabas. The infant Jesus is presented in the Temple, and Simeon is inspired to come to the Temple himself, to see the messiah (Luke 2:22–8). His song is also inspired by God, and is not a matter of citing Scripture (Luke 2:29–32):

Master, now release your servant,
    according to your word, in peace;
because my eyes have seen your salvation,
    which you have prepared before the face of all peoples:
a light for the revelation of the Gentiles,
    and the glory of your people Israel.

Simeon functions in the manner of the prophets, in order to identify Israel's glory as the extension of the revelation of God to non-Jews. Such is the certainty of that christological stance, it does not need the words of Scripture to be confirmed; it rather produces its own Scripture, designed for devotional repetition.

Simeon's prophecy in fact extends beyond the song which has so deeply influenced the liturgy. His prediction, in a separate statement to Mary, explicitly includes reference to division *within Israel* as a result of Jesus (2:34–3):

Lo, he is set for the falling and rising of many in Israel,
    and for a sign which is spoken against –
and even through your soul shall a sword pass –
    so that the thoughts of many hearts shall be revealed.

What is cast as a prediction by means of God's own spirit, which is also a narrative key to the events of the Gospel (and of Acts), links Jesus' death in particular (the sword through Mary's soul) with the ambivalent response of Israel. Many shall fall, and many rise, because "Israel" is in the process of being redefined according to one's response to Jesus. A positive response extends the divine promises to non-Jews and is for the glory of Israel, while a negative response divides Israel against itself into those who fall and those who rise.[32]

John's Gospel

John's Gospel, written in Ephesus around 100 CE, presupposes that its readers have been baptized, following a catechesis such as the Synoptics represent. It is a far more reflective work than the first three Gospels, and it develops in its prologue (John 1:1–18) as full a statement of the relationship between Jesus and Scripture as the Gospels ever offer. It explores a distinctive vocabulary in order to articulate Jesus' impact upon humanity, and this is largely derived from the theological language of the Targumim.

Jesus is explained in terms of God's "word," *logos* in Greek, *memra*

119

in Aramaic. *Memra*, a nominal form of the verb "to speak" (*'amar*), is the way the Targums refer to God's activity of commanding. God might simply be thought of as commanding what is ordered when the term is used, but the emphasis might fall on the intention behind the divine order. Then again, the usage might call attention to how and why people respond to the order. *Memra* might therefore refer to the primordial "word" of God in creating the Heavens and the earth, to the revelation of the Torah, or to the disobedient response God's commands sometimes encounter. It is no coincidence that John's Gospel explains the relationship between Jesus and Scripture by means of a term whose exact significance was determined by the context in which it was used.[33]

John's presentation of the relationship between Jesus and God's word is demanding, as is to be expected from an advanced work such as the fourth Gospel. But when we reduce the poetics of Johannine interpretation to the underlying theory, we find a simple formulation: Jesus makes the divine *logos* known which is also attested in Scripture, and he makes it known more truly than does Scripture, because he personally embodies God (above all, see John 1:14–18). The poetics of John are complex and moving; the hermeneutics of John are fundamentally what we find in the Synoptics.

John the baptist is a key figure in the prologue. It is said that, although he himself was not the light, he came to bear witness to Jesus as the true light of God (John 1:6–9). That function is precisely and self-consciously accepted by John later in the first chapter of John.[34] John declares that Jesus is the lamb of God, the one on whom God's spirit rests, God's own son (John 1:29–34). The key to the realization is the descent of the spirit upon Jesus as a dove, which fulfills the promise of God to John, "'On whom you see the spirit descend and remain on him, he is the one baptizing with holy spirit'" (John 1:33).

John is made to testify to the release of God's spirit through Jesus, rather than through the baptism John himself practiced. Specifically Christian baptism, baptism in the name of Jesus, is what John attests, and his own function is purely introductory. He is aware of his own limitation (John 1:31): "I did not know him, but in order that he might be revealed to Israel, for this purpose I came baptizing with water." "Israel" here seems to be used in a less inclusive sense than in the Synoptics, in order to refer to Jesus' manifestation during his activity in and among the Jews of Palestine. But that usage needs to be understood within the dominant pattern of the Gospel.

As he enters Jerusalem shortly before his crucifixion, Jesus will be hailed in John as "king of Israel" (John 12:13), an acclamation which does not appear in the Synoptics.[35] John's Gospel is deliberate in its use of the title; within chapter 1, it is used by Nathanael in association with "son of God" in order to identify Jesus (John 1:49). One of Jesus' first disciples in John, Nathanael says to him, "Rabbi, you are the son of God, you are the king of Israel."

That statement summarizes the christology of John's Gospel as a whole: directly related to God, as the incarnation of the divine word, Jesus is also the true regent of Israel. Jesus' response to Nathanael indicates the depth of the importance of "Israel" as a term of reference within John. He tells Nathanael (John 1:51): "You[36] will see Heaven opened, and the angels of God ascending and descending upon the son of man." For the biblically literate hearers for whom the Gospel is intended, the allusion is unmistakable.

At Bethel, the patriarch Jacob dreamed, and in his vision he saw the angels of God ascending and descending (Genesis 28:12). God spoke to Jacob, and told him that all the families of the earth would bless themselves through Jacob's descendants (Genesis 28:14). That Jacob was the same patriarch whom God would later rename "Israel" (in Genesis 32:28). John's meaning is plain: Jesus is the true Israel, attested by the angels of God, by whom all the families of the earth will be blessed. Where Paul had argued that Jesus effectuated the universal promise to Abraham (by means of Genesis 12:3; see Galatians 3:8), John's Gospel makes Jesus the new Jacob in his extension of God's promise to new people. Jesus becomes the divinely warranted guarantee of the promise of Israel for all people.

The main lines of John's principal definition of Israel are therefore straightforward: all that is to be realized in the promise to the patriarchs occurs in Jesus. But alongside that evident definition, a shadow is cast. As we saw, the first usage of "Israel" in John is *not* a reference to the true Jacob, warranted by God, but a reference to the people to whom Jesus is presented by John the baptist (1:31). Those people – the historical, Jewish contemporaries of Jesus – are repeatedly represented as unwilling or unable to grasp his teaching. The theme of the Jewish rejection of Jesus is sounded in the prologue with the words, "He came into his own, and his own received him not" (John 1:11).

The body of the Gospel persistently reminds us that "the Jews" were seeking over a long period to kill Jesus (John 5:18; 7:1, 11; 10:31; 11:8, 49–50; 18:14; 19:7, 12). John's Jesus is in an alien environment,[37] because he is known from the outset as "the son of God" (and so

121

Nathanael says in 1:49), while "the Jews" would kill anyone who claimed to be such (John 5:18; 19:7).

The Jewish resistance to Jesus is within John not a historical happenstance, but a theological necessity. No Israel can accept Jesus which does not embrace him as God's son and Israel's king. Even sincere efforts to understand Jesus by Jews are doomed to failure if they are conducted on any other terms. Nicodemus, a ruler of the Jews, comes by night and tries to appreciate Jesus as a teacher come from God (John 3:1–2). Jesus replies with riddles which befuddle Nicodemus, and Jesus taunts him, "You are a teacher of Israel, and you do not understand this?" (John 3:10). Johannine irony is not simply a question of style. What Jesus says to Nicodemus effectively claims the term "Israel" for those who seen the reality of Jesus as the true Jacob, while all others who claim to be Israel are relegated to the status of "the Jews," the deadly opposition.

JESUS' ISRAEL AND THE GENERATION OF CHRISTIANITY

Jesus' concern was to address local Israel, particular communities (especially in Galilee), on the supposition of the purity of those who heard him. From his perspective, it was necessary to assert that they were clean until their actions proved them otherwise. That is precisely what Jesus did in a saying whose authenticity is widely accepted (Mark 7:14–15):

> Hear me, all of you, and understand:
> There is nothing outside the man, entering into him,
> which defiles him,
> but those things coming out of the man
> are what defile him.

The "Jesus Seminar" is representative both of the conventional wisdom of the saying's authenticity, and of what is usually done with the consensus. The saying is accepted as "a categorical challenge to the laws governing pollution and purity," and is attributed to Jesus.[38]

All such interpretations ignore the issue of substance: the saying is an assertion *concerning* defilement, not a general denial of defilement. The assertion is easily construed in Aramaic attested from Jesus' period and place,[39] and is more attractive when it is so rendered:

la' demin bar bar-'enasha'/da'teh bey demtamohi
bera' min da'tan min/bar-'enasha' 'elen demtamohi.

The English representation might be:

nothing that is outside a person/entering one defiles one,
except that things coming from/a person, these defile one.

The stroke (/) is used to help describe the poetics of the assertion, which divides into two lines, each of four beats followed by three beats. Using *bar* for "outside"[40] (in the phrase *demin bar*), produces a repetition of sound with "person" (*bar-'enasha'*). "Person" itself is repeated in the last line, so as to emphasize closure. The use of *bar* is continued in "except that" (*bera' mi*n),[41] linking the two lines by the same device which opens the first line strikingly. The participle "defile" (from *tema'*; here rendered with a finite verb)[42] dominates the sense of the entire saying; it is clearly an example of a *mashal*, the Hebrew term for a proverbial or parabolic teaching.

Rendering the aphorism into Aramaic obviously makes it no more and no less a saying of Jesus. That it can be so rendered, and is memorable in Aramaic, simply helps to confirm the suggestion that the circle of Jesus confronted the issue of defilement. The circle was centered in Galilee, and was characterized by fellowship at meals involving various people with different practices of purity. That description applies to the period of Jesus' own activity, and to the period after his death when the movement continued to engage in the practice of fellowship at meals. Before and after Jesus' death, the celebration of the kingdom's purity in such fellowship was the hallmark of the movement.

In either phase, the circle of Jesus needed to cope with the social issue of possible defilement as one member of Israel (with one set of practices) met another member of Israel (with a different set of practices). The "Jesus Seminar" uncritically accepts the present context of the saying, limited to a dispute about foods, as the generative concern of the saying.[43] If it is a *mashal* from the circle of Jesus, its setting cannot be determined from the literary context which later circles associated the aphorism with.

Had Jesus taken any other stance in regard to purity than the acceptance of each local community as Israel, he would have committed himself to engage in specific procedures of purification (such as John the baptist's) prior to preaching the message of the kingdom.[44] His argument here in Mark 7:15 is as simple as an aphoristic assertion, just as his practice generally was straightforward: the purity of generic Israel is acknowledged as true purity. On that assumption, the promulgation of the kingdom by word and deed, by Jesus and by his disciples, could and should proceed. The statement concerning defilement represents a policy of treating all of Israel *as Israel*, pure by means of its customary practice.

The point of such sayings as Mark 7:15 (see also Matthew 15:11 and Luke 11:39–41) is that there is a link between integrity and cleanness: that Israelites are properly understood as pure, and that what extends from a person, what he is and does and has, manifests that purity. Paul was to write some twenty-five years later (and for his own purposes), "*Do you not know* that your body is a temple of the holy spirit within you, which you have from God?" (1 Corinthians 6:19a, b; italics added). Paul may be alluding to a particular saying of Jesus' (cf. John 2:21) or to what he takes to be a theme of Jesus'; in either case, he refers his readers to what he assumes to be elementary knowledge of the gospel.

That Jesus and especially Paul (who identified himself as a Pharisee; cf. Philippians 3:5) speak from such a perspective is not unusual. It is said that Hillel took a similar point of view, and expressed it in a more heterodox manner. He defended an Israelite's right to bathe in Roman installations on the grounds that, if gentiles deem it an honor to wash the idols of their gods, Israelites should similarly deem it an honor (indeed, a duty) to wash their bodies, the image of God (Leviticus Rabbah 34.3). In other words, bathing does not make one pure, but celebrates the fact of purity; in their quite different ways, Hillel and Paul demonstrate that representatives of the Pharisaic movement – contrary to its repute in the Gospels – conceived of purity as a condition which Israelites could be assumed to enjoy, and out of which they should act. Fundamentally, Jesus' concern appears similarly to have been with cleanness as a matter of production, rather than of consumption.

Jesus' perspective in regard to purity is attested within a passage which is also common to the Synoptics, but which is particularly articulated in the source called "Q." The source consists for the most part of distinct statements of Jesus, reflected best in some 200 verses of Matthew and Luke which are not fully present in Mark. "Q" arranges the sayings of Jesus as if they were the teachings of a rabbi; it approximates to a mishnah, arranged by topic and the association of ideas and words.

In the commission to his twelve followers (and, in Luke, seventy followers) to preach and heal, Jesus specifically commands them to remain in whatever house they are received within a given village until they depart (Matthew 10:11–13; Mark 6:10; Luke 9:4; 10:5–7). That commandment by itself is a notable development compared with a Pharisaic construction of purity, because it presupposes that what the disciples eat, within any house that might receive them, is clean. Jesus' itinerary and that of his disciples, treated in much recent literature as if it were an obviously Graeco-Roman practice, was a profound statement of the general purity of food in Israel.

The mishnaic source underscores that statement by having the disciples pronounce their peace upon the house in question (Matthew 10:12, 13; Luke 10:5, 6), and Luke's Jesus particularly insists that the disciples should eat what is set before them in whatever town they might enter (10:7, 8).[45] The pronouncement of peace and the injunction not to go from house to house within a given community (cf. Luke 10:7), but to stay put until the visit is over, had obvious utility within the missionary concerns of the mishnaic source. But the particular focus upon purity, all but obscured in "Q" with missionary directives, appears to have been Jesus'.

A last peculiarity of the commission in "Q," which has long seemed incomprehensible, finds its sense under our analysis. Although Mark's Jesus has the disciples without bread, bag, money, or a change of clothes, he does permit them a staff and sandals (6:8, 9). In the mishnaic source, however, just those obviously necessary items are singled out for *exclusion*: no staff should be carried, no sandals worn (cf. Matthew 10:9, 10; Luke 9:3; 10:4). The traditional attempt to explain differences within the lists as the result of missionary practices within the early Church is reasonable superficially, but that attempt only diverts attention from the obvious fact that the commission makes extremely poor sense as a missionary instrument. Why tell people not to take what on any journey they, practically speaking, might need?

But if we understand the commission to treat every village they might enter as clean, as pure territory such as that in which sacrifice might be offered,[46] the perplexing structure of the commission makes eminent sense. The disciples are to enter villages exactly as pilgrims were to enter the Temple within Pharisaic teaching: without the food, the sandals, the staffs, the garments, the bags, and the money (cf. Berakhoth 9:5; b. Yebamoth 6b) which would normally accompany a journey. "Q" makes Jesus' commission into a missionary discourse; within his ministry, it was designed to be an enacted parable of Israel's purity.

Whether in the triply attested material of the Synoptics (a probable reflection of Petrine tradition) or in the doubly attested mishnaic source known as "Q," a circle of concern associated with Jesus is held to see purity as proceeding from Israel. Once one is identified with Israel, it is not that which is without which defiles, but those things which come from oneself. Separation from that which is outside one does not therefore assure purity, and non-Jews in the mixed environment of Galilee pose no particular danger to Israel. The circle of Jesus frames its rhetoric for its specific, social circumstance, of Israel in the midst of the nations.[47] Defilement here is a matter of failing to recognize the others of Israel, refusing to produce from within and to contact on that basis the pure Israel which those others represent.

Jesus' definition was unlike that of his followers, because it was not systematic. His policy of fellowship with others of Israel, the assumption that their practices were to be accepted as pure, implied that they were indeed Israel, but there is no statement attributed (or attributable) to Jesus that establishes the boundaries of Israel. Boundaries were precisely among those things which were melting away in his eschatological imagination.

A characteristic claim is attested in the source of Jesus' sayings called "Q" (Matthew 8:11; Luke 13:28, 29):[48]

> Many shall come from east and west
> and recline in feasting
> with Abraham and Isaac and Jacob . . .

There can be no doubt of the emphasis upon a future consummation in the saying, involving a particular (but unnamed) place, the actions and material of festivity (including the luxurious custom of reclining, not sitting, at a banquet), and the incorporation of the many who shall rejoice in the company of the patriarchs.

Jesus' use of the imagery of feasting in order to refer to the kingdom, a characteristic of his message, is resonant both with early Judaic language of the kingdom and with his own ministry. The picture of God offering a feast on Mount Zion "for all peoples," where death itself is swallowed up, becomes an influential image from the time of Isaiah 25:6–8. Notably, the Targum of Isaiah refers to the divine disclosure on Mount Zion which includes the image of the feast as "the kingdom of the LORD of hosts" (24:23).[49] Sayings such as the one cited from "Q" invoke that imagery, and Jesus' practice of fellowship at meals with his disciples and many others amounted to a claim that the ultimate festivity had already begun.

The development of systematic definitions of the Israel implied by the movement of Jesus became a necessity in the period after the resurrection. The two forces which produced the necessity were, first, the acceptance of Jesus' message – including the claim he had been raised from the dead – among non-Jews, and, second, the increasing hostility of Jewish authorities, both the priesthood in Jerusalem and Pharisaic leaders there and abroad. It is vital to appreciate, however, that those two forces of systematization, powerful as they were, were further developments of constitutional characteristics of the new movement: the followers of Jesus were willing to include more people in "Israel" than was conventional, and they claimed that their authority to do so exceeded any other authority. In their readiness to redefine "Israel," they perpetuated the substance of Jesus' policy of eschatological inclusion.

The book of Acts portrays the circle of Peter in Jerusalem as organized into households, for the breaking of bread and worship in the Temple (see Acts 1:12–26; 2:44–7; 3:1–26; 4:1–37). As long as only Jews were involved, the practice of meals – and the demarcation of boundaries by means of meals – must have made the group seem to be a version of Pharisaic fellowship. The participation of non-Jews, whether in Caesarea (where Cornelius is located in Acts 10) or as far afield as Antioch (so Galatians 2), would obviously strain that appearance of Pharisaic piety to the breaking-point. The Christian Judaism of the Petrine circle, whether from the point of view of Jews or of non-Jews, appeared to be a contradiction in terms. The rejection of Peter's social policy by James and Paul (attested in Galatians 2) demonstrates that the contradiction was unacceptable to principal leaders within the Church.

James and Paul represent diametrically opposed responses to the conceptual failure of Petrine Christianity. James insisted upon the leadership of the movement from Jerusalem, the continuation of sacrifice in the Temple, the purity of all those (Jews and non-Jews) associated with him, and the separation of Jews and non-Jews at meals. Hegesippus reports that, like the Essenes, James refused to anoint himself with oil.[50] That has been taken as evidence that James actually was an Essene.[51] But abstinence from oil was not a trademark of the Essenes; rather, it expressed doubt as to the purity of the oil one might acquire. What James shares with the Essenes is only a desire to define Israel by means of the specifics of purity.

As Peter may be compared with Pharisees and James with Essenes, Paul is reminiscent of those whom Philo of Alexandria described as

127

scrupulous for the intellectual reference of laws to the exclusion of their expressed meaning.[52] Educated and speculative thinkers in the Diaspora, they held that the Torah was to be mined for its symbolic meaning, and that, so understood, it no longer regulated practice. They anticipated Paul's argument that circumcision could be dispensed with; Philo attacks the view that, since circumcision represents the excision of passion, the practice itself need not be followed once one's passions are controlled. Paul, too, was a product of the Diaspora,[53] from Tarsus (a prominent city within philosophical discussion).[54] The Israel he saw realized in Christ accords with the character of his background.

Paul's allegorical Israel would finally prevail within Christianity, as John's Gospel attests. But in his own time, the prevalent views were those of James and Peter and Barnabas. The Synoptic Gospels represent Barnabas' perspective better than any other source. They take up a policy akin to Philo's: although allegorical meaning is acknowledged, the continuation of practice is also defended. Just as Philo's readers are to circumcise their sons, so those who attend to the Synoptics are to accept that Christian Jews and non-Jewish Christians will find ways to live together.

6

PRACTICE: JESUS AND THE TORAH

The Gospels' Judaic way of life

KNOWING GOD, IMITATING GOD

The Judaism represented by the Mishnah and later writings offers knowledge of God through the Torah and instruction on the right conduct of life through learning in the Torah. God enters the world through the Torah, and the way of life of that Judaism finds its definition in thoughtful study of the Torah and the practice of its teachings. For Christians, Jesus Christ the Incarnation of God accords that same knowledge and instruction, the record of his days on earth in the Gospels forming a narrative of what happens when God is made flesh. The way of life set forth by both Judaisms found its definition in imitating God. Humanity has been made "in our image, after our likeness" (Genesis 1:26; 9:6). The task of Israel is to show what it means, then, to be "like God." The individual and "Israel" serve as examples of the same thing, namely, God's love, which is all the greater because the person and the social entity are informed of that love:

Tractate Abot 3:14

A He would say, "Precious is the human being, who was created in the image [of God]. It was an act of still greater love that it was made known to him that he was created in the image [of God] as it is said, 'For in the image of God he made man' " (Genesis 9:6).

B Precious is Israel [that is, are Israelites], who are called children to the Omnipresent. It was an act of still greater love that it was made known to them that they were called children to the Omnipresent, as it is said, "You are the children of the Lord your God" (Deuteronomy 14:1).

C Precious are Israelites, to whom was given the precious thing. It was an act of still greater love that it was made known to them that to them was given that precious thing with which the world was made, as it is said, "For I give you a good doctrine. Do not forsake my Torah" (Proverbs 4:2).

"Israel" here means "Israelite," not the social entity viewed as a collectivity, but those who belong to the entity – and therefore constitute that entity, even one by one. These are the children of the Lord, as Scripture says; "Israel[ites]" are shown to be beloved because the Torah was given to them and because that fact was made known to them. In making these statements, the central issue is the Torah, not Israel. What is celebrated is the gift of the Torah, here, the information therein.

We take the measure of what is at stake, therefore, in the formulation of the system's way of life when we ask large questions about fundamental matters. For the Christian Judaism that is given expression in the New Testament, an account of the life and teachings of God Incarnate conveyed those principles of the godly life that, in small detail, would animate the everyday life of ordinary people. Others rightly find in the Gospels different points of critical concern, but for us, in our effort to describe the Christian Judaism that forms the counterpart to other Judaisms of the age, the heart of the matter once more concerns Christ and the Torah. Here again, if in the Torah we know God and how God wants us to live, finding there the specifics entailed in the imitation of God, then what need for Torah learning endures once God has walked among us and instructed us in person?

The issue plays itself out in Jesus' own teaching about the Torah and of the Torah. The Gospels portray Jesus as a master with a circle of disciples, like any other sage. They further present Jesus as the source of instruction on the godly way. But the critical focus of the stories is reached when the Gospels show how Jesus proposes to mediate between the Torah of Sinai and his own instruction, presented not in the name of Sinai's Torah but his own. Here, once again, we find the key to the system: what does it mean to know God Incarnate? The issue becomes, when God walks among us, what of the Torah God revealed long ago?

Jesus' profession is not to destroy but to fulfill the Torah given by God to Moses as he himself states in so many words:

"Think not that I have come to abolish the Torah and the prophets; I have come not to abolish them but to fulfill them. For truly I say to you, till and earth pass away, not an iota, not a dot, will pass from the Torah until all is accomplished. Whoever then relaxes one of the least of these commandments and teaches men so shall be called least in the kingdom of , but he who does them and teaches them shall be called great in the kingdom of heaven. For I tell you, unless your righteousness exceeds that of the scribes and Pharisees, you will never enter the kingdom of heaven."

(Matthew 5:17–20)

God Incarnate affirms the Torah – but at the same time brings the Torah to fulfillment, which, in context, would come to mean closure and conclusion. God Incarnate takes priority, God is the authority that validates the Torah.

The language of "the kingdom of Heaven" invokes for other Israelites the dominion of God. Declaring the unity of God is taken to accept "the yoke of the kingdom of Heaven" and "the yoke of the commandments." So at issue here is how this Judaism, like others, will form a way of life that expresses God's rule over the everyday realm of the here and the now. When in the Judaism of our sages, people accept the yoke of the commandments of the Torah and do them, they accept God's rule. Israel then lives not only in the natural world but in the kingdom of God, which is to say, in the dominion of Heaven, here on earth. That is what it means to live a holy life: to live by the will of God in the here and now. And, it is clear, one fundamental point in the Incarnate God's instruction affirms that life in the here and now takes place before God.

TRANSCENDING SINAI, SURPASSING THE TORAH

But Christian Judaism bears its special Torah, too: knowledge of God Incarnate bears Torah that surpasses Sinai's. This claim is explicit; other, prior masters teach a lesser truth, but Jesus, a greater one. Speaking with the authority of Sinai, Jesus revises the received commandments, imposing a higher standard for the Christian way of life. These are what is meant by not abolishing but fulfilling the Torah and the prophets, and among them five important ones capture our attention.

1 "You have heard that it was said, 'You shall not kill.'... But I say to you that everyone who is angry with his brother shall be liable" (Matthew 5:21–2).

2 "You have heard that it was said, 'You shall not commit adultery.' But I say to you that every one who looks at a woman lustfully has already committed adultery with her in his heart" (Matthew 5:27–8).

3 "You have heard that it was said to the men of old, 'You shall not swear falsely but shall perform to the Lord what you have sworn.' But I say to you, 'Do not swear at all'" (Matthew 5:33–4).

4 "You have heard that it was said, 'An eye for an eye and a tooth for a tooth.' But I say to you, 'Do not resist one who is evil, but if any one strikes you on the right cheek, turn to him the other also'" (Matthew 5:38–9).

5 "You have heard that it was said, 'You shall love your neighbor and hate your enemy.' But I say to you, love your enemies and pray for those who persecute you.... You must be perfect as your heavenly father is perfect" (Matthew 5:43–4, 48).

The Christian Judaic way of life set forth by God walking among us enhances the received commandments at each point. Specifically, Jesus sets forth as his demonstration of how not to abolish the Torah and the prophets but to fulfill them a set of teachings that, all together, point to a more profound demand – on the Torah's part – than people have realized. Not only must we not kill, we must not even approach that threshold of anger that in the end leads to murder. Not only must we not commit adultery, we must not even approach the road that leads to adultery. Not only must we not swear falsely by God's name, we should not swear at all. These formulations represent an elaboration of three of the Ten Commandments. In the language of a text of Judaism attributed to authorities long before Jesus' own time, "Make a fence around the Torah." That is to say, conduct yourself in such a way that you will avoid even the things that cause you to sin, not only sin itself.

By seeking reconciliation, we make a fence against wanting to kill; by chastity in thought, against adultery in deed; by not swearing, against not swearing falsely. Here is a message well worth hearing, one that makes plausible the somewhat odd contrast between what we have heard and what we now hear. To be sure, rabbis in the great

Rabbinic documents would in time come to the same conclusion, to avoid anger, to avoid temptation, to avoid vowing and swearing, but that fact is not germane to our argument. What is relevant is that many of the teachings of the wisdom writings and prophecy, Proverbs for example, will lead to these same laudable conclusions; for example, the Lord hates a false witness, not to desire the beauty of an evil woman in your heart and not to let her capture you with her eyelashes (Proverbs 6:16–19, 25–6), and the like.

Nothing in this distinct revision of the Torah represents an intent to nullify, let alone to violate, the received revelation. The Christian way of life meant to reaffirm the Torah's entire moral and ethical message. Jesus' teaching of the Torah by a paraphrase of the Torah would form a staple of rabbis' teaching later on in the same century. For we have access to a great master, Yohanan ben Zakkai, who in teaching Torah also meant to add to the glory of Sinai. In sayings associated with him and his disciples, we have exactly the same program: restate in concrete terms, and in a more profound setting, the requirements of the Torah of Sinai. A brief glimpse at how he taught his disciples, and how they too paraphrased the teachings of the Torah in such a way as to make them more concrete and more profound at the same time, will show the congruence of Jesus' and sages' conception of the right way of living:

> Rabban Yohanan b. Zakkai received [the Torah] from Hillel and Shammai. He would say, "If you have learned much Torah, do not puff yourself up on that account, for it was for that purpose that you were created."
>
> He had five disciples, and these are they: Rabbi Eliezer b. Hyrcanus, Rabbi Joshua b. Hananiah, Rabbi Yosé the priest, Rabbi Simeon b. Netanel, and Rabbi Eleazar b. Arakh.
>
> He said to them, "Go and see what is the straight path to which someone should stick."
>
> Rabbi Eliezer says, "Good will."
> Rabbi Joshua says, "A good friend."
> Rabbi Yosé says, "A good neighbor."
> Rabbi Simeon says, "Foresight."
> Rabbi Eleazar says, "A generous spirit."
>
> He said to them, "I prefer the opinion of Rabbi Eleazar b. Arakh, because in what he says is included everything you say."
>
> He said to them, "Go out and see what is the bad road, which someone should avoid."

Rabbi Eliezer says, "Envy."

Rabbi Joshua says, "A bad friend."

Rabbi Yosé says, "A bad neighbor."

Rabbi Simeon says, "Defaulting on a loan."

Rabbi Eleazar says, "An ungenerous spirit."

He said to them, "I prefer the opinion of Rabbi Eleazar b. Arakh, because in what he says is included everything you say."

They [each] said three things.

Rabbi Eliezer says, "Let the respect owing to your fellow be as precious to you as the respect owing to you yourself. And don't be easy to anger. And repent one day before you die."

Rabbi Yosé says, "Let your fellow's property be as precious to you as your own. And get yourself ready to learn Torah, for it does not come as an inheritance to you. And may everything you do be for the sake of Heaven."

(Mishnah-tractate Abot 2:8ff.)

If we wanted to explain the meaning of the great commandment of Leviticus 19:18, "You will love your neighbor as yourself," we could not do better than turn to the disciples of Yohanan ben Zakkai. The final sayings draw us closest to that amplification: "loving my neighbor as myself" means that we have to take care of our neighbor's honor as much as the honor owing to us, our neighbor's property as much as our own. Neither Jesus nor the disciples of Yohanan ben Zakkai cite verses of Scripture or proof-texts. The disciples simply state their own propositions in response to the master's question; the operative verse of Scripture, Leviticus 19:18, is not quoted, but it is very present. Represented as Matthew presents Jesus, we should have something like this:

> You have heard it said, "You will love your neighbor as yourself," but I say to you, "Let the respect owing to your fellow be as precious to you as the respect owing to you yourself."
>
> You have heard it said, "You will love your neighbor as yourself," but I say to you, "Let your fellow's property be as precious to you as your own."

In calling upon the Torah and explaining how a true understanding of its intent requires more than people now understand, Jesus's torah meets the challenge that sages set for themselves, which was not only to receive the Torah, but also to hand it on. And that means, not only to repeat or to paraphrase, but to teach, explain, extend, amplify, enrich. And in these sayings, that is precisely what Jesus accomplishes. For the community formed around him and in response to him as the Incarnate God, the Torah of Sinai gained renewed authority.

Jesus nonetheless intended much more than to reinforce the received Torah, and Christian Judaism would frame a way of life that not only enhanced but also revised the requirements, "for he taught them as one who had authority, and not as their scribes." Moses alone had authority. The scribes teach the message and meaning of what Moses had set down as the Torah on the authority of God. Only God Incarnate can have proposed not only to affirm but also to revise, not only to intensify but also to excise, the ancient teachings.

"COME TO ME, ALL WHO LABOR AND ARE HEAVY-LADEN, AND I WILL GIVE YOU REST." "FOR THE SON OF MAN IS LORD OF THE SABBATH"

The Sabbath celebrates creation and commemorates God's completion of the work of creation with the sanctification of the day of rest, the paramount celebration in the way of life set forth by the Torah. Jesus instructs the Christian community that he is the Lord of the Sabbath, meaning, acts of service take precedence over the requirements of sanctification of that day. But that is because Christ gives rest and restoration: he is the Sabbath.

> At that time Jesus went through the grainfields on the Sabbath; his disciples were hungry, and they began to pluck ears of grain and to eat. But when Pharisees saw it, they said to him, "Look, your disciples are doing what is not lawful to do on the Sabbath." He said to them, "Have you not read what David did when he was hungry and those who were with him, how he entered the house of God and ate the bread of the presence, which it was not lawful for him to eat nor for those who were with him but only for the priests? Or have you not read in the law how on the Sabbath the priests in the Temple profane the Sabbath and are guiltless? I tell you, something greater than the temple is here. And if you had known what this means, 'I desire mercy and not sacrifice' [Hosea 6:6] you would not have condemned the guiltless. For the son of man is Lord of the Sabbath."
> (Matthew 12:1–8)

In the everyday life of the Torah, the Sabbath marked the climax and fulfillment. Remembering the Sabbath day to keep it holy formed, and

135

now forms, what eternal Israel does together: it is what makes eternal Israel what it is, the people that, like God in creating the world, rest from creation on the Seventh Day. The Sabbath has both positive and negative sides; on that day, we do not do servile work; on that day, we do celebrate creation. For six days we make things, on the seventh, we appreciate them.

The stakes for the Sabbath are very high, and that is precisely why Jesus and his disciples would set forth their doctrine, also, in the setting of Sabbath-life and holiness. For not working on the Sabbath stands for more than nit-picking ritual. It is a way of imitating God. God rested on the Sabbath day and declared the Sabbath day holy (Genesis 2:1–4). And that explains why we who form eternal Israel rest on the Sabbath day, enjoy it, make it a holy day. We do on the Seventh Day what God did on the Seventh Day of creation. And that makes all the more striking Jesus' presentation of the matter. In choosing the Sabbath as a point of dispute, he identifies a critical issue. In particular, and of greatest interest, Jesus treats the Sabbath in two statements, which stand side by side. The two statements, appropriately, deal with the Sabbath first in the setting of our relationship with God, and only second in the context of the things we do, and do not do, on that particular day. So Jesus stands well within the framework of the Torah in his presentation of what he wishes to say about the Sabbath: a this-worldly moment that bespeaks eternity. The Sabbath forms the centerpiece of our life with God, and Jesus treats it as the centerpiece of his teaching; only as a second thought do the do's and don't's matter.

These statements on the Sabbath (as Matthew tells us about them) appropriately stand in close sequence. First Jesus speaks about rest from work, and then, and only then, about the Sabbath. Putting the two together we find a remarkable message:

> All things have been delivered to me by my Father, and no one knows the Son except the Father, and no one knows the Father except the Son, and any one to whom the Son chooses to reveal him. Come to me, all who labor and are heavy-laden, and I will give you rest. Take my yoke upon you, and learn from me; for I am gentle and lowly in heart, and you will find rest for your souls; for my yoke is easy and my burden is light.
>
> (Matthew 11:27–30)

Since, on the Sabbath, we rest as God rested on the seventh day of creation, we find entirely appropriate the focus here: how do we come to God? And how do we find rest?

These two questions in any other context but that of the Torah will appear disconnected. But the Ten Commandments include the one that says, "Remember the Sabbath Day to keep it holy: for in six days the Lord made heaven and earth, the sea and all that is in them and rested on the Sabbath Day. Therefore the Lord blessed the Sabbath Day and hallowed it." Now, when we remember we keep the Sabbath because God rested on the Sabbath, we realize that keeping the Sabbath makes us like God. Then the theme of labor and heavy burdens, on the one side, rest on the other, forms a close fit with, "Come to me, and I will give you rest."

Standing by itself, Jesus' statement speaks only about rest. But in the very same context, he speaks of the Sabbath. So, hearing what he said, one thinks only of the Sabbath, which is how eternal Israel finds rest for its soul: "Six days you shall labor and do all your work, but the seventh day is a Sabbath to the Lord your God; in it you shall not do any work" (Exodus 20:9–10). The issue is not trivial and is not to be treated as a matter of some silly ritual. The stakes are very high.

God told us through Isaiah, "If you . . . call the Sabbath a delight . . . if you honor it, not going your own ways or seeking your own pleasure or talking idly, then you shall take delight in the Lord" (Isaiah 58:13–14). When we hear about rest for our soul, surcease for our labor, Jesus speaks of exchanging the heavy burden for his and so finding rest. And in that same context, about how Jesus' disciples picked food on the Sabbath, Jesus declares that "the son of man is lord of the Sabbath." This teaching stands alongside an action, that "it is lawful to do good on the Sabbath:"

> And he went on from there and entered their synagogue. And behold there was a man with a withered hand. And they asked him, "Is it lawful to heal on the Sabbath?" so that they might accuse him. He said to them, "What man of you, if he has one sheep and it falls into a pit on the Sabbath, will not lay hold of it and lift it out? Of how much more value is a man than a sheep! So it is lawful to do good on the Sabbath."
>
> (Matthew 12:9–12)

But, we see that what is at issue in the Sabbath is not a question of ethics ("it is lawful to do good"). Now when we remember why we rest on the Sabbath, we must find somewhat jarring the allegation, "It is lawful to do good on the Sabbath." The reason is that that statement is simply beside the point; the Sabbath is not about doing good or not doing good; the issue of the Sabbath is holiness, and, in the Torah, to be holy is to be like God.

To be sure, the commandment on the Sabbath is explicit, giving two distinct, equally valid accounts of the Sabbath:

> For in six days the Lord made heaven and earth, the sea and all that is in them and rested on the Sabbath day. Therefore the Lord blessed the Sabbath day and hallowed it.
>
> (Exodus 20:11)

> Observe the Sabbath day to keep it holy. . . . You shall remember that you were a servant in the land of Egypt, and the Lord your God brought you out thence with a mighty hand and an outstretched arm, therefore the Lord your God commanded you to keep the Sabbath day.
>
> (Deuteronomy 5:12, 15)

The Sabbath celebrates creation: Israel rests on that day from its everyday labor of creation because God rested on that day in creating the world; Israel rests on that day to remember that "I am not a slave, and my slave rests that day too, to be reminded that the slave is not a slave." In both aspects, the Sabbath imposes itself upon the social order: the defining moment of society, in particular a social order that organizes itself around the days of the week.

In addressing the issue of the Sabbath, therefore, Jesus and his disciples strike squarely at the critical issue: what do we do to imitate God? How do we so live as to make ourselves into that "eternal Israel" that God through the Torah has brought into being? Like the honor owing to father and mother, therefore, the celebration of the Sabbath defines what makes Israel Israel. The entire way of life of the community centers on that day. Here is an example of how every moment of the week points toward that one holy day:

> Eleazar ben Hananiah ben Hezekiah ben Garon says, " 'Remember the Sabbath day to keep it holy:'
>
> you should remember it from Sunday, so that if something nice comes to hand, you should set it aside for the sake of the Sabbath."
>
> Rabbi Isaac says, "You should not count the days of the week the way others do, but rather, you should count for the sake of the Sabbath [the first day, the second day, upward to the seventh which is the Sabbath]."
>
> (Mekhilta attributed to Rabbi Ishmael LIII:II.7)

The first point is that the six working days point toward the Seventh Day, and, throughout the week, we are to remember the Sabbath, even counting the days toward the seventh. How then are we to celebrate the Sabbath? It is an attitude of mind, to give ourselves release from the very thought of work:

"Six days you shall labor and do all your work:"
But can a mortal carry out all of one's work in only six days?
But the nature of Sabbath rest is such that it should be as though all of your labor has been carried out.
Another teaching [as to "Six days you shall labor and do all your work:"]
"Take a Sabbath rest from the very thought of work."
And so Scripture says, "If you turn away your foot because of the Sabbath" (Isaiah 58:13), and then, "Then you shall delight yourself in the Lord" (Isaiah 58:14).
(Mekhilta attributed to Rabbi Ishmael LIII:II.9, 10)

No one completes the work of creation in six days; even God's work of creation goes on continually. That then is not the point of the Sabbath. What is the point is that, on that day, we think about not creation but the celebration of creation: it is a day of appreciation. And the concluding line is the key: if you turn away from work on the Sabbath, then you have delight in God. So, once more, we appreciate that the Sabbath is our way of taking delight in God. And, not surprisingly, the Sabbath is God's gift to humanity, since God did not need the rest, but we do:

"and rested on the seventh day:"
And does fatigue affect God? Is it not said, "The creator of the ends of the earth does not faint and is not weary" (Isaiah 40:28); "He gives power to the faint" (Isaiah 40:29); "By the word of the Lord the heavens were made" (Psalms 33:6)?
How then can Scripture say, "and rested on the seventh day"?
It is as if [God] had it written concerning himself that he created the world in six days and rested on the seventh.
Now you may reason *a fortiori*:
Now if the One who is not affected by fatigue had it written concerning himself that he created the world in six days and rested on the seventh, how much the more so should a human

being, concerning whom it is written, "but man is born to trouble" (Job 5:7) [also rest on the Sabbath]?

(Mekhilta attributed to Rabbi Ishmael LIII:II.17)

In all of these statements, we gain a grasp of the issues of the Sabbath day, and, in that context, we see that Heaven and earth meet on the Sabbath, God and humanity join together, with humanity imitating God in a very concrete and specific way.

The social order of eternal Israel takes shape not in the division of time alone. It concerns also the delineation of space, for society becomes concrete both in time and in place. When, therefore, we see the Sabbath as the defining moment in the life of eternal Israel, we anticipate that that statement tells only part of the tale. The other part concerns where Israel locates itself, and not only when the Sabbath takes over to sanctify Israel. The definition of where Israel is to be found receives a concrete definition on the Sabbath, because of a simple rule of the Torah.

God told Moses to tell the people to stay home on the Seventh Day:

See, the Lord has given you the Sabbath, therefore on the sixth day he gives you bread for two days; remain every man of you in his place, let no one go out of his place on the Seventh Day; so the people rested on the Seventh Day.

(Exodus 16:29–30)

So to keep the Sabbath, one remains at home. It is not enough merely not to work. One also has to rest. And resting means, re-forming one day a week the circle of family and household, everyone at home and in place; re-entering the life of village and community, no matter how life is lived on the other six days of creation. Here we discern the interplay of time and space on an enchanted day: the day that turns us into something other than what we think we are. In the context of the cited verse, which tells people not to go out into the fields on the Sabbath to collect mana, it follows that people are not supposed to carry burdens from place to place. They are supposed to stay home, and they also are supposed not to transport things from place to place: two sides to the same coin. What we understand is that we are not to labor on the Sabbath, not to gather food or carry burdens. But, by contrast, Israel remains in place. What it means to "remain in place" is that we are to enjoy the rest in our own village. The locative quality of the Sabbath – stay home, rest – serves to restore authentic community: the people we see in the everyday and the here and now.

The prohibition against carrying or moving objects around from one place to another on the Sabbath day takes effect at the advent of the Sabbath, which marks the end of the time of bearing burdens. In this law of the Torah, therefore, we are told about a day that defines Israel in time and in place. Accordingly, the Torah lays the foundations for the construction of the holy life of eternal Israel on the Sabbath day. Exodus 16:29–30 require each person to stay where he is on the Seventh Day.

To be sure, remaining in one's place does not mean that one may not leave his house, but it does mean that one should remain in his own village, which consists of the settled area of the village as well as its natural environs.

Isaiah alludes to the importance of celebrating the day of rest by "not going your own ways:" "if you turn back your foot from the Sabbath, from doing your pleasure on my holy day," "I will make you ride upon the heights of the earth" (Isaiah 58:13, 14). We stay at home in our own villages, and, with God, we ride upon the heights. When the holy day comes, therefore, it enchants and changes us. We were heavy-laden and now we leave off our burden. With the setting of the sun all is changed; we are changed. The Sabbath is when God's kingdom comes. Rightly, then, did Jesus link the two messages: take up my yoke, the son of man is Lord of the Sabbath. He could not have made the matter clearer. That justifies our insistence upon the notion that the New Testament's Judaism systematically addresses the issues and categories that every Judaism is going to have to take up, and meets these issues head on. Lacking statements that the son of man is Lord of the Sabbath, that we are to take up Jesus' burden and he will give us rest – lacking statements of precisely that character, the Gospels' account will have lacked the main point that they should address!

Jesus' disciples pick crops on the Sabbath, which is servile labor within creation, rather than the celebration of creation. Has he then abrogated the Sabbath for Christian Judaism? Not at all, but he has redefined its focus. Jesus' argument appeals to the fact that David's followers took food – reserved for the priests. What follows is that if we are hungry, we can do what we have to to get food. But the Sabbath requires preparation in advance, not cooking food on that day; that is the meaning of the statement we noted earlier, prepare each day of the week for the Seventh Day. Not kindling a flame, not carrying objects, not cooking food – these are not silly prohibitions; they form the this-worldly expressions of that act of sanctification that imitates God's act of sanctification of the Seventh Day.

When Jesus further justifies his followers' actions by pointing out that, in the Temple, the priests perform the rites of the cult, so it is all right to do so here, he introduces a very profound argument, making a claim about himself that in its monumental quality parallels what he has said about abandoning father and mother and following him. To understand what he says you have to know that the Temple and the world beyond the Temple form mirror-images of one another. What we do in the Temple is the opposite of what we do everywhere else.

The Torah is explicit that sacrifices are to be offered on that day. For example, an additional offering for the Sabbath is prescribed at Numbers 28:9–10; the show bread of the Temple was replaced on the Sabbath day (Leviticus 24:8). So it was clear to everybody that what was not to be done outside of the Temple, in secular space, was required to be done in holy space, in the Temple itself. When, therefore, Jesus says that something greater than the Temple is here, he can only mean, he and his disciples may do on the Sabbath what they do because they stand in the place of the priests in the Temple: the holy place has shifted, now being formed by the circle made up of the master and his disciples.

What troubles me, therefore, is not that the disciples do not obey one of the rules of the Sabbath. That is trivial and beside the point. What captures our attention is Jesus' statement that at stake in their actions is not the Sabbath but the Temple, a truly fresh formulation of matters. His claim, then, concerns not whether or not the Sabbath is to be sanctified, but where and what is the Temple, the place where things are done on the Sabbath that elsewhere are not to be done at all. Not only so, but just as on the Sabbath it is permitted to place on the altar the food that is offered up to God, so Jesus' disciples are permitted to prepare their food on the Sabbath, again a stunning shift indeed.

Jesus does not propose to abolish but to fulfill the Torah, and, also, Jesus is Lord of the Sabbath. Then in keeping the Sabbath in the way in which Jesus represents it, we fulfill the Torah – in the way in which Jesus means it to be fulfilled. We recall that at the issue of the Sabbath and its rest is our coming home to God: "All things have been delivered to me by my Father, and no one knows the Son except the Father, and no one knows the Father except the Son, and any one to whom the Son chooses to reveal him." These words, by themselves, bear no clear connection to the Sabbath. But these words do not stand by themselves. They lead directly into the appeal to come to the father through the son, and then:

> Come to me, all who labor and are heavy-laden, and I will give you rest. Take my yoke upon you, and learn from me; for I am gentle and lowly in heart, and you will find rest for your souls; for my yoke is easy and my burden is light.

Sinai's message for the Sabbath scarcely echoes over the distant horizon. And yet, if on the Sabbath we do what God did on the first Sabbath, then in very different terms to be sure, Jesus says to his disciples what Moses has said to all Israel. On the Sabbath day we remember and do what God did: "Remember the Sabbath Day ... for in six days the Lord made Heaven and earth . . . and rested on the Seventh Day; therefore the Lord blessed the Sabbath Day and hallowed it." Those who seek rest, in Jesus' radical revision, seek God as we seek God; but instead of leaving off their burdens, they take on a new burden: a yoke that is easy and light.

No wonder, then, that the son of man is Lord of the Sabbath! The reason is not that he interprets the Sabbath restrictions in a liberal manner, nor yet that he gives good arguments for allowing people to harvest and eat their crops that day, or heal the sick and otherwise do good on that day. Jesus was not just another reforming rabbi, out to make life "easier" for people. And no one who keeps the Sabbath so as to imitate God pays much mind to considerations of "lenient" or "strict," except so far as we want to know what God through the Torah wants of us. No, the issue is not that the burden is light. The issue is another one altogether.

At issue in the Sabbath is neither keeping nor breaking this one of the Ten Commandments. At issue here as everywhere else is what it means to imitate God Incarnate, who gave the Torah at Sinai and is Lord of the Sabbath: the person of Jesus himself, in Christian language, Jesus Christ. What matters most of all is the simple statement, no one knows the Father except the Son, and any one to whom the Son chooses to reveal him. There, startling and scarcely a consequence of anything said before or afterward, stands the centerpiece of the Sabbath-teaching: my yoke is easy, I give you rest, the son of man is Lord of the Sabbath indeed, because the son of man is now Israel's Sabbath. This is how we act like God.

In the very context of the Sabbath, when in sacred space and holy time, Israel acts like God, we grasp that Jesus addresses that very issue (what does it mean to know God?), and does so in precisely the context in which Israel, from Sinai, knows God and acts like God: the Sabbath. Jesus has chosen with great precision the message he wishes to set forth with regard to the Sabbath, both the main point, which comes first, and then the details and consequences of that same point, which follow. What is God's stake in remembering the Sabbath day? The Torah teaches that it is celebrating creation, acting on the Sabbath day as God acts on the day when creation ceases; blessing the Sabbath day and sanctifying it. Jesus too teaches that the Sabbath day brings the gift of rest – but it is the rest that God gives through the son. So we find ourselves precisely where we were when we wondered what is at stake in honor of father and mother: keeping the Sabbath forms a this-worldly act of imitation of God. The Lord of the Sabbath forms a this-worldly model, in the language of the Torah: "for in six days the Lord made Heaven and earth . . . therefore the Lord blessed" and therefore "remember the Sabbath day to keep it holy," by not working, as God stopped working.

"IF YOU WOULD BE PERFECT, GO, SELL ALL YOU HAVE AND GIVE TO THE POOR, AND YOU WILL HAVE TREASURE IN HEAVEN, AND COME, FOLLOW ME"

The key question answered by the account of the holy way of life is: what does God want of me? And how can I – an Israelite of this time and place – make myself into what God wants me to be, made me to be?

> And behold, one came up to him saying, "Teacher, what good deed must I do to have eternal life?"
>
> And he said to him, "Why do you ask me about what is good? One there is who is good. If you would enter life, keep the commandments."
>
> He said to him, "Which?"
>
> And Jesus said, "'You shall not kill. You shall not commit adultery. You shall not steal. You shall not bear false witness. Honor your father and mother' (Exodus 20:12–16), and, 'You shall love your neighbor as yourself'" (Leviticus 19:18).
>
> The young man said to him, "All these I have observed, what do I still lack?"
>
> Jesus said to him, "If you would be perfect, go, sell all you

144

have and give to the poor, and you will have treasure in heaven, and come, follow me."

When the young man heard this, he went away sorrowful, for he had great possessions.

(Matthew 19:16–22)

The young man's question is a mature and proper one. Jesus here responded and taught a message of the Torah, telling people what Israel's sages found in the Torah, what the Torah required them to say:

"Teacher, which is the great commandment in the law?"

And he said to him, "You shall love the Lord your God with all your heart and with all your soul and with all your mind. This is the great and first commandment. And a second is like it: you shall love your neighbor as yourself. On these two commandments depend the whole Torah and the prophets."

(Matthew 22:36–40)

Here we have what is familiar and authentic: to love God, as the *Shema*, the prayer proclaiming God's unity and Israel's submission to God's rule, demands; and to love your neighbor as yourself. No sage could take exception to these teachings. But in how they are elaborated, there is room for argument and exception. To understand why, we have first of all to examine the context in which the second of the two commandments is set:

And the Lord said to Moses, "Say to all the congregation of the people of Israel, You shall be holy, for I the Lord your God am holy. . . ."

(Leviticus 19:1–2)

"You shall not hate your brother in your heart, but you shall reason with your neighbor, lest you bear sin because of him. You shall not take vengeance or bear any grudge against the sons of your own people, but you shall love your neighbor as yourself: I am the Lord."

(Leviticus 19:17–18)

What Jesus does not say, rather than what he says, bears a message as well; silence on the matter of sanctification conveys his message of a way of life in which imitation of God covers some matters that the Torah has taught but omits others.

Leviticus chapter 19, which teaches Israel to be Holy, goes over the

Ten Commandments. They will demonstrate that in the commandments of Leviticus 19 are the Ten Commandments of Exodus 20. So
there is a good reason to keep the Ten Commandments, and that is,
so that we, Israel, shall be holy, because God is holy. We want to be
like God, and the Ten Commandments, restated in Leviticus 19, teach
us how to be like God.

Rabbi Hiyya taught, "[The statement, 'Say to all the congregation of the people of Israel' (Leviticus 19:2)] teaches that the
entire passage was stated on the occasion of the gathering [of the
entire assembly].

And what is the reason that it was stated on the occasion of
the gathering [of the entire assembly]? Because the majority of
the principles of the Torah depend upon [what is stated in this
chapter of the Torah]."

Rabbi Levi said, "It is because the Ten Commandments are
encompassed within its [teachings].

'I am the Lord your God' (Exodus 20:2), and here it is
written, 'I am the Lord your God' (Leviticus 19:2).

'You shall have no [other gods] (Exodus 20:3) and here it is
written, 'You shall not make for yourselves molten gods'
(Leviticus 19:4)

'You shall not take [the name of the Lord your God in vain]'
(Exodus 20:7) and here it is written, 'You shall not take a lying
oath by my name' (Leviticus 19:12)

'Remember the Sabbath day' (Exodus 20:8), and here it is
written, 'You will keep my Sabbaths' (Leviticus 19:3).

'Honor your father and your mother' (Exodus 20:12) and
here it is written, 'Each person shall fear his mother and his
father' (Leviticus 19:3).

'You shall not murder' (Exodus 20:13) and here it is written,
'You shall not stand idly by the blood of your neighbor'
(Leviticus 19:16).

You shall not commit adultery' (Exodus 20:13) and here it is
written, 'Do not profane your daughter by making her a harlot'
(Leviticus 19:29).

'You shall not steal' (Exodus 20:13), and here it is written,
'You shall not steal and you shall not deal falsely' (Leviticus
19:11).

'You shall not bear false witness (against your neighbor)'

(Exodus 20:13), and here it is written, 'You shall not go about as a talebearer among your people' (Leviticus 19:16).

'You shall not covet' (Exodus 20:14), and here it is written, 'And you shall love your neighbor as yourself'" (Leviticus 19:18)

(Leviticus Rabbah 24:5)

Jesus wants his disciples to follow him and be like him: "You shall be holy, for I the Lord your God am holy." Then what is life about? What makes life worth living? Christ and the Torah concur that God answers that question, Christ and the Torah agree that to be perfect, I must strive to be holy like God, or I must give up everything for Christ. When Israel forms a social world that conveys the sanctity of life, then Israel sanctifies God:

"You shall be holy, for I the Lord your God am holy:"

That is to say, "if you sanctify yourselves, I shall credit it to you as though you had sanctified me, and if you do not sanctify yourselves, I shall hold that it is as if you have not sanctified me."

Or perhaps the sense is this: "If you sanctify me, then lo, I shall be sanctified, and if not, I shall not be sanctified"?

Scripture says, "For I . . . am holy," meaning, I remain in my state of sanctification, whether or not you sanctify me.

Abba Saul says, "The king has a retinue, and what is the task thereof? It is to imitate the king."

(Sifra CXCV:I.2–3)

We do well to hear what Israel's sages make of this commandment to be like God. Here is how our sages of blessed memory read some of the critical verses before us:

"You shall not take vengeance [or bear any grudge]:"
To what extent is the force of vengeance?
If one says to him, "Lend me your sickle," and the other did not do so.
On the next day, the other says to him, "Lend me your spade."
The one then replies, "I am not going to lend it to you, because you
  didn't lend me your sickle."
In that context, it is said, "You shall not take vengeance."
"or bear any grudge:"
To what extent is the force of a grudge?
If one says to him, "Lend me your spade," but he did not do so.

147

The next day the other one says to him, "Lend me your sickle," and the other replies, "I am not like you, for you didn't lend me your spade [but here, take the sickle]!"
In that context, it is said, "or bear any grudge."
"but you shall love your neighbor as yourself: [I am the Lord]:"
Rabbi Aqiba says, "This is the encompassing principle of the Torah."

(Sifra CC:III.4, 5, 7)

Being holy like God means not taking vengeance in any form, even in words, not pointing out to the other that I have not acted in the nasty way he did. In many ways, we find ourselves at home. This counsel recalls, after all, the message that if the Torah says not to murder, then we must not even risk becoming angry. Loving God means going the extra mile. Aqiba has the climax and conclusion "love your neighbor as yourself" as the great commandment, the encompassing principle, of the entire Torah. And that brings us to the next question. Precisely what then does it mean to be "like God"? Here is one answer:

Abba Saul says, "O try to be like him:
'Just as he is gracious and merciful,' you too be gracious and merciful" [add: for it is said, "The Lord, God, merciful and gracious" (Exodus 34:6)].

(Mekhilta attributed to Rabbi Ishmael XVIII:II.3)

To be like God means to imitate the grace and mercy of God: these are what make God God, and these are what can make us like God. So to be like God is to be very human. But to be human in a very special way: it is, after all, the grace of God that in the end accords to us the strength to be merciful and gracious – the grace, but also the example. Not a few followers of Jesus will point to him in this way, just as we point to God in this way.

And here is another pointer along the same lines. In what follows a sage asks how we can follow God or be like God, that is, what does it mean to be holy, like God? And the answer is, it means to imitate God, to do the things that God does, as the Torah portrays God's deeds:

And Rabbi Hama ben Rabbi Hanina said, "What is the meaning of the following verse of Scripture: 'You shall walk after the Lord your God' (Deuteronomy 13:5)?
Now is it possible for a person to walk after the Presence of

God? And has it not been said, 'For the Lord your God is a consuming fire' (Deuteronomy 4:24)?

"But the meaning is that one must walk after the traits of the Holy One, blessed be he.

Just as he clothes the naked, as it is written, 'And the Lord God made for Adam and for his wife coats of skin and clothed them' (Genesis 3:21), so should you clothe the naked.

[Just as] the Holy One, blessed be he, visited the sick, as it is written, 'And the Lord appeared to him by the oaks of Mamre' (Genesis 18:1), so should you visit the sick.

[Just as] the Holy One, blessed be he, comforted the mourners, as it is written, 'And it came to pass after the death of Abraham that God blessed Isaac his son' (Genesis 25:11), so should you comfort the mourners.

[Just as] the Holy One, blessed be he, buried the dead, as it is written, 'And he buried him in the valley' (Deuteronomy 34:6), so should you bury the dead."

(Babylonian Talmud-tractate
Sotah 14A=M. 1:8.LXXXVIA–G)

So to be holy like God, we must clothe the naked, visit the sick, comfort the mourner, bury the dead – "love my neighbor as myself." These again are very human traits, loving traits. It is not for nothing that, in the Torah, we are told that we are made in God's image, after God's likeness: "So God created man in his own image, in the image of God he created him; male and female he created them" (Genesis 1:27). No wonder, then, that the Torah's sages would find the holiness of God in clothing the naked, visiting the sick, comforting the mourner, burying the dead – maybe even teaching Torah to prisoners (see Matthew 25:31–46).

THE WEIGHTIER MATTERS OF THE LAW

Clearly the Christian way of life coincided with that set forth by the Torah of Sinai only where and as Jesus so mediated matters. God Incarnate stood above the Torah, and his teachings not only affirmed but also reformed, and not only improved but also abrogated. At one critical point, the Christian way would insist upon establishing a hierarchy of observance, with ethics given priority over ritual, just as the prophets had said time and again. Moses says, "You shall tithe all the yield of your seed" (Deuteronomy 14:22) and Jesus says, do that but don't neglect more important things. No one doubts that there are more important things, for instance, "Love your neighbor as yourself" and "You shall be holy." But part of holiness is tithing, along with the other teachings of the Torah. No one would claim that everything is as important as everything else, and everyone would agree with Jesus: do the major commandments – the Ten Commandments, for instance – without neglecting the lesser ones.

But Jesus takes for granted that right conflicts with rite. He repeatedly draws a contrast between inner corruption and outer piety, or between inner uncleanness and external signs of cleanness. True, he concedes, tithing is part of the Torah. But if you tithe but neglect "weightier matters of the law," then you are "blind guides." The remarkable saying of Rabbi Pinhas ben Yair, "holiness leads to modesty, modesty leads to the fear of sin, the fear of sin leads to piety, piety leads to the Holy Spirit," calls into question the certainty that we are one thing or another: either pious or moral:

> Woe to you, scribes and Pharisees, hypocrites! For you tithe mint and dill and cumin and have neglected the weightier matters of the law, justice and mercy and faith; these you ought to have done, without neglecting the others. You blind guides, straining out a gnat and swallowing a camel!
>
> (Matthew 23:23–4)

> Woe to you, scribes and Pharisees, hypocrites! For you cleanse the outside of the cup and of the plate, but inside they are full of extortion and rapacity. You blind Pharisee! First cleanse the inside of the cup and of the plate, that the outside also may be clean.
>
> (Matthew 23:25–6)

But while many share that prejudice, many more find self-evident the prophet's denunciation of those who are ritualistic but unrighteous, for instance, the prophet Nathan's confrontation with King David: "Have you murdered and also inherited?" or Amos' contention that those who sell the needy for a pair of shoes can never be right with God. And when we affirm the prophetic insistence on right, we also affirm that rite must lead to right, and that the purpose of doing the commandments, as the Talmud says, "is to purify the human heart." So there is a place in God's scheme for rite and also right, though of course what God most wants of us is righteousness.

For Jesus in Matthew there is no conflict between rite and right,

150

because, in his opinion, rites are null; rituals mean nothing; all that matters is obedience to the moral and ethical teachings of the Torah:

> And he called the people to him and said to them, "Hear and understand: not what goes into the mouth defiles a man, but what comes out of the mouth, this defiles a man. . . . Do you not see that whatever goes into the mouth passes into the stomach and so passes on? But what comes out of the mouth proceeds from the heart, and this defiles a man. For out of the heart come evil thoughts, murder, adultery, fornication, theft, false witness, slander. These are what defile a man, but to eat with unwashed hands does not defile a man."
>
> (Matthew 15:10, 11, 17–20)

If what I eat does not make me "unclean," then the rules of the Torah about what to eat and what not to eat are null. In drawing a contrast between right and rite and saying that eating with unwashed hands doesn't mean a thing, or what you eat doesn't make you unclean, then Jesus has abolished some of the dots and iotas of the Torah. So the master makes it clear that there really is a contrast to be drawn between the commandments that tell us to love our neighbor as ourselves and the commandments that tell us about eating and drinking. Here is certainly one of earliest Christianity's most distinctive positions in the setting of other Judaisms. For, as a matter of fact, the Torah devotes much attention to food. Right from the story of creation onward, one important focus is on what people eat. The Garden of Eden is an orchard; Noah offered up sacrifices of animals; all of the patriarchs of Israel did the same.

Israel serves God by offering up animal sacrifices as well as grain, wine, and other produce of the Holy Land. So, in the Torah, one form of divine service – sacrifice – takes the earthly form of food. It did not have to be that way; one may offer God a gift of flowers, or incense, or the gesture of a sacred dance, for example. But the Torah wants food. Second, the priesthood is supplied with food as well. The priests get a share of the sacrifices in the Temple. They also stand in for God, who owns the Holy Land, and God's share of the crop is set aside for the priests and Levites as well as for the poor and indigent. Third, all Israel is instructed on certain foods that may not be eaten as "unclean," and others that may be eaten. So these are not concerns that the Pharisees have made up for themselves, not at all. In fact, how life is sustained – through raising crops and herds in the Holy Land

151

– forms one central issue in the Torah's conception of the life of the kingdom of priests and the holy people.

When it comes to considerations of purity, the Torah is explicit that, when they come to the Temple courtyard to do their holy work, the priests and others who work with them, including the people as a whole, are to be "pure." The word "pure" translates the Hebrew word, *tahor*, and "impure" translates "*tamé*." But the meaning of "purity" in context is not conveyed by that translation. We think of "pure" in very general terms. But in the Torah, "pure" and "impure" in the main refer to a particular context, and that is the Temple and its service to God. When something is called "pure," in general it is acceptable to the holy rite, and if it is "impure," it is not. So the word "pure" in this context has a very limited and particular meaning indeed. In fact, an alternative translation for "pure" in many contexts would be "acceptable in the holy place," and "impure," "unacceptable." "Purity" is simply not a category that has anything to do with ethics. Not only is there no tension between rite and right, there is no point of intersection. Contrasting "inner" impurity with "outer" purity, meaning an unethical private life joined to a ritually correct external life, is incomprehensible.

The issue of "purity" does not concern ethics, does not intersect with ethics, and does not stand in tension with ethics when one has attained "acceptability in the holy place" even though guilty of a lack of mercy. Why not? Because what makes one acceptable in the holy place is one set of considerations, while what makes the same person morally upright or unacceptable is simply another set of considerations. "Purity" means "acceptability for the Temple and its cult," as set forth in the books of Leviticus and Numbers. Sources of uncleanness are spelled out at Leviticus 11–15 and elsewhere. These readings of the Torah's rules are not the only way to understand why what is unclean is classified in that way; they are just a way of suggesting that in matters of cleanness and uncleanness – food that we eat and food we do not eat, washing hands to rid them of uncleanness, and washing dishes for the same purpose – we are not engaged in actions that have any bearing on ethics, but, on the other hand, these things do matter. Not everything matters because it has a bearing on right action, on ethics, even on human relationships. Some things matter because they bear on our relationship with God, and while that involves loving our neighbor as ourselves, it also requires us to try to be "holy" because God is holy; and in the Torah, holiness bears very concrete and specific meanings, not all of them having to do with human relationships by any means. The upshot is simple: when Jesus makes the statements before us, he removes from the Christian way of life both the palpable reality of the Temple and the matter of the counterpart to the Temple's altar, which is the table of the family at home.

What has changed should be seen not only in a negative light, for, once more, the presence of God Incarnate defines the Christian perspective. In keeping the laws of purity as these affect food and the Temple alike, those who keep the laws are acting out the rites of sanctification of the Temple and the priesthood. So they are pretending that every place in the holy land is as holy as the Temple. They are acting as if every Israelite is a priest. They are so behaving as if to say that everyday food at home is subject to the same rules of "purity" ("cultic acceptability") as the priest's holy food in the Temple. In all of these ways, they are responding to the commandment of holiness. This is what the Torah means when it says, "You shall be holy, for I the Lord your God am holy," and it is what God said in so many words to Moses:

> "You have seen what I did to the Egyptians and how I bore you on eagles' wings and brought you to myself. Now therefore if you will obey my voice and keep my covenant, you shall be my own possession among all peoples; for all the earth is mine, and you shall be to me a kingdom of priests and a holy people."
>
> (Exodus 19:4–6)

So, the point is, when they keep these rules, which the Torah lays down for the holy place, they act as though every place is holy. When they eat meals in accord with the rules that govern the priests when they eat holy food, they are acting as though they were priests and as though the food came from the altar. It is one way of being holy, one way of acting out what it means to be a kingdom of priests and a holy people. No wonder Jesus Christ dismissed the entire matter, having a different mode of imitation of God in mind, with a different result.

For, in the end, in the Torah one important opposite of *unclean* is *holy*. Israel's natural condition, pertinent to the three dimensions of life – Land, people, and cult – is holiness. To be God's people is to be like God in order to have access to him. Accordingly, impurity is what causes Israel to cease to be holy; in the present context it is uncleanness which is abnormal, and, to state the reverse, what is abnormal is unclean. Cleanness thus is a this-worldly expression of the conception of the holiness and the set-apartness of all three – people, Land, and cult. By keeping oneself apart from what affects and afflicts other lands, peoples, and cults ("the Canaanites who were here before you"), the Israelite attains that separateness that is expressive of holiness and reaches the holiness that is definitive also of the natural condition of Israel. The processes of nature correspond to those of supernature, restoring in this world the datum to which this world corresponds. The disruptive sources of uncleanness – unclean foods and dead creeping things, persons who depart from their natural condition in sexual and reproductive organs (or, later on, in their skin condition and physical appearance), and the corpse – all of these affect Israel and necessitate restorative natural processes.

For Jesus, clean or unclean pertained not to the Temple but to matters of right or wrong conduct. They meant virtuous or sinful; hence cleanness is a moral category. It says what kind of person you are. For the Pharisees, clean or unclean meant "able to go to the holy Temple" or "not able to go to the holy Temple." It says what kind of place you can go to, what kind of deed you can do (at that particular moment). But it has no bearing at all on what kind of a person you are or are not. It is not a moral category at all. It describes the state of being in which, at that moment, you find yourself.

For the Pharisees, the antonym of uncleanness is holiness. And virtue and holiness constitute distinct classifications, the one having to do with morality, the other with what it means to be a human being in God's image and after God's likeness: "you shall be holy, for I the Lord your God am holy." Uncleanness formed a theological and cultic category, not a moral one at all. To be able to become unclean formed a measure of the capacity to become holy. That statement clearly bears no implications whatever for whether or not an unclean person was a sinner, or a clean person not a sinner. For in the classification of uncleanness at hand, the opposite of unclean is holy, precisely as, throughout the priestly code, e.g. the book of Leviticus, the antonym of unclean is "holy," far more than it is merely "clean" ("unclean" as against "holy," appears far more regularly than "unclean" as against "clean"). We are used to thinking that to be "holier than thou" means to be more virtuous than the other. But that is far from what holiness means and monumentally irrelevant to why holiness is important to us. That is why, as we shall see, representing uncleanness as sin and a sign of wickedness hardly represents a conception generated by the Torah. This brings us back to the wonderful passage at Mishnah-tractate Sotah 9:15, which shows how cleanness relates to purity and purity to morality or holiness – upward to the coming of the Messiah and the resurrection of the dead:

Rabbi Pinhas ben Yair says, "Heedfulness leads to cleanliness, cleanliness leads to cleanness, cleanness leads to abstinence, abstinence leads to holiness, holiness leads to modesty, modesty leads to the fear of sin, the fear of sin leads to piety, piety leads to the Holy Spirit, the Holy Spirit leads to the resurrection of the dead, and the resurrection of the dead comes through Elijah, blessed be his memory, Amen."

(Mishnah-tractate Sotah 9:15)

In this context, we see how a variety of virtues form a ladder, upwards to Heaven. We start with attentiveness or heedfulness, paying close attention to what we do. An excess of attentiveness can lead to: too much of a good thing. That then should lead to personal cleanliness, and that proceeds to the "cleanness" that is at stake here. From there, that is, from cleanness (or purification, for a reason I'll spell out in a minute), we get to holiness, and that leads us from these virtues of holiness to the more important virtues of ethics and morality: modesty, fear of sin, piety, and upward to the resurrection of the dead.

Clearly, the unclean person is not on that account wicked, and so we cannot contrast uncleanness with morality. The capacity to become clean, a stage on the route to holiness as we saw, finds a counterpart in the capacity to become unclean; the more "holy" something may become, the more susceptible it is to uncleanness. Sanctification marks a step on the path to salvation, and Jesus took the position that in his person, he had resolved matters and saved Israel. Hence the Christian disagreement in details of the way of life flowed from that more fundamental conviction that Jesus Christ is God incarnate.

Jesus preaches the kingdom, the end of time, a moment in very public history, and we who follow the Pharisees focus our attention upon the private establishment of the home and heart. Jesus addresses a one-time, unique *event*, but, given the ordinariness of these meals that concern us, the rest of eternal Israel focus upon "eternity." Our interest is in the recurrent and continuing patterns of life – birth and death, planting and harvest, the regular movement of the sun, moon, stars in Heaven, night and day, Sabbaths, festivals, and regular seasons on earth.

The issue when we take up the Christian way of life concerns not the practical as against the heavenly; it concerns another conception of what Heaven wants, of where Heaven must be brought to earth. The Torah has told me how to build a kingdom of priests and a holy people. So the Torah speaks of God's kingdom. But it speaks of the goring ox and the breach of trust. Real people live real lives in God's kingdom. The Torah teaches them how to build that kingdom where they are, how they are. Nothing that Jesus has said about the kingdom of Heaven affirms that here, where we are, we can build, that we can obey the Torah and so form a kingdom of priests and holy people. He speaks of Heaven, not earth; his rules are rules for his time, his yoke is easy and his burden is light – up there.

THE REFORMATION OF THE FAMILY

In formulating a Judaic way of life, the critical social component of Israel, the family, demands sustained attention, and we may hardly find surprising that the advent of God Incarnate imposed a new definition upon that formative social category. Specifically, a new, supernatural relationship replaced the old, natural one: Christ over father and mother, Christ imposing his own family upon the established, given framework of everyday life, with its mother and father, brother and sister, son and daughter. So Jesus states in so many words:

> Do not think that I have come to bring peace on earth; I have not come to bring peace but a sword. For I have come to set a man against his father and a daughter against her mother and a daughter-in-law against her mother-in-law and a man's foes will be those of his own household. He who loves father or mother more than me is not worthy of me; and he who loves son or daughter more than me is not worthy of me.
>
> (Matthew 10:34–7)

In so stating the social datum of everyday life – the life with Christ, in the mystical body, in preference to life in the family – the Christian way of life brought into being what no one knew before, the conception that a social unit might ever take priority, in Israel, over the family unit on which, for all time, the social order had been constructed. For until then, Israel had been a family of families, a community of families, all with the same parents and grandparents, Abraham and Sarah, Isaac and Rebecca, Jacob and Leah and Rachel. Of the three dimensions of human existence, community, family and home, and individual, first comes the family, then the village, and only then does the individual find his or her position in the scheme of things.

Now in the representation of the Torah, "Israel" forms a family, that is to say, "Israel" here and now – "Israel after the flesh," in later

Christian language – the actual, living, present family of Abraham and Sarah, Isaac and Rebecca, Jacob and Leah and Rachel. So to explain eternal Israel, sages appeal to the metaphor of genealogy, because to begin with they point to the fleshly connection, the family, as the rationale for Israel's social existence. And Jesus would do the same, turning the metaphor on its head: the family is made up of people who do what God wants, turning genealogy into the effect of true piety. For his part, in setting forth his doctrine of the family, Jesus calls into question the primacy of the family in the priority of one's responsibilities, the centrality of the family in the social order. Not only so, but Jesus says so explicitly:

> While he was still speaking to the people, behold, his mother and his brothers stood outside, asking to speak to him. But he replied to the man who told him, "Who is my mother, and who are my brothers?" And stretching out his hand toward his disciples, he said, "Here are my mother and my brothers! For whoever does the will of my Father in heaven is my brother and sister and mother."
>
> (Matthew 12:46–50)

To follow Jesus, the Christian Judaic way of life requires abandoning home and family. Yet, fundamental to the kingdom of Heaven that the Torah asks eternal Israel to bring about is the formation of an enduring society in sanctification.

The same issue faced the Torah's masters and disciples later on, and in time to come masters would call disciples away from home and family, and they would leave their wives and children for long periods of time, so as to study the Torah. In that context, it is not alien for Jesus to ask that disciples place their love of him over their love of family. And is he not forming a family built on the intangible beams of loyalty and love – a supernatural family, in that love in the end resonates what is beyond the merely natural? And is that not, too, a family, indeed, the building block of the kingdom of Heaven, the new house of Israel? So the disciple might say on the master's behalf.

In the Torah as it would be interpreted by other sages, Israel would be instructed to place honor for the Torah, in the person of the sage, even above honor for the father and the mother. In the formulation of sages later on, we find precisely the same contrast between genealogy and another bond, besides the one of family, namely, a supernatural tie, in an exact sense of the word, "a holy family," that is, a family founded on holiness, on love that surpasses understanding, so, in secular, descriptive terms, on supernatural love. In what follows, first of all, learning in the Torah is contrasted with genealogical status, a matter important to Israel in that time. Therefore while the castes of the Temple, the priests, and Levites were recognized, took precedence, and while these castes derived their status from their genealogy – going back to Aaron and Moses, respectively – so the Torah said, nonetheless, a disciple of a sage took precedence. Thus:

> A priest takes precedence over a Levite, a Levite over an Israelite, an Israelite over a person whose parents were not legally permitted to marry. . . .
> Under what circumstances?
> When all of them are equivalent.
> But if the person whose parents were not legally permitted to marry was a disciple of a sage and a high priest was an unlettered person, then the person whose parents were not legally permitted to marry who is a disciple of a sage takes precedence over a high priest who is an unlettered person.
>
> (Mishnah-tractate Horayot 3:8)

Since a person whose parents were not legally permitted to marry (e.g. brother and sister, among various possibilities) bequeathed a most difficult genealogical, and also (by the way) social, status, the statement that such a person took precedence over a high priest represents a considerable claim. The master takes precedence over the father; but the father and the master and the disciple remain bound into a single bond, a social order that endures. For example:

> [If he has to choose between seeking] what he has lost and what his father has lost, his own takes precedence. [If he has to choose between seeking] what he has lost and what his master has lost, his own takes precedence. [If he has to choose between seeking] what his father has lost and what his master has lost, that of his master takes precedence. For his father brought him into this world. But his master, who taught him wisdom, will bring him into the life of the world to come. But if his father is a sage, that of his father takes precedence. [If] his father and his master were carrying heavy burdens, he removes that of his master, and afterward removes that of his father. [If] his father and his master were taken captive, he ransoms his master, and afterward he

ransoms his father. But if his father is a sage, he ransoms his father, and afterward he ransoms his master.

(Mishnah-tractate Baba Mesia 2:11)

First, one is responsible to begin with for himself or herself. But what is striking here is, first, that the master and the father compete – but only if the latter is not a master of the Torah; if he is, then the master who teaches the Torah does not take precedence over the father who enjoys the same status.

We are now able to place in a single continuum the centerpiece of the Judaic way of life, the doctrine of the family, as defined by the New Testament's system of Judaism and that of the later sages. The doctrine in each case makes provision for a supernatural relationship that exceeds the natural family. On the one side, Christ, on the other side, the Torah, imposes its measure. It is knowledge of the Torah that endows a person with standing. Now, in the passage just now cited, either man, father or master, has the power to gain the standing conferred by the knowledge of the Torah; but if both of them enjoy the same standing, then the father takes precedence. Can Jesus' saying be read in an analogous manner? In no way, because the discipleship to Christ is unique. It is not discipleship to the Torah, which anyone may master, which will endow with supernatural status the relationship of any two persons, master and disciple. It is discipleship to Jesus Christ, uniquely, that is at issue, and to that standing, the standing of Christ, only Jesus is called. "Whoever does the will of my Father in Heaven is my brother and sister" is simply not the same thing as "whoever becomes a sage, master of the Torah, enters into the standing of the Torah." The one is particular, specific to Jesus, the other general, applicable to anyone. The Torah stands in one world, Christ in another. Yet, viewing the systems within the same structural framework, we find grounds for comparison and appropriate points of comparison and contrast. And that validates our basic notion of seeing Christianity as a Judaism.

7

THE TRANSFORMATION OF JUDAISM: FROM SALVATION TO SANCTIFICATION

The Letter to the Hebrews' Judaic world-view

THE REQUIREMENT OF A JUDAIC SYSTEM'S WORLD-VIEW

In the context of a Judaism a world-view will take over, recast, and make its own the entire scriptural inheritance of Israel. Scripture will be reread in light of the systemic message, a self-evident truth will impose itself on the details of the ancient narratives and prophecies and laws, and the whole will emerge renewed. In this way the Israel that comes into being within the nascent system situates itself in time and eternity, defining the stakes of the group's existence in supernatural terms. The power is generated to impose upon the received Torah an entirely fresh set of meanings, new issues, unanticipated possibilities. So the mark of a successful system will emerge with its power to draw upon its unique systemic perspective in order to recast the received heritage of Scripture, to rewrite the sacred history of Israel.

Before turning to the New Testament Judaism's most encompassing statement of the Christian world-view, let us briefly consider how the Judaism of sages formulated matters, for, in context, the Christian rereading of Scripture will emerge as a hermeneutic entirely congruent in mode of thought with other Judaisms' way of seeing the world. For that purpose we turn to sages' formulation of a theology of history by appeal to the lives of the patriarchs and matriarchs of Genesis, seen to embody the future history of their children, who are Israel. The basic hermeneutic derives from the principle that if Israel is a family, then families have histories, and "Israel" as family found in the record of its family history those points of coherence that transformed events into meaningful patterns, that is, the history of the social unit, the nation-family, as a whole. Sages looked in the facts of history for the laws of history. They proposed to generalize, and, out of generalization, to explain their own particular circumstance.

The urgent question facing the Judaism of sages – in writings produced in the century after Rome became Christian, that is, from the fourth century forward – addressed the question of Rome, with special attention to explaining how the competing scriptural faith, Christianity, can have achieved such remarkable success, while Israel, awaiting the Messiah the Christians claimed had come, found itself in despair. Matters reached their climax when the apostate emperor, Julian, in 360 gave permission to rebuild the Temple in Jerusalem and to restore the holy rites, only to die shortly afterward, the promise unkept. The Christians were quick to point out the meaning of that event and adduced it in evidence that the Messiah had already come and that there would be no other Messiah for Israel after the fiasco of the unrestored Temple. Now the formulation of a theology of history presented an acute crisis of thought, not merely a chronic problem for ongoing reflection.

It is in this context that we see how a system rereads Scripture, placing into perspective the achievement of the Christian counterpart in forming the New Testament system of Judaism several centuries earlier. Specifically, this is what happened. Genesis provided facts concerning the family. Careful sifting of those facts will yield the laws that dictated why to that family things happened one way, rather than some other. Among these social laws of the family history, some took priority: the laws that explained the movement of empires upward and downward and pointed toward the ultimate end of it all. Scripture provided the model for the ages of empires, yielding a picture of four monarchies, to be followed by Israel as the fifth. In reading Genesis, in particular, sages found that time and again events in the lives of the patriarchs prefigured the four monarchies, among which, of course, the fourth, last, and most intolerable was Rome. Israel's history falls under God's dominion. Whatever will happen carries out God's plan, and that plan for the future has been laid out in the account of the origins supplied by Genesis. The fourth kingdom, Rome, is part of that plan, which we can discover by carefully studying Abraham's life and God's word to him:

Genesis Rabbah XLIV:XVIII

1 A "Then the Lord said to Abram, 'Know of a surety [that your descendants will be sojourners in a land that is not theirs, and they will be slaves there, and they will be oppressed for four hundred years; but I will bring judgment on the nation which they serve, and afterward they shall come out with great possessions']" (Genesis 15:13–14):

   B "Know" that I shall scatter them.

   C "Of a certainty" that I shall bring them back together again.

   D "Know" that I shall put them out as a pledge [in expiation of their sins].

   E "Of a certainty" that I shall redeem them.

   F "Know" that I shall make them slaves.

   G "Of a certainty" that I shall free them.

Number 1 parses the cited verse and joins within its simple formula the entire history of Israel, punishment and forgiveness alike. Not only the patriarchs, but also the matriarchs, so acted as to shape the future life of the family, Israel. One extended statement of the matter suffices.

Here, in number 2, is how sages take up the detail of Abraham's provision of a bit of water, showing what that act had to do with the history of Israel later on. The intricate working out of the whole, involving the merit of the patriarchs, the way in which the deeds of the patriarchs provide a sign for proper conduct for their children, the history and salvation of Israel – the whole shows how, within a single metaphor, the entire system of the Judaism of the dual Torah could reach concrete expression:

Genesis Rabbah XLVIII:X

2 A "Let a little water be brought" (Genesis 18:4):

   B Said to him the Holy One, blessed be he, "You have said, 'Let a little water be brought' (Genesis 18:4). By your life, I shall pay your descendants back for this: 'Then sang Israel this song,' spring up O well, sing you to it" (Numbers 21:7).

   C That recompense took place in the wilderness. Where do we find that it took place in the Land of Israel as well?

   D "A land of brooks of water" (Deuteronomy 8:7).

E   And where do we find that it will take place in the age to come?

F   "And it shall come to pass in that day that living waters shall go out of Jerusalem" (Zechariah 14:8).

G   ["And wash your feet" (Genesis 18:4)]: [Said to him the Holy One, blessed be he,] "You have said, 'And wash your feet.' By your life, I shall pay your descendants back for this: 'Then I washed you in water' " (Ezekiel 16:9).

H   That recompense took place in the wilderness. Where do we find that it took place in the Land of Israel as well?

I   "Wash you, make you clean" (Isaiah 1:16).

J   And where do we find that it will take place in the age to come?

K   "When the Lord will have washed away the filth of the daughters of Zion" (Isaiah 4:4).

L   [Said to him the Holy One, blessed be he,] "You have said, 'And rest yourselves under the tree' (Genesis 18:4). By your life, I shall pay your descendants back for this: 'He spread a cloud for a screen' " (Psalms 105:39).

M   That recompense took place in the wilderness. Where do we find that it took place in the Land of Israel as well?

N   "You shall dwell in booths for seven days" (Leviticus 23:42).

O   And where do we find that it will take place in the age to come?

P   "And there shall be a pavilion for a shadow in the day-time from the heat" (Isaiah 4:6).

Q   [Said to him the Holy One, blessed be he,] "You have said, 'While I fetch a morsel of bread that you may refresh yourself' (Genesis 18:5). By your life, I shall pay your descendants back for this: 'Behold I will cause to rain bread from heaven for you' " (Exodus 16:4).

R   That recompense took place in the wilderness. Where do we find that it took place in the Land of Israel as well?

S   "A land of wheat and barley" (Deuteronomy 8:8).

T   And where do we find that it will take place in the age to come?

U   "He will be as a rich grain field in the land" (Psalms 82:16).

V   [Said to him the Holy One, blessed be he,] "You ran after the herd ['And Abraham ran to the herd' (Genesis 18:7)]. By your life, I shall pay your descendants back for this:

'And there went forth a wind from the Lord and brought across quails from the sea' " (Numbers 11:31).

W   That recompense took place in the wilderness. Where do we find that it took place in the Land of Israel as well?

X   "Now the children of Reuben and the children of Gad had a very great multitude of cattle" (Numbers 32:1).

Y   And where do we find that it will take place in the age to come?

Z   "And it will come to pass in that day that a man shall rear a young cow and two sheep" (Isaiah 7:21).

AA [Said to him the Holy One, blessed be he,] "You stood by them: 'And he stood by them under the tree while they ate' (Genesis 18:8). By your life, I shall pay your descendants back for this: 'And the Lord went before them' " (Exodus 13:21).

BB That recompense took place in the wilderness. Where do we find that it took place in the Land of Israel as well?

CC "God stands in the congregation of God" (Psalms 82:1).

DD And where do we find that it will take place in the age to come?

EE "The breaker is gone up before them . . . and the Lord at the head of them" (Micah 2:13).

Everything that Abraham did brought a reward to his descendants. The enormous emphasis on the way in which Abraham's deeds prefigured the history of Israel, both in the wilderness, and in the Land, and, finally, in the age to come, provokes us to wonder who held that there were other children of Abraham, beside this "Israel." The answer – from the triumphant Christians in particular, who right from the beginning, with Paul and the Evangelists, imputed it to the earliest generations of Jesus' followers and said it in so many words – then is clear. We note that there are five statements of the same proposition, each drawing upon a clause in the base verse. The extended statement, moreover, serves as a sustained introduction to the treatment of the individual clauses that now follow, item by item. Obviously, it is the merit of the ancestors that connects the living Israel to the lives of the patriarchs and matriarchs of old.

If we ask, precisely what lessons about history or social rules of Judaism the sages derived for the descendants of Abraham and Sarah, we come upon a clear answer. The lessons concern God's conduct with Israel – then and now. One important example concerns God's threats to punish Israel. In the polemic of the age, with the Christians accusing Israel of having sinned and citing the prophets for evidence, the following could have provided a striking response. God can change the plan originally conceived. None of the prophetic warnings lay beyond God's power of revision, should Israel's repentance warrant.

Genesis Rabbah LIII:IV

1 A "For ever, O Lord, your word stands fast in heaven" (Psalms 119:89):

   B But does God's word not stand fast on earth?

   C But what you said to Abraham in heaven, "At this season I shall return to you" (Genesis 18:14) [was carried out:]

   D "The Lord remembered Sarah as he had said and the Lord did to Sarah as he had promised" (Genesis 21:1).

2 A R. Menahamah and R. Nahman of Jaffa in the name of R. Jacob of Caesarea opened discourse by citing the following verse: " 'O God of hosts, return, we beseech you' (Psalms 80:15).

   B 'Return and carry out what you promised to Abraham: "Look from heaven and behold" (Psalms 80:15). "Look now toward heaven and count the stars"' (Genesis 15:5).

   C 'And be mindful of this vine' (Psalms 80:15). 'The Lord remembered Sarah as he had said and the Lord did to Sarah as he had promised' " (Genesis 21:1).

3 A R. Samuel bar Nahman opened discourse with this verse: "God is not a man, that he should lie" (Numbers 23:19).

   B Said R. Samuel bar Nahman, "The beginning of this verse does not correspond to its end, and the end does not correspond to its beginning.

   C 'God is not a man that he should lie' (Numbers 23:19), but the verse ends, 'When he has said, he will not do it, and when he has spoken, he will not make it good' (Numbers 23:19).

   D [That obviously is impossible. Hence:] When the Holy One, blessed be he, makes a decree to bring good to the world: 'God is not a man that he should lie' (Numbers 23:19).

   E But when he makes a decree to bring evil on the world:

'When he has said, he [nonetheless] will not do it, and when he has spoken, he will not make it good' (Numbers 23:19).

F   When he said to Abraham, 'For through Isaac shall your descendants be named,' 'God is not a man that he should lie' (Numbers 23:19).

G   When he said to him, 'Take your son, your only son' (Genesis 22:2), 'When he has said, he will not do it, and when he has spoken, he will not make it good' (Numbers 23:19).

H   When the Holy One, blessed be he, said to Moses, 'I have surely remembered you' (Exodus 3:16), 'God is not a man that he should lie' (Numbers 23:19).

I   When he said to him, 'Let me alone, that I may destroy them' (Deuteronomy 9:14), 'When he has said, he will not do it, and when he has spoken, he will not make it good' (Numbers 23:19).

J   When he said to Abraham, 'And also that nation whom they shall serve will I judge' (Genesis 15:14), 'God is not a man that he should lie' (Numbers 23:19).

K   When he said to him, 'And they shall serve them and they shall afflict them for four hundred years' (Genesis 15:13), 'When he has said, he will not do it, and when he has spoken, he will not make it good' (Numbers 23:19).

L   When God said to him, 'I will certainly return to you' (Genesis 18:10), 'God is not a man that he should lie' (Numbers 23:19).

M   'The Lord remembered Sarah as he had said and the Lord did to Sarah as he had promised' " (Genesis 21:1).

The main point is that God will always carry out his word when it has to do with a blessing, but God may well go back on his word when it has to do with punishment. The later events in the history of Israel are drawn together to make this important point.

The single most important paradigm for history therefore emerged from the binding of Isaac, the deed at Moriah, portrayed on synagogue mosaics, e.g. at Beth Alpha, and reflected upon as the source for knowledge of the laws of the history of Israel, heirs and continuators of Abraham and Isaac. Sages drew one specific lesson. Future Israel would live from the model and merit of that moment:

Genesis Rabbah LVI:I

1 A "On the third day Abraham lifted up his eyes and saw the place afar off" (Genesis 22:4):

     B "After two days he will revive us, on the third day he will raise us up, that we may live in his presence" (Hosea 6:2).

     C On the third day of the tribes: "And Joseph said to them on the third day, 'This do and live'" (Genesis 42:18).

     D On the third day of the giving of the Torah: "And it came to pass on the third day when it was morning" (Exodus 19:16).

     E On the third day of the spies: "And hide yourselves there for three days" (Joshua 2:16).

     F On the third day of Jonah: "And Jonah was in the belly of the fish three days and three nights" (Jonah 2:1).

     G On the third day of the return from the Exile: "And we abode there three days" (Ezra 8:32).

     H On the third day of the resurrection of the dead: "After two days he will revive us, on the third day he will raise us up, that we may live in his presence" (Hosea 6:2).

     I On the third day of Esther: "Now it came to pass on the third day that Esther put on her royal apparel" (Esther 5:1).

     J She put on the monarchy of the house of her fathers.

     K On account of what sort of merit?

     L Rabbis say, "On account of the third day of the giving of the Torah."

     M R. Levi said, "It is on account of the merit of the third day of Abraham: 'On the third day Abraham lifted up his eyes and saw the place afar off' " (Genesis 22:4).

2 A " . . . lifted up his eyes and saw the place afar off" (Genesis 22:4):

     B What did he see? He saw a cloud attached to the mountain. He said, "It would appear that that is the place concerning which the Holy One, blessed be he, told me to offer up my son."

The third day marks the fulfillment of the promise, at the end of time of the resurrection of the dead, and, at appropriate moments, of Israel's redemption. The reference to the third day at Genesis 22:2 then invokes the entire panoply of Israel's history. The relevance of the composition emerges at the end. Prior to the concluding segment, the passage forms a kind of litany and falls into the category of a liturgy.

Still, the recurrent hermeneutic which teaches that the stories of the patriarchs prefigure the history of Israel certainly makes its appearance.

While Abraham founded Israel, Isaac and Jacob carried forth the birthright and the blessing. This they did through the process of selection, ending in the assignment of the birthright to Jacob alone. The importance of that fact for the definition of "Israel" hardly requires explication. The lives of all three patriarchs flowed together, each being identified with the other as a single long life. This immediately produced the proposition that the historical life of Israel, the nation, continued the individual lives of the patriarchs. The theory of who is Israel, therefore, is seen once more to have rested on genealogy: Israel is one extended family, all being children of the same fathers and mothers, the patriarchs and matriarchs of Genesis. This theory of Israelite society, and of the Jewish people in the time of the sages of Genesis Rabbah, made of the people a family, and of genealogy, a kind of ecclesiology. The importance of that proposition in countering the Christian claim to be a new Israel cannot escape notice. Israel, sages maintained, is Israel after the flesh, and that in a most literal sense. But the basic claim, for its part, depended upon the facts of Scripture, not upon the logical requirements of theological dispute. Here is how those facts emerged in the case of Isaac:

Genesis Rabbah LXIII:III

1 A "These are the descendants of Isaac, Abraham's son: Abraham was the father of Isaac" (Genesis 25:19):

B Abram was called Abraham: "Abram, the same is Abraham" (1 Chronicles 1:27).

C Isaac was called Abraham: "These are the descendants of Isaac, Abraham's son, Abraham" (Genesis 25:19)

D Jacob was called Israel, as it is written, "Your name shall be called no more Jacob but Israel" (Genesis 32:28).

E Isaac also was called Israel: "And these are the names of the children of Israel, who came into Egypt, Jacob and his" (Genesis 46:8).

F Abraham was called Israel as well.

G R. Nathan said, "This matter is deep: 'Now the time that the children of Israel dwelt in Egypt' (Exodus 12:40), and in the land of Canaan and in the land of Goshen 'was four hundred and thirty years' " (Exodus 12:40).

The polemic at hand, linking the patriarchs to the history of Israel, claiming that all of the patriarchs bear the same names, derives proof, in part, from the base verse. But the composition in no way rests upon the exegesis of the base verse. Its syllogism transcends the case at hand. The importance of Isaac in particular derived from his relationship to the two nations that would engage in struggle, Jacob, who was and is Israel, and Esau, who stood for Rome.

By himself, as a symbol for Israel's history, Isaac remained a shadowy figure. Still, Isaac plays his role in setting forth the laws of Israel's history. To understand what is to follow, we recall that Esau, in sages' typology, always stands for Rome. Later we shall see that the representation of Esau as sibling, brother, and enemy, distinguishes Esau/Rome from all other nations. Esau is not an outsider, not a gentile, but also not Israel, legitimate heir. We once more recall the power of the social theory to hold all together all of the middle-range components of society: all nations within a single theory. The genealogical metaphor here displays that remarkable capacity.

Genesis Rabbah LXV:XIII

1 A "[He said, 'Behold I am old; I do not know the day of my death.] Now then take your weapons, [your quiver and your bow, and go out to the field and hunt game for me, and prepare for me savory food, such as I love, and bring it to me that I may eat; that I may bless you before I die']" (Genesis 27:2–4):

   B "Sharpen your hunting gear, so that you will not feed me carrion or an animal that was improperly slaughtered.

   C Take your *own* hunting gear, so that you will not feed me meat that has been stolen or grabbed." [Italics added.]

Isaac's first point is that Esau does not ordinarily observe the food laws, e.g. concerning humane slaughter of animals. He furthermore steals, while, by inference, Jacob takes only what he has lawfully acquired. This prepares the way for the main point:

2 A "Your quiver:"

   B [Since the word for "quiver" and the word for "held in suspense" share the same consonants, we interpret the statement as follows:] he said to him, "Lo, the blessings [that I am about to give] are held in suspense. For the one who is worthy of a blessing, there will be a blessing."

3 A Another matter: "Now then take your weapons, your quiver and your bow and go out to the field:"

   B "Weapons" refers to Babylonia, as it is said, "And the weapons he brought to the treasure house of his god" (Daniel 1:2).

   C "Your quiver" speaks of Media, as it says, "So they suspended Haman on the gallows" (Esther 7:10). [The play on the words is the same as at number 2.]

   D "And your bow" addresses Greece: "For I bend Judah for me, I fill the bow with Ephraim and I will stir up your sons, O Zion, against your sons, O Javan [Greece]" (Zechariah 9:13).

   E "and go out to the field" means Edom: "Unto the land of Seir, the field of Edom" (Genesis 32:3).

Once more the patriarchs lay out the future history of their family, and, in dealing with their own affairs, prefigure what is to come. The power of the metaphor of family is not exhausted in its capacity to link household to household; quite to the contrary, as with any really successful metaphor, it draws everything into one thing and makes sense of the whole all together and all at once. Here the households that are joined are today's to yesterday's to those of the entirety of past and future.

5 A "And Rebecca was listening when Isaac spoke to his son Esau. So when Esau went to the field to hunt for game and bring it . . ." (Genesis 27:5):

   B If he found it, well and good.

   C And if not, " . . . to bring it" even by theft or violence.

The matter of the blessing is represented as more conditional than the narrative suggests. Isaac now is not sure who will get the blessing; his sense is that it will go to whoever deserves it. Number 3 then moves from the moral to the national, making the statement a clear reference to the history of Israel (as though, by this point, it were not obvious). What the author of the item at hand contributes, then, is the specific details. What the compositor does is move the reader's mind from the philological to the moral to the national dimension of exegesis of the statements at hand. Esau steals, but Jacob takes only what is lawful.

Now we see, not surprisingly, how Isaac foresaw the entire history of Israel.

Genesis Rabbah LXV:XXIII

1 A ["See the smell of my son is as the smell of a field which the Lord has blessed" (Genesis 27:27):] Another matter: this teaches that the Holy One, blessed be he, showed him the house of the sanctuary as it was built, wiped out, and built once more.

      B "See the smell of my son:" This refers to the Temple in all its beauty, in line with this verse: "A sweet smell to me shall you observe" (Numbers 28:2).

      C " . . . is as the smell of a field:" This refers to the Temple as it was wiped out, thus: "Zion shall be ploughed as a field" (Micah 3:12).

      D " . . .which the Lord has blessed:" This speaks of the Temple as it was restored once more in the age to come, as it is said, "For there the Lord commanded the blessing, even life for ever" (Psalms 133:3).

The conclusion explicitly links the blessing of Jacob to the Temple throughout its history. The concluding proof-text presumably justifies the entire identification of the blessing at hand with what was to come. Whatever future history finds adumbration in the life of Jacob derives from the struggle with Esau. Israel and Rome – these two contend for the world. Still, Isaac plays his part in the matter. Rome does have a legitimate claim, and that claim demands recognition – an amazing, if grudging concession on the part of sages that Christian Rome at least is Esau – different from the gentiles, but also not Israel.

Jacob's contribution to knowledge of the meaning and end of Israel's history, as sages uncovered it, is exemplified in the following:

Genesis Rabbah LXX:VI

1 A " . . . so that I come again to my father's house in peace, then the Lord shall be my God" (Genesis 28:20–2):

      B R. Joshua of Sikhnin in the name of R. Levi: "The Holy One, blessed be he, took the language used by the patriarchs and turned it into a key to the redemption of their descendants.

C Said the Holy One, blessed be he, to Jacob, 'You have said, "Then the Lord shall be my God." By your life, all of the acts of goodness, blessing, and consolation which I am going to carry out for your descendants I shall bestow only by using the same language:

D "Then in that day, living waters shall go out from Jerusalem" (Zechariah 14:8). "Then in that day a man shall rear a young cow and two sheep" (Isaiah 7:21). "Then, in that day, the Lord will set his hand again the second time to recover the remnant of his people" (Isaiah 11:11). "Then, in that day, the mountains shall drip down sweet wine" (Joel 4:18). "Then, in that day, a great horn shall be blown and they shall come who were lost in the land of Assyria" ' " (Isaiah 27:13).

The union of Jacob's biography and Israel's history yields the passage at hand. It is important only because it says once again what we have now heard throughout our survey of Genesis Rabbah – but makes the statement as explicit as one can imagine. Now the history of the redemption of Israel is located in the colloquy between Jacob and Laban's sons.

Genesis Rabbah LXX:XV

1 A "Now Laban had two daughters, the name of the older was Leah, and the name of the younger was Rachel" (Genesis 29:16):

B They were like two beams running from one end of the world to the other.

C This one produced captains and that one produced captains, this one produced kings and that one produced kings, this one produced lion-tamers and that one produced lion-tamers, this one produced conquerors of nations and that one produced conquerors of nations, this one produced those who divided countries and that one produced dividers of countries.

D The offering brought by the son of this one overrode the prohibitions of the Sabbath, and the offering brought by the son of that one overrode the prohibitions of the Sabbath.

E   The war fought by this one overrode the prohibitions of the Sabbath, and the war fought by that one overrode the prohibitions of the Sabbath.

F   To this one were given two nights, and to that one were given two nights.

G   The night of Pharaoh and the night of Sennacherib were for Leah, and the night of Gideon for Rachel, and the night of Mordecai was for Rachel, as it is said, "On that night the king could not sleep" (Esther 6:1).

The metaphor encompasses not only "Israel" but also "Rome." It makes sense of all the important social entities, for in this metaphor, "Israel" is consubstantial with other social entities, which relate to "Israel" just as "Israel" as a society relates to itself, present and past. Accordingly, "Rome" is a family just as is "Israel," and, more to the point, "Rome" enters into "Israel's" life in an intelligible way precisely because "Rome" too is a part of that same family that is constituted by "Israel." That is a stunning claim, working itself out time after time so smoothly, with such self-evidence, as to conceal its daring.

Again we see how the metaphor that joins past to present, household to household to "all Israel," in fact encompasses the other noteworthy social entity and takes it into full account – a powerful, successful field-theory indeed. The contrast to the taxonomic metaphor is clear. "Non-Israel" accommodates, it classifies, but it does not explain. Then, ironically, neither does "Israel." Here we have explanation, which, after all, is the purpose of natural philosophy in its social aspect. It is no surprise, therefore, that much that Jacob said serves to illuminate Israel's future history.

Genesis Rabbah LXXVIII:XIII

1   A   "[Then Esau said, 'Let us journey on our way, and I will go before you.'] But Jacob said to him, 'My lord knows [that the children are frail, and that the flocks and herds giving suck are a care to me; and if they are over-driven for one day, all the flocks will die. Let my lord pass on before his servant, and I will lead on slowly, according to the pace of the cattle which are before me and according to the pace of the children, until I come to my lord in Seir']" (Genesis 33:12–14):

173

B   Said R. Berekhiah, " 'My lord knows that the children are frail' refers to Moses and Aaron.

C   . . . and that the flocks and herds giving suck are a care to me' speaks of Israel: 'And you, my flock, the flock of my pasture, are men' "(Ezekiel 34:31).

D   R. Huna in the name of R. Aha: "If it were not for the tender mercies of the Holy One, blessed be he, 'and if they are over-driven for one day, all the flocks will die' in the time of Hadrian."

E   R. Berekhiah in the name of R. Levi: " 'My lord knows that the children are frail' speaks of David and Solomon.

F   '. . . the flocks and herds' refers to Israel:' 'And you, my flock, the flock of my pasture, are men' "(Ezekiel 34:31).

G   Said R. Huna in the name of R. Aha, "If it were not for the tender mercies of the Holy One, blessed be he, 'and if they are over-driven for one day, all the flocks will die' in the time of Haman."

The event at hand now is identified with other moments in the history of Israel. The metaphor of family makes a place for women as much as men, matriarchs and much as patriarchs, in a way in which the gender-neutral, but in fact masculine, metaphors of the mishnaic system do not.

The metaphorical role of the matriarchs, imputed in the case of Rachel, is as follows:

Genesis Rabbah LXXXII:X

1   A   "So Rachel died and she was buried on the way to Ephrath, [that is, Bethlehem, and Jacob set up a pillar upon her grave; it is the pillar of Rachel's tomb, which is there to this day. Israel journeyed on and pitched his tent beyond the tower of Eder]" (Genesis 35:16–21):

    B   Why did Jacob bury Rachel on the way to Ephrath?

    C   Jacob foresaw that the exiles would pass by there [en route to Babylonia].

    D   Therefore he buried her there, so that she should seek mercy for them: "A voice is heard in Ramah. . . . Rachel weeping for her children. . . . Thus says the Lord, 'Keep your voice from weeping . . . and there is hope for your future' "(Jeremiah 31:15–17).

174

We see no differentiation between matriarch and patriarch; both components of the family accomplish the same purpose, which is to link the whole together, providing for the descendants.

The deeds of the patriarchs and matriarchs aim at the needs of Israel later on. The link between the lives of the patriarchs and the history of Israel forms a major theme in the exegetical repertoire before us. These propositions really laid down a single judgment for both the individual and the family in the form of the community and the nation. Every detail of the narrative of Genesis therefore served to prefigure what was to be, and "Israel" as extended family found itself, time and again, in the revealed facts of the family record of Abraham, Isaac, and Israel. A survey of how sages read Genesis has brought us time and again to a clear perception of sages' thinking about "Israel." We see how they thought and therefore understand the positions they reached. Imagining the group to constitute a family, they organized the entire social world – Israel's part, the nations' share – within the single metaphor at hand. That mode of thought gave them a rich resource for interpreting in the context of world politics the everyday history of Israel and also explaining the future to be anticipated for Israel. And, in the present setting, it goes without saying, none of this corresponds to that ethnic conception of "Israel after the flesh" that the family-metaphor ought to have brought to expression. And this brings us to the counterpart program of the Epistle to the Hebrews, in framing a world-view out of the received Scripture, its history, law, prophecy, and sacred service in light of the fact that God had taken human form and walked on earth. How did that fact impose itself upon the rereading of Israel's entire heritage?

FROM SALVATION TO SANCTIFICATION

The Epistle to the Hebrews has long stood as an enigma within the New Testament. "Who knows who wrote the epistle?" asked Origen in the third century; he answered the question himself, "God knows!"[1] But the enigma of Hebrews goes beyond the question of who wrote it; when and where it was written, and to whom, are also issues of lively debate.[2]

It is natural to wish to answer such questions as clearly as possible, but it is even more vital not to permit them to obscure the essential clarity of Hebrews' contribution. Origen himself valued the epistle as the work of a follower of Paul's (such as Luke or Clement of Rome).[3] In North Africa a common view was that the epistle was written by

Brooke Foss Westcott

B. F. Westcott (1825–1901) was born and educated in Birmingham,[1] before he went on to Trinity College, Cambridge. At Cambridge, he taught J. B. Lightfoot and F. J. A. Hort. Together, the three scholars – each of whom was to become famous in his own right – conceived of a project of work on the New Testament. Lightfoot was to address himself to Paul, Hort to the Synoptic Gospels and certain non-Pauline letters, and Westcott to John and Hebrews.[2]

Westcott left Cambridge to take up a position at the Harrow School, where he wrote *A General Survey of the History of the Canon of the New Testament* (Cambridge: Macmillan 1855), in which he argued that the early Church consciously referred in its documents to the apostolic faith as authoritative. Then came his *Introduction to the Study of the Gospels* (Cambridge: Macmillan 1860), one of the most influential books of its time. Westcott set out a vigorous defense of the relative independence of the Gospels; against theories of literary dependence, he insisted that each Gospel reflects a particular form of the oral gospel in distinct places. Sadly, Westcott's contemporary at Oxford, William Sanday, did not have his seminar consider Westcott's position. Because Sanday's group has been taken as canonical by some scholars since, the hypothesis of orality in the early Church is widely treated as if it were something new. In fact, it is a reasonable inference from the Synoptic relationship among the Gospels, as Westcott proved.[3]

Westcott returned to Cambridge as Regius Professor in 1870, and the period saw the harvest of his scholarship. The text of the New Testament he prepared with Hort was published in 1881, and continues as a standard point of reference to this day. Both the results of their study and their method of analysis are taken as a matter of course. His commentary on John (*The Gospel According to St John* (London: Murray, 1890)) approached the Gospel as a conscious deviation from the Synoptics, in the interests of christology, and his classic work on Hebrews (*The Epistle to the Hebrews* (London: Macmillan, 1889)) presented the epistle as a boldly creative theology which discovered principles in the early preaching which would serve the Church for all time.

Westcott's own theology was always incarnational. In his mind, the presence of the son of God in the midst of humanity set off a coherent response, from the oral preaching of the apostolic faith, through its written expressions in the Synoptic Gospels and the meditative synthesis of John, and on to the discovery of a christology for the future in Hebrews. His convictions as well as his talent led him to become bishop of Durham, where his involvement in social issues came as a surprise to those unfamiliar with his theology. He was an activist because he was a pastor, a bishop because he was a scholar; he was all four because the incarnation in his belief changed the very substance of human nature.

1   See A. Westcott, *Life and Letters of Brooke Foss Westcott* (London: Macmillan, 1903).
2   See C. K. Barrett, *Westcott as Commentator* (Cambridge: Cambridge University Press, 1959), 3–8.
3   For a treatment of the question, see B. D. Chilton, *Profiles of a Rabbi. Synoptic Opportunities in Reading about Jesus*, Brown Judaic Studies 177 (Atlanta: Scholar's Press, 1989).

Barnabas, not Paul, but Tertullian reported it was "more widely received among the Churches than the Shepherd [of Hermas]," one of the most popular works among Christians of the second century.[4] B. F. Westcott, perhaps the greatest commentator in English on Hebrews, provides the key to why the epistle was accepted as canonical, doubts regarding its authorship aside, "no Book of the Bible is more completely recognised by universal consent as giving a divine view of the facts of the Gospel, full of lessons for all time, than the Epistle to the Hebrews."[5] "A divine view of the facts of the Gospel" is just what Hebrews purports to deliver, and by understanding its purpose and achievement, the epistle comes into a clear focus.

The epistle has been compared to a homily,[6] and calls itself a "word of exhortation" in 13:22. "Word" here (*logos*, as in John's Gospel) bears the meaning of "discourse," and the choice of diction declares Hebrews' homiletic intent. It is a sustained argument on the basis of authoritative tradition which intends to convince its readers and hearers to embrace a fresh position and an invigorated sense of purpose in the world. Hebrews engages in a series of scriptural identifications of Jesus: both Scripture (in the form of the Septuagint) and God's son are the authoritative points of departure.

Scripture is held to show that the son, and the son's announcement of salvation, are superior to the angels and their message (1:1–2:18, see especially 2:1–4). Jesus is also held to be superior to Moses and Joshua, who did not truly bring those who left Egypt into the rest promised by God (3:1–4:13). Having set up a general assertion of the son's superiority on the basis of Scripture, the author proceeds to his main theme (4:14):

Having, then, a great high priest who has passed into the heavens, Jesus the son of God, let us hold the confession fast.

That statement is the key to the central argument of Hebrews, and therefore to an understanding of the epistle.

Two terms of reference in the statement are used freshly and – on first acquaintance with the epistle – somewhat unexpectedly. Jesus, whom we have known as son, is now "great high priest." The term "high priest" is in fact used earlier, to speak of his having expiated sin (2:17),[7] and in that role Jesus is also called the "apostle and high priest of our confession" (3:1). But now, in 4:14, Jesus is the *great high priest*," whose position is heavenly. Now, too, the single confession of his heavenly location is the only means to obtain divine mercy.

Jesus' suffering is invoked again in 4:15 in order to make the link to what was said earlier, of Jesus' expiation. But then 4:16 spells out the ethical point of the entire epistle:

> Let us then draw near with assurance to the throne of grace, so that we might receive mercy and find grace in time of need.

With bold calculation, Jesus is presented as the unique means of access to God in the only sanctuary which matters, the divine throne in Heaven.

The portrayal of Jesus as great high priest, exalted in Heaven, proves to be the center of the epistle (Hebrews, chapters 4–7). At first, the argument may seem abstruse, turning as it does on Melchizedek, a relatively obscure figure in Genesis 14. In Genesis, Abram[8] is met by Melchizedek after his defeat of the king of Elam. Melchizedek is identified as king of Salem, and as priest of God Most High (Genesis 14:18). He brings bread and wine, and blesses Abram; in return, Abram gives Melchizedek one tenth of what he has in hand after the victory (Genesis 14:18–20).

The author of Hebrews hammers out a principle and a corollary from this narrative. First, "It is beyond all dispute that the lesser is blessed by the greater" (Hebrews 7:7). From that straightforward assertion, the superiority of Melchizedek to Levitical priests is deduced. Levi, the founding father of the priesthood, was still in Abram's loins at the time Abram paid his tithe to Melchizedek. In that sense, the Levitical priests who were to receive tithes were themselves tithed by the greater priest (Hebrews 7:8–10).

The importance of Melchizedek to the author of Hebrews, of course, is that he resembles Jesus, the son of God. His very name means "king of righteousness," and he is also "king of *peace*," Salem. He does not bear a genealogy, and his birth and death are not recorded (Hebrews 7:2b-4). In all these details, he adumbrates Jesus, true king of righteousness and peace, from a descent which is not priestly in a Levitical sense, of whom David prophesied in the Psalms, "You are a priest *for ever*, after the order of Melchizedek" (Hebrews 7:11–25, citing Psalm 110:4 on several occasions, cf. 7:11, 15, 17, 21[9]). Jesus is the guarantor by God's own promise of a better, everlasting covenant (7:22). His surety is linked to Melchizedek's as clearly as the bread and wine which both of them use is the seal of God's promise and blessing.[10]

The superiority of the better covenant is spelled out in what follows in Hebrews through chapter 9, again relying on the attachment to Jesus of God's promise in Psalm 110 (Hebrews 7:28):

> For the law appoints men having weakness as high priests, but the word of the oath which is after the law appoints a son for ever perfected.

Perfection implies that daily offerings are beside the point. The son was perfect "once for all, when he offered himself up" (7:26–7). The author leaves nothing to implication: Moses' prescriptions for the sanctuary were a pale imitation of the heavenly sanctuary which Jesus has actually entered (8:1–6). Accordingly, the covenant mediated by Jesus is "better," the "second" replacing the "first," the "new" replacing what is now "obsolete" (8:6–13).

Chapter 9 simply puts the cap on an argument which is already clear. In its elaboration of a self-consciously christological interpretation, Hebrews turns the Synoptic approach to the relationship between Jesus and Scripture into an actual theory. The devotion to detail involved attests the concern to develop that relationship fully.

Chapter 9 of Hebrews begins with the "first" covenant's regulations for sacrifice, involving the Temple in Jerusalem. The passage begins with an attention to detail that characterizes the entire discussion. The objects of worship are used to set the scene: specific mention is made of the menorah, the table and presented bread in the holy place, with the holy of holies empty, but for the gold censer and the ark.[11] The reference to the censer as being in the holy of holies fixes the point in time of which the author speaks: it can only be the day of atonement, when the high priest made his single visit of the year to that sanctum, censer in hand.[12]

That precise moment is only specified in order to be fixed, frozen forever. For Hebrews, what was a fleeting movement in the case of the high priest was an eternal truth in the case of Jesus. The movement of ordinary priests, in and out of the holy place, the "first tabernacle"

(9:6) while the high priest could only enter "the second tabernacle," the holy of holies (9:7), once a year, was designed by the spirit of God as a parable: the way into the holy of holies could not be revealed while the first Temple, the first tabernacle and its service, continued (9:8–10). That way could only be opened, after the Temple was destroyed, by Christ, who became high priest and passed through "the greater and more perfect tabernacle" of his body (9:11) by the power of his own blood (9:12) so that he could find eternal redemption in the sanctuary.

Signal motifs within the Gospels are developed in the passage. The identification of Jesus' death and the destruction of the Temple, which the Gospels achieve in narrative terms, is assumed to be complete.[13] Moreover, the passage takes it for granted that Jesus' body was a kind of "tabernacle," an instrument of sacrifice (9:11), apparently because the Gospels speak of his offering his body and his blood in the words of institution. (And John, of course, actually has Jesus refer to "the temple of his body," 2:21.)[14] "Body" and "blood" here are Jesus' self-immolating means to his end as high priest. The Temple in Jerusalem has in Hebrews been replaced by a purely ideological construct. The true high priest has entered once and for all (9:12) within the innermost recess of sanctity, so that no further sacrificial action is necessary or appropriate.

In Hebrews the homiletic conviction of Luke, that Scripture finds its purpose in Jesus, is elevated to the status of a theory. Hermeneutics which had attested the resurrection (for example, in Luke 24:25–7) have now become the hermeneutics of pre-existence. Jesus lives because he was always alive, and in the light of his activity one can finally understand what Scripture was speaking of. The destruction of the Temple in 70 CE was an advantage, because it enables us to distinguish the image from the reflection.

In the conception of Hebrews, the Temple on earth was a copy and shadow of the heavenly sanctuary, of which Moses had seen "types."[15] A type (*tupos* in Greek) is an impress, a derived version of a reality (the anti-type). Moses had seen the very throne of God, which was then approximated on earth. That approximation is called the "first covenant" (Hebrews 9:1), but the heavenly sanctuary, into which Christ has entered (9:24), offers us a "new covenant" (9:15) which is the truth which has been palely reflected all along.

The concluding three chapters of Hebrews point to what has preceded in order to influence the behavior of those who read and hear the epistle. Literal sacrifice is to be eschewed (10:1–18), and the approach to God in purity is now by means of Jesus (10:19–22). The confession of faith is to be maintained, love and good works are to be encouraged, communal gatherings are to continue as the day of the Lord approaches (10:23–5).

Above all, there is to be no turning back, no matter what the incentives (10:26–39). Faith in that sense is praised as the virtue of the patriarchs, prophets, and martyrs of old, although they were not perfected (11:1–39). Jesus alone offers perfection, as "the pioneer and perfecter of our faith" (12:1–3). Many incidental commandments follow: do not be afraid of shedding your blood (12:4), do not become immoral or irreligious in leaving old ways behind (12:16), provide hospitality and care for prisoners and those who are mistreated (13:1–3), honor marriage and do not love money (13:4–5), respect leaders and beware false teaching (13:7, 9, 17), remember to share and to pray (13:16, 18). Interesting as those commands are individually (especially in drawing a social profile of the community addressed (see pp. 185–7), the over-riding theme is evident and carries the weight of the argument (12:14):

> Pursue peace with all, and sanctification, apart from which no one will see God.

Divine vision, the sanctification to stand before God, is in Hebrews the goal of human life, and the only means to such perfection is loyalty to Jesus as the great high priest.

The sense of finality, of a perfection from which one must not defect, is deliberately emphasized (12:22–4):

> But you have come to Mount Zion and the city of the living God, the heavenly Jerusalem, and to myriads of angels in festal gathering, and to the assembly of first-born enrolled in heaven, and to a judge – God of all, and to the spirits of the just who are made perfect, and to Jesus the mediator of a new covenant, and to sprinkled blood which speaks better than the blood of Abel.

Jesus, the only mediator of perfection, provides access to that heavenly place which is the city of the faithful, the heart's only sanctuary.

HEBREWS' NEW RELIGION

The themes of Hebrews were to become the themes of Catholic Christianity. The son of God would be understood as inherently and obviously superior to the angels, to Moses and Joshua, as the great high priest who alone provides access to the only sanctuary that matters. Framing a single confession of his heavenly location in relation to the divine throne was to require literally centuries of discussion within the Church, but the necessity of such a confession was axiomatic.

Because Hebrews' themes became widespread, their development in the epistle will strike most readers as needlessly elaborate. But those themes were only discovered because the author maintained his rigorously christological focus on Melchizedek, so that the bread, the wine, and the blessing he gave Abraham became the key to Jesus' superiority in the bread and the wine of a new and better covenant. Moses' prescriptions are shadows, imitations of the heavenly sanctuary which Jesus has actually entered. The Temple in Jerusalem has in Hebrews been replaced by a conception of the divine throne in heaven and the faithful congregation on earth, and Jesus' perfect sacrifice is the unique and perfect link between the two.

Hebrews does not entertain the question of how Jesus, as the perfect link between the heavenly sanctuary and a world in need of forgiveness, can relate to both God and people. In one breath, the author portrays Jesus as learning from and being perfected by his suffering (Hebrews 5:7–10); indeed, here his suffering obedience is held to be the precedent of his designation by God as a high priest after the order of Melchizedek. But in another breath, even as he assures us that "we do not have a high priest who is unable to sympathize with our weaknesses," the author cannot resist observing that in Jesus we have a high priest who was "tempted in everything in the same way, *apart from sin*" (Hebrews 4:15; italics added). Jesus is both like people and not like people, because he is the great high priest in the divine sanctuary.

So is Jesus human, divine, or some combination of the two natures? And did Jesus' human experience actually teach him anything he did not already know? Catholic Christianity, in councils, creeds, persecutions, and more councils, addressed just such issues. Commentators, usually functioning as theologians, have naturally taken them up in discussing Hebrews,[16] but in so doing they overlook the achievement of the epistle. Hebrews so centrally locates Jesus as the locus of revelation that it became inevitable to ask about his nature(s) and his consciousness in a way which was not current before, because Hebrews develops a religious system which derives completely from Jesus.

Comparison with the systems of Christian Judaism which we have seen earlier enables us clearly to characterize the achievement of

Hebrews. Where the obvious question in Christian Judaism was the nature of Israel, the natural question which emerges from Hebrews is the nature(s) of Christ. We can see an indication of that change immediately by placing the "Israel" of Hebrews in the context of the often fraught, generative concern to define Israel within the movement of Jesus from its earliest phases (see Chapter Five).

Jesus had insisted upon a policy of treating all of Israel *as Israel*, pure by means of its customary practice to accept and enter the kingdom of God. For Peter, this made Jesus a new Moses: just as there is an implicit analogy between the followers of Jesus and the Israel which followed Moses out of Egypt, the prophetic covenant of Moses and the divine sonship of Jesus stand side by side. James' point of departure was David, rather than Moses. Here, the belief of gentiles achieves, not the redefinition of Israel, but the *restoration* of the house of David, which is committed to preserve Israel in its purity. But Paul began with Abraham, who in Pauline theology embodied a principle of believing which was best fulfilled by means of faith in and through Jesus Christ. The Synoptic Gospels, in their variety, posit an *analogy* between Jesus and the figures of the Hebrew Bible: Christ becomes the standard by which Israel's Scripture is experienced, corrected, and understood to have been fulfilled. John's nuance is sophisticated, but plain: Jesus is the true Israel, attested by the angels of God, by whom all the families of the earth will be blessed.

All such options are brushed aside in Hebrews. The author understands Israel, literally, as a thing of the past, the husk of the first, now antiquated covenant. He says the word "Israel" just three times. Twice in chapter 8, he refers to Israel, but simply as part of his quotation of Jeremiah 31:31–4, where to his mind a completely new covenant is promised (Hebrews 8:8, 10). The point of that citation, as elaborated by the author, is that the new covenant makes the former covenant obsolete (8:13). Accordingly, when the author speaks of Israel in his own voice, it is simply to refer to "the sons of Israel" in the past, at the time of the exodus from Egypt (11:22).[17] Melchizedek is a positive, theological category. Israel is no longer, and remains only as a cautionary tale from history.

The ability of the author of Hebrews to relegate Israel to history is related to the insistence, from the outset of the epistle, that the son's authority is greater than that of the Scripture. Once, God spoke in many and various ways through the prophets; now, at the end of days, he speaks to us by a son (Hebrews 1:1, 2). The comparative judgment is reinforced when the author observes that, if the word delivered by angels (that is, the Torah[18]) carried with it retribution for transgression, how much more should we attend to what we have heard concerning the son (Hebrews 2:1–4). The implication of both statements is clear: Scripture is only authoritative to the extent that it attests the salvation mediated by the son (1:14; 2:3–4). The typology which is framed later in the epistle between Jesus and the Temple derives directly from the conviction of the prior authority of the son of God in relation to Scripture.[19]

The dual revaluation, of Israel and Israel's Scripture, is what permits Hebrews to trace its theology of Christ's replacement of every major institution, every principal term of reference, within the Judaisms of its time. Before Hebrews, there were Christian Judaisms, in which Christ was in various ways conceived of as the key to the promises to Israel. Hebrews' theology proceeds from those earlier theologies, and it remains a Christian Judaism in the sense that all of its vocabulary of salvation is drawn from the same Scriptures that were axiomatic within the earlier circles.

But the Christian Judaism of Hebrews is also and self-consciously a system of Christianity, because all that is Judaic is held to have been provisional upon the coming of the son, after which point it is no longer meaningful on its own. There is a single center within the theology of Hebrews. It is not Christ with Moses, Christ with Temple, Christ with David, Christ with Abraham, Christ with Scripture, Christ with Israel. In the end, the center is not really even Christ with Melchizedek, because Melchizedek disappears in the glory of his heavenly archetype. Christ is the beginning, middle, and end of theology in Hebrews, just as he is the same yesterday, today, and forever (Hebrews 13:8). Everything else is provisional – and expendable – within the consuming fire which is God (12:29).

The intellectual achievement of Hebrews may be gauged by comparing its insistence upon Christ as the unique center of faith with the presentations of previous circles of thought and practice (as discussed in Chapter Five). The care with which the Petrine circle had presented Jesus *with* Moses in the Transfiguration (see Mark 9:4) is simply abandoned when the author of Hebrews remarks, as if in passing, that Jesus was counted worthy of more glory than Moses was (Hebrews 3:2–6). Similarly, James' emphasis on the Davidic promise in Jesus (see Acts 15:13–21) is all but ignored in Hebrews, as David appears only as the author of Psalms (Hebrews 4:7) and as one of a string of heroes from the past (11:32). And chapter 9 of Hebrews, of course, sets aside any continuing interest in the Temple in Jerusalem, where James' authority was centered (see Acts 21:17–26).

Comparison between Paul and Hebrews is natural.[20] Paul presented Jesus as the fulfillment of God's promises to Abraham (Galatians 3:6–9), and argued that the fulfillment of the promise meant that Torah could no longer be looked upon as a requirement (Galatians 3:19–29). Paul brands any attempt to require non-Jews to keep the Torah as a consequence of their baptism as "Judaizing" (Galatians 2:14). That theology is obviously a precedent for the author of Hebrews, who proceeds to refer openly to a new covenant superseding the old (8:13).

But for Paul "all Israel" was the object of God's salvation (Romans 11:26), just as the covenant fulfilled by Jesus was nothing other than the covenant with Abraham (so Galatians 3:15–18). For that reason, Scripture in Paul's thought is a constant term of reference; from it derives the coherent narrative of a covenant revealed to Abraham, guarded under Moses and fulfilled in Christ. By contrast, Christ is the only coherent principle in Hebrews, and Scripture is a mine from which types may be quarried.

Hebrews' technique of argumentation is a logical extension of the allegorical and symbolic readings presented in the Synoptics and in John. But the Synoptics and John accept, in the manner of Philo of Alexandria, that Scripture is to be used – at least for some – to regulate behavior, as well as to uncover divine truth. When the Synoptics compare Jesus to Elijah (see Matthew 16:14; Mark 8:28; Luke 9:19), and when John presents him as Jacob (John 1:51), the assumption is that Elijah and Jacob have their own meaning, and that some people will live loyally within their understandings of Elijah's or Jacob's presentation of the God of Israel. In Hebrews, the past is of interest principally as a counter-example to the city that is to come (see Hebrews 13:14), and old ways are to be left behind (Hebrews 10:1–18).

It is possible to compare (provided one also contrasts, as in Chapter Five) Peter with Pharisees, James with Essenes, Paul with Philo's allegorists, Barnabas with Philo himself. The author of Hebrews resists such comparison, because nothing within Judaism has a value independent of Jesus within the Epistle to the Hebrews. Of all of the previous associations, the one with Philo is most viable, since the allegorical or symbolic interpretation of Scripture is clearly developed even further than it is in the Synoptics and John. Particularly, the theory of "types" is redolent of Philo's approach and vocabulary.[21]

185

But, even when confronted with what he takes to be ethical lapses, the author of Hebrews does *not* rely on *any* argument on the basis of the authority of Scripture. The contrast with Philo could not be plainer.

Instead of invoking Scripture, or even an account (such as Paul's) of the covenantal meaning of Scripture, the author of Hebrews ties his ethical imperatives directly to the example of Jesus. The community is to overcome its fear of shedding blood (Hebrews 12:4) by considering the perfection of Jesus (12:1–3). That perfection is held to exclude immoral or irreligious ways, because they are not compatible with the grace of God (12:15–17). The perspective upon social policy reflects a greater degree of assurance than anything we have seen: the author of Hebrews can say precisely and without argument, when most of his predecessors could not, just how Jesus' example is to be followed and what behavior causes God to withdraw his grace.

The anticipated agreement in regard to mandated behavior is pursued in the next chapter of Hebrews. Urban virtues, of hospitality as well as the care for prisoners and those who are mistreated (Hebrews 13:1–3), seem to reflect an awareness that Jesus had taught such duties (see Matthew 25:31–46; compare Luke 7:22–3 and Matthew 11:4–6). For the same reason, the honor of marriage (Hebrews 13:4), the injunction not to love money (Hebrews 13:5), the call to respect leaders and to beware false teaching (Hebrews 13:7, 9, 17), and the reminder to share and to pray (Hebrews 13:16, 18), all can come as a matter of course.

Hebrews is written to a community which views the teaching of Jesus alone as regulative. Scripture, the Old Testament (the only form of Scripture then available[22]), is simply the foreshadowed truth of what Jesus the great high priest fully reveals. The community is addressed as a whole; most of its people have received baptism (6:1–3), and they know right from wrong in the light of Jesus' teaching. They need to be urged to continue meeting together (10:25), despite what is called "the custom of some." Factions within a community in which there is general consensus are therefore intimated, and that impression is confirmed by the particular appeal to obey leaders (13:17).

In his recent commentary on Hebrews, William L. Lane relates the epistle to the "Hellenists" described in the book of Acts (6:1; 9:29). The term refers to "Jews living in Jerusalem but originally connected with Diaspora Judaism and characterized by the use of Greek as their principal language, especially for worship and scripture."[23] Lane suggests that those Hellenistic Jews who accepted baptism in Jesus' name became trenchant in their criticism of the Temple.[24] Their position is reflected in the speech of Stephen (see Acts 7:2–53). But where Stephen in Acts assumes the continuing validity of the Torah because it is mediated by angels (7:53), Hebrews cites the mediation of angels to qualify the standing of the Torah in relation to the son (2:2–4). On the whole, the sophistication of the epistle marks it, as Lane argues, as a considerable advance in the position of Hellenistic Jews who had become Christians.

The connection of the Hellenists to a form a Judaism in which the importance of the Temple was relativized[25] is reminiscent of the people Philo described as scrupulous for the intellectual reference of laws to the exclusion of their expressed meaning, those who saw the point of Scripture as being symbolic, rather than regulative.[26] But Hebrews takes a conceptual step beyond attributing an allegorical meaning to the Temple. Rather than portraying the cult as the direct counterpart of the heavenly sanctuary (which is Philo's conception[27]), all Levitical regulations are dissolved in the single sacrifice of the great high priest. The Epistle to the Hebrews represents Hellenistic Judaism, as reflected by Philo, after its conversion into a form of Christian Judaism by means of a consciously symbolic interpretation of Scripture and of Scripture's contents.

Martin Luther suggested that the author of Hebrews was Apollos, described in Acts as a Jew from Alexandria, learned and powerful in the Scriptures (see Acts 18:24–8). Neither Westcott[28] nor Lane[29] accords the suggestion much sympathy, probably because they both locate the community of the epistle in Jerusalem prior to the destruction of the Temple. But the advanced technique of interpretation, the formal denial of the efficacy of worship in Jerusalem, the stilted description in chapter 9 concerning the arrangement of the sanctuary, all are indications against a local knowledge of the Temple prior to 70 CE. Luther's suggestion is probably incorrect because Apollos, a contemporary of Paul's, is too early a figure to have written Hebrews. The author and community were probably Alexandrian,[30] but by the time the epistle was written circumcision was not even an issue. It was assumed the readership had long known it was not a requirement.[31] The period assumed is well after the council of 49 CE and the confrontation between Peter and Paul at Antioch.

The oldest form of the title of the epistle, "To Hebrews," sums up the perspective which is represented. Westcott, with his usual skill, articulated the orientation succinctly:

The arguments and reflections in their whole form and spirit, even more than in special details, are addressed to "Hebrews," men, that is, whose hearts were filled with the thoughts, the hopes, the consolations, of the Old Covenant. . . .[32]

The epistle does not deal with circumcision, with a Temple which is standing, or in particular with any contemporary synagogue of Judaism. Its orientation is global. The author works out Christian Judaism as a religion which replaces every major institution with Christ, their heavenly archetype, who now offers his perfection to humanity.

With Hebrews a Christian Judaism becomes a closed system, Christianity complete within its own terms of reference. Primitive Christianity here becomes, before the reader's eyes, early Christianity. After Hebrews, it will be apparent to Christians that any loyalty to Judaism is a throwback, to be tolerated or not, but always off the center of the religious system. Before Hebrews, there were Christian Judaisms; after Hebrews, the appearance of any institution of Judaism within the Church was seen to be a form of Jewish Christianity.

The achievement of Hebrews is systemic, and the result of the intellectual effort of what appears to be a single author. The skill of the rhetoric, the relatively high level of the Greek, the originality and coherence of the argument, all suggest the contribution of a single mind. Westcott's conclusion, once again, is telling:

> On the one side we see how the Spirit of God uses special powers, tendencies and conditions, things personal and things social, for the expression of a particular aspect of the Truth; and on the other side we see how the enlightened consciousness of the Church was in due time led to recognise that teaching as authoritative which was at first least in harmony with prevailing forms of thought.[33]

What Westcott saw, and struggled to express, was that in Hebrews the ambient Christian Judaism of the author became a Christianity. It was not yet in the classical mode that emerged during the second century, within the terms of reference of popular, philosophical discussion. Hebrews' Christianity is "early," not classical. Although it replaces the institutions of Israel with Christ, that replacement is taken to be complete in itself, without the addition of other forms of thought. Interpretation here makes an early Christianity out of the Christian Judaism of its community, and offers the result to those who followed, and wrestled in philosophical terms with this son of God whose suffering was for humanity as a whole.

NOTES

1 JUDAISM IN THE NEW TESTAMENT OR THE NEW TESTAMENT'S PARTICULAR JUDAISM?

1 Philadelphia: Trinity Press International, 1991. On this book see Jacob Neusner, *Rabbinic Literature and the New Testament. What We Cannot Show, We Do Not Know* (Philadelphia: Trinity Press International, 1993), *idem, Judaic Law from Jesus to the Mishnah. A Systematic Reply to Professor E. P. Sanders* (Atlanta: Scholars Press for South Florida Studies in the History of Judaism, 1993) and *idem, The Documentary Foundation of Rabbinic Culture. Mopping Up after Debates with Eliezer Segal, Peter Schaefer, Gerald L. Bruns, Christine Hayes, E. P. Sanders, James Kugel, S. J. D. Cohen, Lawrence H. Schiffman, and Susan Handelman* (Atlanta: Scholars Press for South Florida Studies in the History of Judaism, 1995).

2 NO ORTHODOX, TRADITIONAL JUDAISM? THE ISSUE OF THE MISHNAH, THE JUDAISM OF ORTHOPRAXY

1 The debate between Walter Bauer and W. E. Turner, the former in *Rechtglaubigkeit und Ketzerei* (English translation, Walter Bauer, *Orthodoxy and Heresy in Earliest Christianity* (Philadelphia: Fortress, 1971)), the latter in *The Pattern of Christian Truth*, leaves no doubt that the same may be said of Christianity, *mutatis mutandis*, thus "all of them calling themselves the Church and their faith Christianity." The situation with Islam requires attention in its own terms, but the varieties of Islam – Sunni and Shi'i being best known just now – surely validate analysis of how diverse Islamic systems of the social order have come to realization over time. True, orthopraxy serves as a valid definition within Islam, in a way in which it does not serve now, and rarely has served in the past, for Judaism. Whether as with Judaism orthopraxy produces results of mere triviality remains to be seen.

2 For the contrary view, which is held by a great many Orthodox Judaic theologians and by some Christian ones as well, cf. Lawrence H. Schiffman, *Sectarian Law in the Dead Sea Scrolls. Courts, Testimony, and the Penal Code* (Chico, Mont.: Scholars Press for Brown Judaic Studies, 1983), 3: "This system [referring to Judaism and its law] composed of

interlocking and re-interlocking parts possessed of an organic connection one to another, is never really divisible." Schiffman does not demonstrate that claim.

3   But before the discovery of synagogues with richly decorated walls, full of images of human beings, no one anticipated that a Jewish place of worship would permit a human image, such as have been found. See Jacob Neusner (ed.), *Goodenough's Jewish Symbols. An Abridged Edition* (Princeton: Princeton University Press, 1988). That is why we must always add, "as matters now appear to have been the case." Otherwise we anachronistically assign contemporary certainties to ancient times.

4   Cf. R. Yaron, *The Law of the Aramaic Papyri* (Oxford: Clarendon, 1961).

5   In addition to Yaron, cf. B. Porten, *Archives from Elephantine. The Life of an Ancient Jewish Military Colony* (Berkeley and Los Angeles: University of California Press, 1968); Y. Muffs, *Studies in the Aramaic Legal Papyri from Elephantine* (Leiden: E. J. Brill, 1969).

6   Compare the view of E. E. Urbach, *The Law. Its Sources and Development* (Jerusalem: Magnes Press of the Hebrew University, 1984) (in Hebrew).

7   Erwin R. Goodenough, *The Jurisprudence of the Jewish Courts in Egypt. Legal Administration by the Jews under the Early Roman Empire as Described by Philo Judaeus* (New Haven, CT: 1929).

8   Porten, *Archives from Elephantine*; Muffs, *Studies*; Yaron, *Law of Aramaic Papyri*.

9   Lawrence H. Schiffman, *The Halakhah at Qumran* (Leiden: E. J. Brill, 1975); *idem*, *Sectarian Law*; Joseph M. Baumgarten, *Studies in Qumran Law* (Leiden: E. J. Brill, 1977).

10 J. Neusner, *Judaism: The Evidence of the Mishnah* (Chicago: University of Chicago Press, 1981).

11 Baruch A. Levine, "Mulugu/Melug. The Origins of a Talmudic Legal Institution," *JAOS*, 1968, 88:271–85.

12 Muffs, *Studies in the Aramaic Legal Papyri*, presents the definitive picture.

13 J. Neusner, "First Cleanse the Inside," *New Testament Studies* 1976, 22:486–95, reprinted in *Method and Meaning in Ancient Judaism. Third Series* (Chico, Mont.: Scholars Press for Brown Judaic Studies, 1981).

14 Cf. M. Gittin 9:10 and Matthew 5:31–2, among numerous well-known points of intersection.

15 That is the argument of Neusner, *Judaism: The Evidence of the Mishnah*.

16 These are summarized in detail in J. Neusner, *Method and Meaning in Ancient Judaism. Second Series* (Chico, Mont.: Scholars Press for Brown Judaic Studies, 1981), 101–214.

3   ANALYZING A JUDAISM: HOW AND WHY

1   E. P. Sanders, "Puzzling Out Rabbinism," in William Scott Green (ed.), *Approaches to Ancient Judaism* (Valley Forge, PA: Trinity Press International, 1980), 2:73.

2   His argument is that those presuppositions time and again contain the

principles of convenantal nomism that figure prominently in his thinking about Judaism in late antiquity. Our argument is not with his position on that Judaism, though we have reservations on the prominence that he accords to those ideas that he finds paramount and are less certain than he that those particular ideas enjoy the disproportionate place that he conceives them to.

4 THEORY OF THE SOCIAL ENTITY: WHO AND WHAT IS "ISRAEL" IN THE JUDAISM OF ST PAUL?

1 A break at 9:24 is more plausible in Greek than in English; cf. the twenty-sixth edition of *Novum Testamentum Graece*, eds E. Nestle and K. Aland (Stuttgart: Deutsche Bibelstiftung, 1979).

2 *Letter Writing in Greco-Roman Antiquity*, Library of Early Christianity (Philadelphia: Westminster, 1986), 25.

3 Stowers, *Letter Writing*, 41–2. Within the Hebrew Bible, Stowers cites 2 Samuel 11:14, 15; 1 Kings 21:8–10; 2 Kings 10:1–6; 19:9–14; Ezra 4–5. The last two passages, of course, relate Assyrian and Persian letters (and the second should be extended to 6:12). Moreover, all of the passages cited concern royal, official, or military communication, rather than the sort of cultural activity which is reflected in the New Testament. Stowers' references to Philo, Josephus, and 1, 2 Maccabees are more on target.

4 Stowers does not, however, make reference to the letters of Bar Kokhba and to the evidence of correspondence between Antioch and Palestine; both sorts of letter are of direct pertinence to his theme. Cf. J. A. Fitzmyer, "Aramaic Epistolography," in *idem, A Wandering Aramean. Collected Aramaic Essays*, SBL Monograph Series 25 (Chico, CA.: Scholars Press, 1979), 183–204; W. A. Meeks and R. L. Wilken, *Jews and Christians in Antioch in the First Four Centuries of the Common Era*, SBL Sources for Biblical Study 13 (Ann Arbor, MI: Scholars Press, 1978).

5 Stowers, *Letter Writing* 113, 114. Cf. also, M. L. Stirewalt, "Appendix: The Form and Function of the Greek Letter-Essay," in K. P. Donfried (ed.),*The Romans Debate* (Minneapolis, MN: Augsburg, 1977), 175–206; and K. P. Donfried, "False Presuppositions in the Study of Romans," in Donfried (ed.), *The Romans Debate,* pp. 120–148.

6 Cf. R. Badenas, *Christ the End of the Law. Romans 10:4 in Pauline Perspective*, Journal for the Study of the New Testament Supplement Series 10 (Sheffield: JSOT, 1985), 90–2.

7 Generally, Paul's text is practically identical with the emerging text of the Septuagint, but he may have been influenced occasionally (as here) by Targumic interpretations, and by the original Hebrew (cf. B. D. Chilton,*God in Strength. Jesus' Announcement of the Kingdom*, The Biblical Seminar (Sheffield: JSOT, 1987), 267, 273, 274.

8 Comparison may be invited with the approach of Jesus to Scripture, in which the kingdom is held to be the hermeneutical center of the Scriptures (cf. B. D. Chilton, *A Galilean Rabbi and His Bible. Jesus' Use of the Interpreted Scripture of His Time,* Good News Studies 8 (Wilmington, Delaware: Glazier, 1984). For Paul, Christ is that center (cf. Romans 10:4).

9 Cf. Badenas, *Christ the End of the Law*, 144–55. Badenas himself does not render τέλος as "point," but such a rendering would be consistent with his case.

10 Notably, this command, in its context, requires separation from the gentiles, which supports the understanding that, as in Galatians 3:12, Paul cites the passage in order to overturn it with a principle of inclusion.

11 Psalm 18:5 in the Septuagint and 19:5 in the Masoretic Text.

12 "Former Prophets," "Latter Prophets," and "Writings" come after the "Torah" in the traditional canon of Judaism, so as to present the Hebrew Bible as a coherent statement of divine "guidance" (which is the basic meaning of the term "Torah"). "Former Prophets" refers to the traditional collection of biblical books between Joshua and 2 Kings. "Latter Prophets" refers to the collection of Prophetic books from Isaiah onward. The term "Writings" was used to speak of works such as Psalms and Proverbs, which were not presented as specifically prophetic.

13 With reverberations with Isaiah 6:9, 10; 29:10.

14 Psalm 68:23, 24 in the Septuagint, and 69:23, 24 in the Masoretic Text.

15 For the present purpose the scriptural allusions in the closing hymn in chapter 11, vs 33–6, are excluded from consideration. The principles of interpretation at work there are nonetheless consistent with those elucidated by the present treatment.

16 Cf. Badenas, *Christ the End of the Law*, 90–2.

17 Cf. W. R. Stegner, "Romans 9:6–29 – A Midrash," *Journal for the Study of the New Testament* 22 (1984), 37–52. Stegner's work is essentially based upon that of E. Earle Ellis, *Paul's Use of the Old Testament* (Edinburgh: Oliver and Boyd, 1957) and *Prophecy and Hermeneutic in Early Christianity* (Tübingen: Mohr, 1978). If recent discussion must qualify the description of Romans 9–11 as Midrash, there is nonetheless no doubt but that Ellis and Stegner contribute signally to our understanding of Paul's manner of thinking scripturally. Indirectly, the Midrashim shed light on the sort of activity Paul was engaged in; it is only the direct equation of Pauline interpretation with the genre of Midrash which needs to be set aside.

18 *Midrash in Context. Exegesis in Formative Judaism*, The Foundations of Judaism 1 (Philadelphia: Fortress, 1983).

19 ibid., 82, 83. It should be noted that these are the modalities of interpretation which Neusner identifies in Talmud, and which he shows were then applied to the Bible in the Midrashim.

20 ibid., 103.

21 For this reason, the procedures for associating disparate passages are important for both Paul and the rabbis. The famous rabbinic rules of interpretation might be regarded as an attempt to specify how the harmony of Scripture may be defined; cf. A. Finkel, *The Pharisees and the Teacher of Nazareth*, Arbeiten zur Geschichte des Spätjudentums und seiner Umwelt (Leiden: Brill, 1964), 123–8; B. D. Chilton and C. A. Evans, "Jesus and the Israel's Scriptures," in B. D. Chilton and C. A. Evans (eds), *Studying the Historical Jesus. Evaluations of the State of Current Research*: New Testament Tools and Studies 19 (Leiden: Brill, 1994), 281–335.

22 The following rendering is that of H. Freedman (*Genesis*, Midrash Rab-
bah (the principal collection of Rabbinic Commentaries on Scripture) eds
H. Freedman and M. Simon (New York: Soncino, 1983) at Genesis
Rabbah 53.12:

> AND GOD SAID UNTO ABRAHAM: LET IT NOT BE
> GRIEVOUS IN THY SIGHT . . . FOR IN ISAAC SHALL
> SEED BE CALLED TO THEE (21:12). R. Judah b. Shilum said:
> Not "Isaac," but IN ISAAC is written here. R. 'Azariah said in the
> name of Bar Ḥutah: The *beth* (IN) denotes two, i.e., [thy seed shall
> be called] in him who recognizes the existence of two worlds. R.
> Judah b. R. Shalum said: It is written, REMEMBER HIS MARVEL-
> OUS WORKS THAT HE HATH DONE, HIS SIGNS, AND THE
> JUDGMENTS OF HIS MOUTH (Psalms 105:5): [God says:] I have
> given a sign [whereby the true descendants of Abraham can by
> known], viz. he who expressly recognizes [God's judgments]: thus
> whoever believes in the two worlds shall be called "thy seed," while
> he who rejects belief in two worlds shall not be called "thy seed."

In order to appreciate the interpretaion, which also appears in Talmud
(Nedarim 31a), it is necessary to realize that ב *(beth)* in Hebrew may mean
both "in" and "two."

23 Cf. B. D. Chilton, "Commenting on the Old Testament (with Particular
Reference to the Pesharim, Philo, and the Mekilta)," in D. A. Carson and
H. G. M. Williamson (eds), *It is Written: Scripture Citing Scripture. Essays
in Honour of Barnabas Lindars, S.S.F.* (Cambridge: Cambridge University Press, 1988), 122–40.

24 Cf. E. P. Sanders, *Paul, the Law, and the Jewish People* (Philadelphia:
Fortress, 1985), 31, 46, 59 n. 75, 97.

25 Cf. Wolfgang Wiefel, "The Jewish Community in Ancient Rome and the
Origins of Roman Christianity," in K.P. Donfried (ed.), *The Romans
Debate* (Minneapolis, MN: Augsburg, 1977), 100–19. Wiefel attempts to
harmonize the accounts of the New Testament, Suetonius, and Dio
Cassius, and in so doing may be reasoning beyond the limits of certainty
imposed by the evidence. He argues that Claudius first expelled Jews from
Rome (so Suetonius and Orosius) and – after many returned – attempted
to prohibit their meeting in public (so Dio Cassius). F. F. Bruce imagines
the precisely opposite scenario: meetings were first banned, and expulsion
followed (*New Testament History* (London: Pickering and Inglis, 1982),
279–83). But the fact of a disturbance involving Jews is well established;
that it had an immediate impact upon Christianity is a sound inference
(cf. Acts 18:2; Cassius Dio, *Roman History* 60.66; Suetonius, *Claudius*
25.4; Orosius, *Seven Books of History against the Pagans* 7.6). In any case,
Wiefel is clearly correct in viewing Romans as an appeal for unity to a
mixed church, in which gentiles were in the majority. For further discussion, cf. E. Mary Smallwood, *The Jews under Roman Rule. From Pompey
to Diocletian*, Studies in Judaism in Late Antiquity 20 (Leiden: Brill,
1976), 210–16; and Francis Watson, *Paul, Judaism and the Gentiles. A
Sociological Approach,* Society for New Testament Studies Monograph

Series 56 (Cambridge: Cambridge University Press, 1986), 91–4 (for positions in support of Bruce's).

26 Paul's position in Romans may be regarded as adumbrated in 1 Corinthians 1:21–5; 9:20–3; 10:32, 33; 12:13; Galatians 3:28.

27 The dates here offered, which are well within the range of the scholarly consensus which has emerged, are those of B. D. Chilton, *Beginning New Testament Study* (Grand Rapids, MI: Eerdmans, 1986; London: SPCK, 1987 (rev.)).

28 A. G. Baxter and J. A. Ziesler, "Paul and Arboriculture: Romans 11:17–24," *Journal for the Study of the New Testament* 24 (1985), 25–32. Their argument is especially telling, in that the purpose of the grafting – which was not considered outlandish in antiquity – was to reinvigorate the tree in which the scion was implanted. The authors cite a contemporary of Paul's, Columella (*De re rustica* 5.11.1–15 and *De arboribus* 26–7); cf. Baxter and Ziesler, "Paul and Arboriculture," 27–9.

29 In "Fences and Neighbors," in W. S. Green (ed.), *Approaches to Ancient Judaism* (Missoula: Scholars Press for Brown Judaic Studies, 1978) 2:1–25 = Jonathan Z. Smith, *Imagining Religion. From Babylon to Jonestown* (Chicago: University of Chicago Press, 1982), 1–18.

30 Geza Vermes, *Dead Sea Scrolls. Qumran in Perspective* (London: Collins, 1977), 88.

31 ibid., 89.

32 ibid, 181.

33 ibid, 181. See also B. Gärtner, *The Temple and the Community in Qumran and the New Testament* (Cambridge: Cambridge University Press, 1965).

34 See Robin Scroggs, *The Last Adam* (Philadelphia: Fortress Press, 1971).

5 PAUL'S COMPETITORS, JESUS' DISCIPLES, AND THE ISRAEL OF JESUS

1 For the dating of documents and the considerations involved in dating, cf. B. D. Chilton, *Beginning New Testament Study* (London: SPCK, 1986; and Grand Rapids, MI: Eerdmans, 1986).

2 Cf. Matthew 16:18.

3 Cf. Acts 4:36–7; 9:26–30; 11:19–26. According to Acts 11:22–4, Barnabas was the designated contact between Jerusalem and the increasingly important community in Antioch.

4 Cf. Matthew 13:55–6; Mark 6:3 and the presentation of James' authority in Acts 15 (as we are about to see). The plain statement in the Gospels that Jesus had brothers and sisters was interpreted at a later period in a loose sense, to be consistent with the doctrine of Mary's perpetual virginity. But two of the brothers, James and Judas, were prominent within the early Church. Their prominence is attested by two great historical resources of the early period, Eusebius from the fourth century and Hegesippus from the second century, cf. Eusebius, *History of the Church* II.23, III.19–20, in each case citing Hegesippus.

5 Paul may have been influenced by the interpretation of some of the

194

Aramaic Targumim at this point. Even so, he would have known that the Septuagint did *not* engage in such a messianic reading.

6 The work of Martin Dibelius, recently updated, is still basic, cf. *Der Brief des Jakobus* (Göttingen: Vandenhoeck und Ruprecht, 1984).

7 Acts often portrays the apostles generally as sharing Paul's position (and his vocabulary). The overall perspective of the document is a development of Pauline theology.

8 The Semitic form of Peter's name, which is usually given as "Simon," following the Greek spelling.

9 The verb in question is *sumphoneo*, which is only used at this point in the New Testament to speak of agreement with Scripture. Usually, the term refers to the concord of people in conversation.

10 The citation is in the form of the Septuagint, in keeping with the usual policy in the book of Acts.

11 His work is cited in the fourth-century *History of the Church* written by Eusebius (II.23).

12 The imagery is inspired by Daniel 7:13–14, where "son of man" is used to refer to an angelic figure in God's heavenly court.

13 The resurrection was the catalyst that prompted his thinking. Prior to that, there was conflict between Jesus and James (as between Jesus and his brothers generally, cf. Mark 3:31–4 and John 7:2–9).

14 Hegesippus goes to great length to describe James' punctilious devotion to the Temple.

15 The irony of the account is that people falsely conclude that Paul was introducing non-Jews into the interior courts, and a riot leads to his final arrest (Acts 21:27–36).

16 Cf. Leviticus 7:27; Deuteronomy 12:16.

17 The letter was composed in Greek well after Paul's position became well known, *c.* 90 CE (long after James' execution in Jerusalem). The denial of a Pauline position is evident in James 2:14–26.

18 At a later period, Talmud would also see the formulation of "Noachic commandments," which gentiles were to keep. Cf. Sanhedrin 56a–b.

19 In contrast, Paul considered Jesus' descent from David as "according to the flesh" (Romans 1:3); he did not cite it as a demonstration of divine authority.

20 At a later period, the letter of James would dispute any such reading, with the statement, "Show me your faith apart from works, and I by my works will show you faith" (2:18).

21 1 Peter and 2 Peter are examples of writings from a later period (no earlier than 90 CE) which attempt to apply the Petrine approach to situations which arose well after Peter's death. A widely accepted tradition has him perish in Rome during the persecution of Nero in 64 CE.

22 The first and most important witness is Papias, whose tradition is quoted in Eusebius' *History of the Church* (III.39).

23 "Glory," of course, is understood to shine, as does Moses' face when he returns from Mount Sinai (Exodus 34:29–35).

24 For what follows, cf. B. D. Chilton, *Profiles of a Rabbi. Synoptic Opportunities in Reading about Jesus,* Brown Judaic Studies 177 (Atlanta: Scholars Press, 1989).

25 John, of course, is presented as a prophetic figure in the Synoptics, see Matthew 3:1–12; Mark 1:1–8; Luke 3:1–18.

26 See Marinus de Jonge, "Messiah," *Anchor Bible Dictionary*, vol. 4 (Garden City, NY: Doubleday, 1992), 777–8.

27 See Matthew 3:15; 5:17; 23:32; 26:54, 56; Mark 14:49; Luke 4:21; 24:44.

28 Cf. Leslie W. Barnard, *Studies in the Apostolic Fathers and Their Background* (Oxford: Blackwell, 1966); Robert A. Kraft, *Barnabas and the Didache* (New York: Nelson, 1965).

29 For examples, see Molly Whittaker, *Jews and Christians. Graeco-Roman Views*, Cambridge Commentaries on Writings of the Jewish and Christian World 200 BC to AD 200 (Cambridge: Cambridge University Press, 1984).

30 It is likely that there were contacts between Matthew's community in Damascus and Essenes who were resident there.

31 The term *ekklesia* also appears in Matthew (16:18; 18:17), and not in the other Gospels.

32 The development of such nuance in Luke is not surprising. In Antioch the continued existence of churches and synagogues in the same city was an incentive to critical reflection.

33 For a technical discussion of the prologue in its relationship to the Targumim, see B. D. Chilton, "Typologies of *memra* and the fourth Gospel," *Targum Studies* 1 (1992), 89–100.

34 That is typical of the relationship of the prologue to the body of the Gospel. The prologue states themes which are taken up by means of narrative and discourse, in the manner of a meditation.

35 When the phrase "king of Israel" appears in Matthew 27:42 and Mark 15:32, it features within the mockery of Jesus, and is far from an acclamation. A better Synoptic counterpart is "king of the Jews;" Pilate wants to know if that is the identity which Jesus is claiming (see Mark 15:2 and parallels, with further references from that point onward).

36 The verbal form is plural, which emphasizes that Nathanael here stands surrogate for the hearers of John as a whole.

37 We are even told that Passover is a "feast of the Jews" (6:4; compare 2:13; 5:1; 7:2; 11:55), as if the liturgical setting might be another people's.

38 Cf. *The Five Gospels. The Search for the Authentic Words of Jesus*, R. W. Funk, R. W. Hoover, and the Jesus Seminar (New York: Macmillan, 1993), 69.

39 Cf. Joseph A. Fitzmyer and Daniel J. Harrington, *A Manual of Palestinian Aramaic Texts*, Biblia et Orientalia 34 (Rome: Biblical Institute Press, 1978), where the forms here used are attested. The pointing, of course, is largely a matter of supposition on the basis of later texts, and a simplified scheme is recommended for that reason.

40 Cf. Fitzmyer and Harrington, *Manual*, 7.8.4.

41 Cf. ibid., 29B.22.23. The result is that *min bar* appears in the first line, and *bera' min* in the second.

42 I have used a form of the *pael*, of which the infinitive appears in Fitzmyer and Harrington, *Manual*, 29B.20.15.

43 For that reason, the version of the saying in *Thomas l.* 14, which specifies what goes into "your mouth" is taken by the "Jesus Seminar" to be as

196

original as what is in Mark. It seems much more likely that the setting in Luke (eating what is given you during missionary journeys; cf. Luke 10:7–9) has influenced the wording in *Thomas. Thomas* frequently gives the appearance of being a pastiche of materials from the Synoptic Gospels, together with other traditions. Cf. B. D. Chilton, "The Gospel According to Thomas as a Source of Jesus' Teaching," in D. Wenham (ed.), *Gospel Perspectives 5. The Jesus Tradition Outside the Gospels* (Sheffield: JSOT, 1985), 155–75.

44 Cf. B. D. Chilton, "John the Purifier," in *idem, Judaic Approaches to the Gospels*, International Studies in Formative Christianity and Judaism 2 (Atlanta: Scholars Press, 1994), 1–37.

45 *Thomas l.* 14 links just this injunction with the saying more primitively attested in Mark 7:15; Matthew 15:11.

46 Of course, within the Pharisaic ethos, purity was held to be consistent with sacrifice, without any assumption that such purity would actually occasion sacrifice each time it was achieved.

47 See Seán Freyne, "The Geography, Politics, and Economics of Galilee and the Quest for the Historical Jesus," in B. D. Chilton and C. A. Evans (eds), *Studying the Historical Jesus. Evaluations of the State of Current Research*, New Testament Tools and Studies 19 (Leiden: Brill, 1994), 75–121.

48 For a detailed analysis of the saying, see B. D. Chilton, *God in Strength. Jesus' Announcement of the Kingdom* (Sheffield: Sheffield Academic Press, 1987) reprinted from Studien zum Neuen Testament und seiner Umwelt 1 (Freistadt: Plöchl, 1979), 179–201. The significant differences between Matthew and Luke here show that "Q" was not the stable source some scholars claim that it was.

49 See the discussion in B. D. Chilton, *A Galilean Rabbi and His Bible* (Wilmington, DE: Glazier; and London: SPCK, 1984), 57–63.

50 See Eusebius' *History* II.23.1–9.

51 Cf. Robert Eisenman, *James the Just in the Habakkuk Pesher*, Studia post-Biblica 35 (Leiden: Brill, 1982).

52 See Philo, *On the Migration of Abraham*, 89–93.

53 For that reason, it seems strange to compare him with Rabbinic Judaism. The historically appropriate question is his relation with his own Judaism in the Diaspora.

54 Cf. W. Ward Gasque, "Tarsus," *Anchor Bible Dictionary*, vol. 6, ed. D. N. Freedman (Garden City, NY: Doubleday, 1992), 333–4.

7 THE TRANSFORMATION OF JUDAISM: FROM SALVATION TO SANCTIFICATION. THE LETTER TO THE HEBREWS' JUDAIC WORLD-VIEW

1 He is quoted in Eusebius' *History of the Church*, VI.25. A discussion of the significance of Hebrews within the development of the canon is available in B. D. Chilton, *Beginning New Testament Study* (London: SPCK, 1987; and Grand Rapids, MI: Eerdmans, 1986), 12–20.

2 A fine, recent commentary is available in William L. Lane, *Hebrews 1–8*

and *Hebrews 9–13*, Word Biblical Commentary 47A, 47B (Dallas: Word, 1991).

3 Also in Eusebius, *History* VI.25.

4 See the helpful discussion in Brooke Foss Westcott, *The Epistle to the Hebrews* (London: Macmillan, 1909 ((first published 1889), lxii–lxxxiv. His quotation of Tertullian is taken from *On Modesty* 20.3).

5 Westcott, *Epistle*, lxxi. See p. 176 for a brief summary of Westcott's contribution to the study of the New Testament.

6 See Lane, *Hebrews*, lxix–lxxxiv.

7 In his recent monograph on Hebrews, Barnabas Lindars considered the possibility that 2:17 presupposed some previous awareness of the theme on the part of the readership of the epistle. But he wisely came to the conclusion that, in fact, the author was simply preparing the way for the closer analysis of Jesus as great high priest which was to come; cf. *The Theology of the Letter to the Hebrews*, New Testament Theology (Cambridge: Cambridge University Press, 1991) 40–1.

8 His name has not yet been changed to Abraham, which is related in Genesis 17:5.

9 See also Hebrews 5:6, 10; 6:20.

10 The link with the practice of eucharist is so obvious in the mind of the author, he does not even elaborate upon it. Cf. the discussion in Lindars, *Theology*, 76–7.

11 For a consideration of the terminological problems, cf. Harold W. Attridge, *The Epistle to the Hebrews*, Hermeneia (Philadelphia: Fortress, 1989), 230; and Westcott, *Epistle,* 244–52.

12 Attridge, *Epistle to the Hebrews*, pp. 232–5, follows other commentators in taking the θυμιατήριον as an altar, and so charges Hebrews with a "minor (*sic*!) anomaly," but he points out himself that "censer" would be the more straightforward rendering, with the diction of the Septuagint.

13 It is not even clear what exactly the author made of the interim between the two events.

14 Cf. Westcott, *Epistle*, 258–60.

15 See Hebrews 8:1–6. Hebrews' usage of the language of typology is quite complex, although the underlying conception is fairly simple. Paul reflects an earlier form of typological interpretation in 1 Corinthians 10.

16 See Lane, *Hebrews*, 114–15, 120–2. Lindars' discussion is far more sensitive to the creativity of Hebrews and to its impact upon subsequent discussion, *Theology*, 38–42.

17 The mention is in reference to Joseph's command for the disposal of his own bones, a fitting context for the attitude toward "Israel" in Hebrews!

18 The angelic mediation of the Torah was a common belief in the period, see Galatians 3:19; Acts 7:53; Josephus' *Antiquities* XV §136. Cf. Lane, *Hebrews*, 37–8.

19 See Lindars, 38. Lindars also presents a careful characterization of *how* Hebrews' approach to Scripture might (and might not) be called typological, ibid., 53–5.

20 Indeed, the epistle in its present form is designed to pass as a late letter of Paul's. His imprisonment is assumed (13:18–19), and the naming of Timothy is an indirect attempt to claim Pauline authorship (13:23). The

famous reference to Italy in 13:24 is similarly part of the strategy of a Pauline presentation, and not a criterion of the actual provenience of the epistle.

21 Cf. his work, *De Opificio Mundi*; and B. D. Chilton, "Commenting on the Old Testament (with particular reference to the pesharim, Philo, and the Mekilta)," in D. A. Carson and H. G. M. Williamson (eds), *It is Written: Scripture Citing Scripture. Essays in Honour of Barnabas Lindars, SSF* (Cambridge: Cambridge University Press, 1988), 122–40. Philo also treated Melchizedek allegorically, and elucidated his name in a way comparable to Hebrews; cf. *Allegory of the Laws*, III.79 and Lindars, *Theology*, 73.

22 Local apostolic writings were clearly available, but the emergence of the canonical New Testament would await the second century, largely under the impetus of the veneration of such traditions that Hebrews displays. Cf. Chilton, *Beginning New Testament Study*, 12–18.

23 The quotation is from Thomas W. Martin, "Hellenists," *Anchor Bible Dictionary*, vol. 3, ed. D. N. Freedman (Garden City, NY: Doubleday, 1992), 135–6. The reading of most manuscripts at Acts 11:20 supports his position, and puts in question Lane's tight association of the Hellenists with Jerusalem.

24 Lane, *Hebrews*, cxlvi–cl.

25 The force of Stephen's speech in Acts becomes anti-cultic, probably in the light of the destruction of the Temple in 70 CE. Luke and Acts are composed with the conviction that the Temple was destroyed and Jerusalem razed in fulfillment of a prophecy of Jesus' (see Luke 19:41–4).

26 Cf. Philo, *On the Migration of Abraham*, 89–93.

27 Cf. Philo, *Questions and Answers on Exodus*, II.52; *On the Life of Moses*, II.71–108. There is a useful description in Peder Borgen, "Philo of Alexandria," *Anchor Bible Dictionary*, vol. 5 (ed. D. N. Freedman, Garden City, NY: Doubleday, 1992), 333–42.

28 Cf. Westcott, *Epistle*, lxxiv–lxxv, lxviii–lxxix.

29 Lane, *Hebrews*, xlix.

30 Lindars details Luther's argument (as accepted by others) as well, and notes the Alexandrian character of the epistle, but claims such an origin "really is excluded by the fact that it was in Alexandria that it was first attributed to Paul" (*Theology*, 15–19). His claim is not convincing, for two reasons. First, the attribution to Paul in Alexandria is late, starting with Clement of Alexandria in the second century (see Eusebius' *History of the Church* VI.14). Second, the epistle passes itself off as a letter of Paul's, so that one would expect the attribution to be accepted wherever the epistle originated (as well as elsewhere). Lindars appears to make a principle out of the epistle's anonymity, much as he indulges in special pleading to suggest that a dating after the destruction of the Temple is not required (ibid. 19–21). The evidence obviously does not "compel" Alexandrian provenience or a dating after 70 CE, to use Lindars' word (ibid. 21), but the place and the tenor of the document are plausibly Alexandrian, and its dating is more likely after 70 than before.

31 The word "circumcision" (*peritome*) does not even appear in the epistle.

32 Westcott, *Epistle*, xxviii.

33 ibid., lxxxiv.

INDEX

INDEX